I0812783

THEN & NOW®

STATEN ISLAND

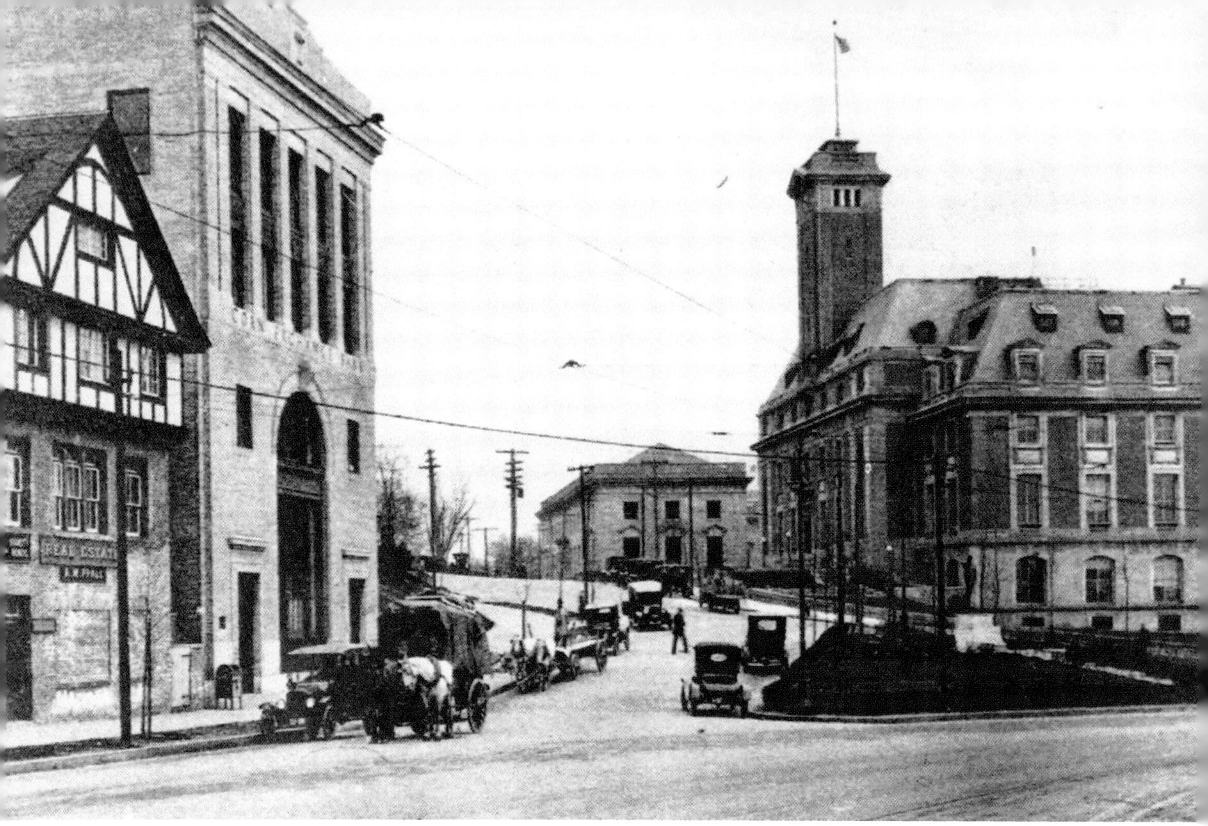

Soon after joining the other boroughs to form the City of New York in 1889, officials planned to move the seat of government from Richmondtown to a location closer to Manhattan. St. George was selected, and on a location overlooking the harbor and the ferry docks, Borough Hall was built. George Cromwell, Staten Island's first borough president, worked with his staff in an office building on the corner of Richmond Terrace and York Avenue until Borough Hall was completed in 1906. Adjacent to Borough Hall, a new courthouse was also built (center of the photograph). The tall building on the left was the Staten Island Branch of the Corn Exchange.

On the cover: Consolidation into the City of New York brought improvements to Staten Island's transportation system. In this 1903 photograph, looking west on Victory Boulevard, workers are seen grading the dirt roadbed at the intersection of Corson Avenue (to the right of the building in the center) and Victory Boulevard. Today the tracks are gone, and the railroad and trolley service has been replaced by the Metropolitan Transit Authority (MTA) bus service, as seen on the back cover. (Front cover, courtesy of the Staten Island Institute of Arts and Sciences; back cover, courtesy of Thomas W. Matteo.)

THEN & NOW®

STATEN ISLAND

Thomas W. Matteo

ARCADIA
PUBLISHING

ISBN 978-0-7385-4495-3

Published by Arcadia Publishing
Charleston, South Carolina

Printed in the United States of America

Then and Now is a registered trademark and is used under license from
Salamander Books Limited

Library of Congress Catalog Card Number: 2005939056

For all general information contact Arcadia Publishing at:
Telephone 843-853-2070
Fax 843-853-0044
E-mail sales@arcadiapublishing.com
For customer service and orders:
Toll-Free 1-888-313-2665

Visit us on the Internet at www.arcadiapublishing.com

This book is dedicated to the one person in my life who instilled in me the love and appreciation of history, my mother Vita.

Contents

ACKNOWLEDGMENTS

This project could not have been successfully completed without the help of many people in the Staten Island community. Whenever I approached someone for information or help, they gave it gladly, without hesitation and with a great sense of pride in the community they love so much.

Anytime you attempt to acknowledge people for their help, there is always someone you forget to mention, and I would like to apologize in advance to them if I do.

The organization that was most helpful not only in providing most of the historical pictures used but also for their wealth of knowledge of the Staten Island community was the Staten Island Institute of Arts and Sciences. It was not always easy identifying locations in a community that has undergone such dramatic changes in the last 40 years. Their patience and cooperation made this project possible. I would like to thank, in particular, Patricia M. Salmon, curator of history; Dorothy D'Eletto, archivist/researcher; and Hugh Powell, historian, for their help. Historic pictures from their collection were used on the following pages: 2, 10, 12–14, 18–22, 26–31, 34–38, 40, 42–54, 56–59, 61–63, 65–66, 68, 70, 72–74, 77, 79, 81, 85–90, 92, and 95.

The Staten Island community is very lucky to have its own newspaper, the *Staten Island Advance.* Its own history goes back to 1886, and Brian LaLine, the editor in chief, opened its archives, which provided a wealth of information that would have otherwise been lost to the community.

Lastly, I would like to thank my family, Diane, my wife, and Andrea and Michelle, my daughters, for putting up with my neurotic behavior as deadlines approached and for their support throughout the project.

Thank you to everyone who made this possible.

INTRODUCTION

The Staten Island Institute of Arts and Sciences is pleased to have worked with Thomas W. Matteo on his latest publication, which features "then and now" photographs of Staten Island. The borough has changed so very much since the earliest of these images was recorded. For this reason, his work is an important reminder of our past and our history, and of the importance of preserving such.

The Staten Island Institute of Arts and Sciences has a long history of preservation through publishing, whether it be environmental or historical. With this book, we are proud to continue our involvement in this field of endeavor. Whether one reads for pleasure, for work, or for scholarship, it is important to the institute's mission to provide worthwhile educational materials for the public. It was in 1883 that the forerunning organization of the Staten Island Institute of Arts and Sciences, the Natural Science Association, began publishing *Proceedings*, a compilation of scholarly articles relating to Staten Island's nature and local history. This tradition continued with the publication of the massive five-volume series *Staten Island and Its People.* Written by Charles W. Leng and William T. Davis, these books continue to be the foremost study volumes for researchers. They have stood the test of time, and for almost eight decades, they have furnished seekers with the answers they have sought. In addition, some of the institute's founders wrote or cowrote such significant volumes as *Days Afield on Staten Island, Church of Saint Andrew's Staten Island, The Conference or Billopp House*, and *Legends, Stories, and Folklore of Old Staten Island: Part I, The North Shore.* The tradition was continued with *A Comparative Flora of Staten Island* by Richard Buegler and Steven Parisio, *The New Field Guide to Staten Island's Rocks and Minerals* by Steven Okulewicz, *Orchids and Orioles: Biodiversity on Staten Island* by Ed Johnson, *New York Metropolitan Ferryboats* by Vince Sweeney, and *Historic Prints of Staten Island, N.Y.* by Hugh Powell. Owing to this legacy, it is with great pleasure that the Staten Island Institute of Arts and Sciences is involved with Matteo's manuscript, as it will no doubt be used for many decades to come.

It is also noteworthy that the majority of the photographs utilized by Matteo are from the collections of the Staten Island Institute of Arts and Sciences. In visiting the archives, he culled through thousands of postcards, photographs, and negatives to select the appropriate images that tell the "then and now" story of Staten Island. Many of the images are taken from the vast holdings of the William T. Davis Collection and the Hugh Powell Postcard Collection. Many are rare, and it has been an even rarer occurrence that they be displayed in this manner. Like the institute founders, particularly William T. Davis, Thomas W. Matteo has painstakingly gone out into the field to document Staten Island as it currently appears, so that we might make comparisons with the past. These photographs will provide an important resource for future researchers, much as Davis's early photograph work captured the life and times of Staten Island for us today. For all of these reasons, the following pages will be enjoyed by generations to come.

—Patricia M. Salmon
Curator of History, Staten Island Institute of Arts and Sciences

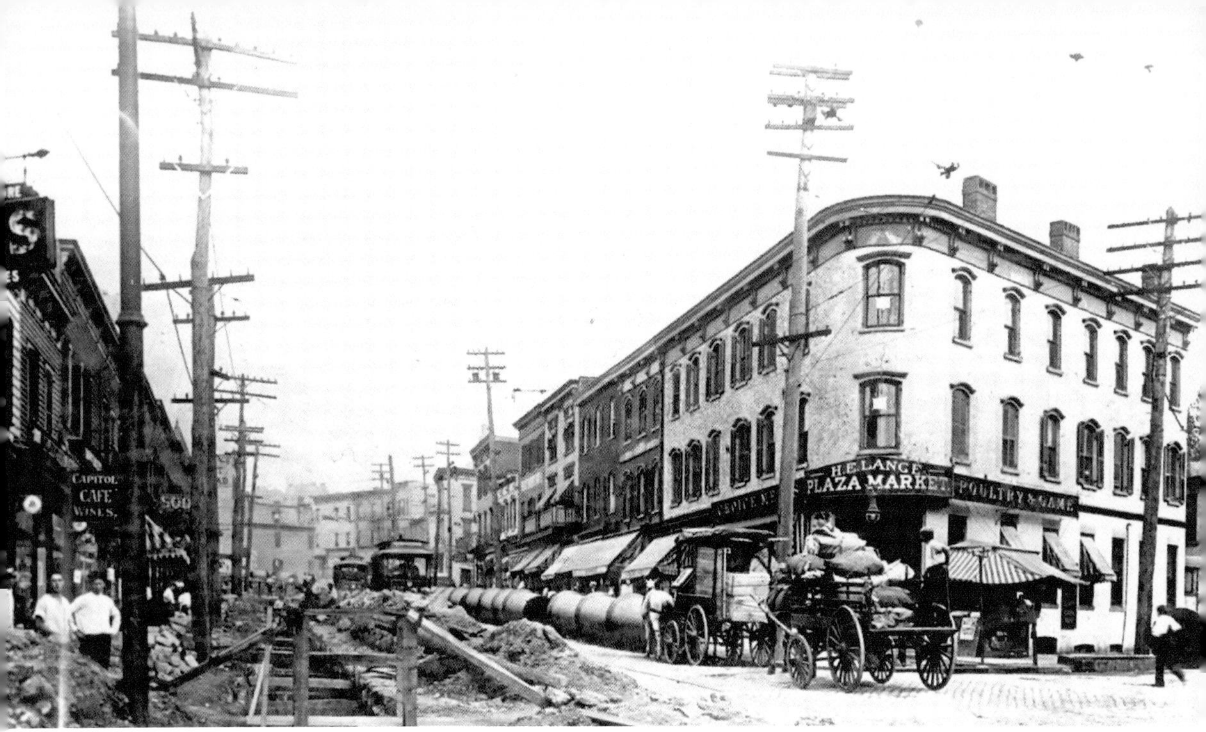

Victory Boulevard, originally named Richmond Turnpike, was privately financed and built by Daniel Tompkins. When the road was completed, it ran from the Watering Place in Tompkinsville to the Carteret Ferry in Travis. This was an important stagecoach route for travelers making their way to Philadelphia. In this 1910 photograph, workmen can be seen working on laying sewer pipes at the intersection of Van Duzer Street and Richmond Turnpike. After World War I, the road was renamed in celebration of the United States' victory over Germany, to Victory Boulevard.

Tottenville is the southernmost part of New York State; however, until the railroad reached Tottenville in 1860, the Westfield town had closer ties to New Jersey then it did to the rest of the island. In this 1920 photograph, Masons are marching in a parade down Main Street, crossing the railroad tracks. Today the West End Hotel pictured here is gone, and the tracks are below grade.

Chapter 1
STREETS AND NEIGHBORHOODS

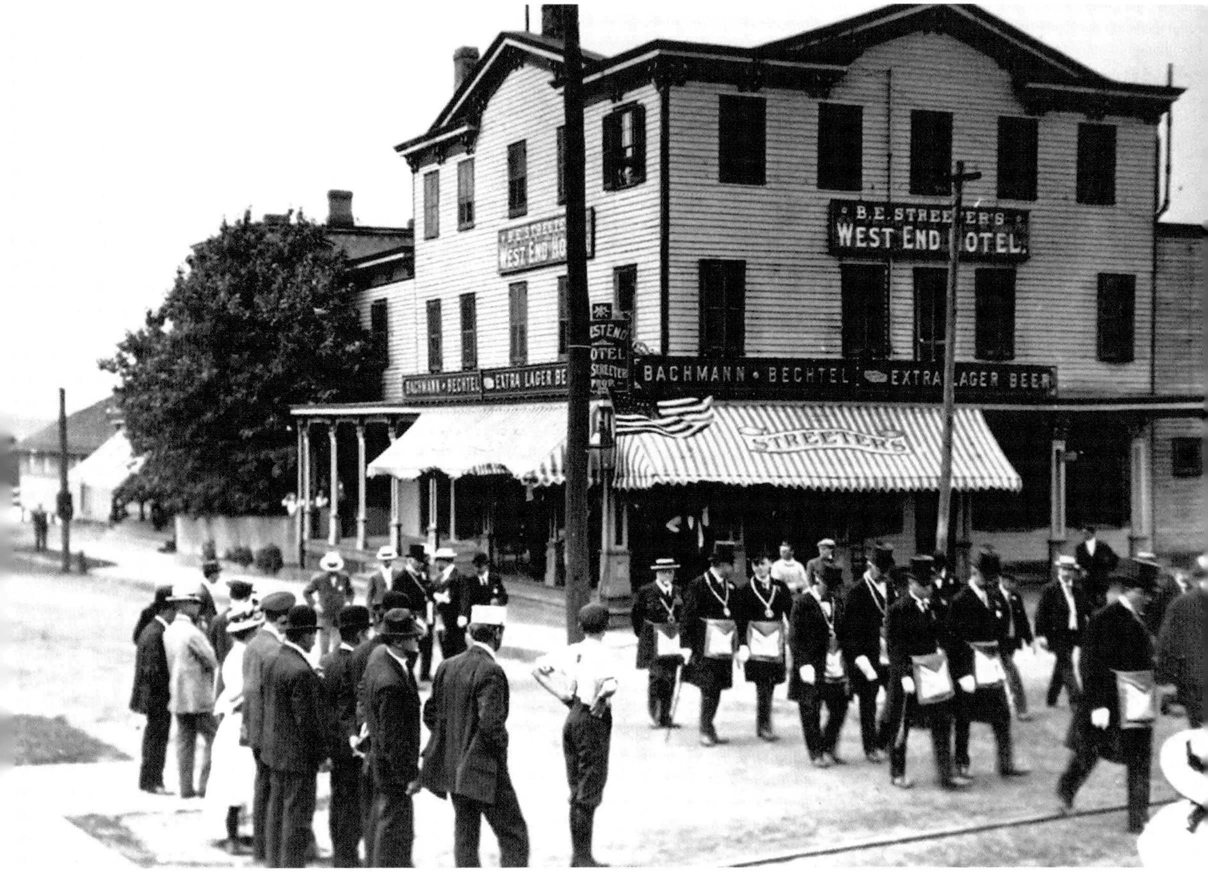

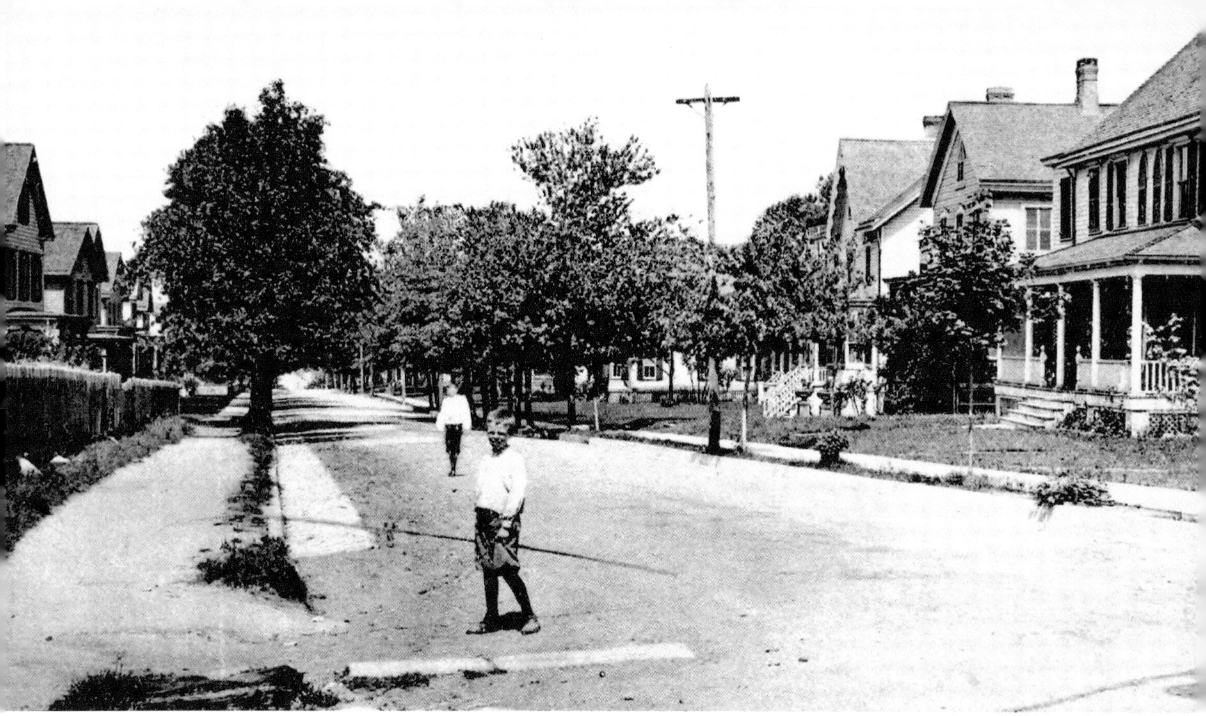

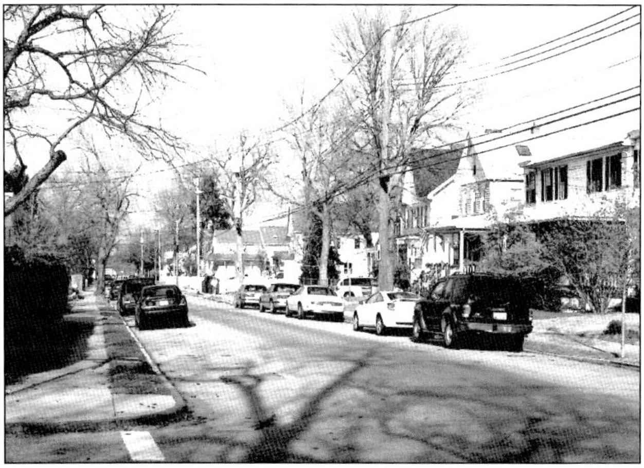

In 1899, the Tottenville Association organized and stocked Tottenville's first public library. The library was located at 208 Johnson Avenue and had 230 books available to the community for lend. In 1904, several community groups came together to petition Andrew Carnegie, who was financing libraries in small communities, for funds to build a larger library. The request was granted, and the first branch of the New York Public Library system was opened on Staten Island in Tottenville. Johnson Avenue was also home to the Tottenville Hat Works, which operated at the foot of Johnson Avenue until 1927. In these photographs of Johnson Avenue (looking north from Craig Avenue), one can see that it has remained a residential community of attractive private homes.

Overdevelopment has long been a problem on Staten Island. Seen in this 1943 photograph is the home of Elizabeth Sukupcac, built by her father on Prescott Avenue. He built the home there because he wanted to live in "the country." The character of Staten Island remained more like a countryside than a city for many years, escaping the sprawl that had consumed the rest of the city. After the Verrazano Bridge was built, people from all over, particularly Brooklyn, flocked to Staten Island. Houses sprang up everywhere, and in 2002, this simple "country" house was torn down and replaced by six semi-attached houses.

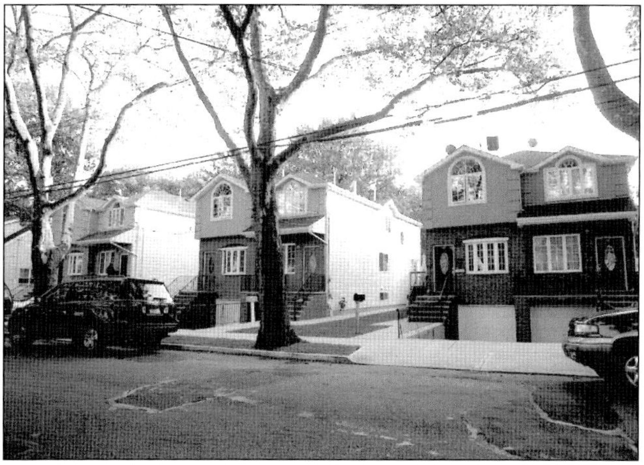

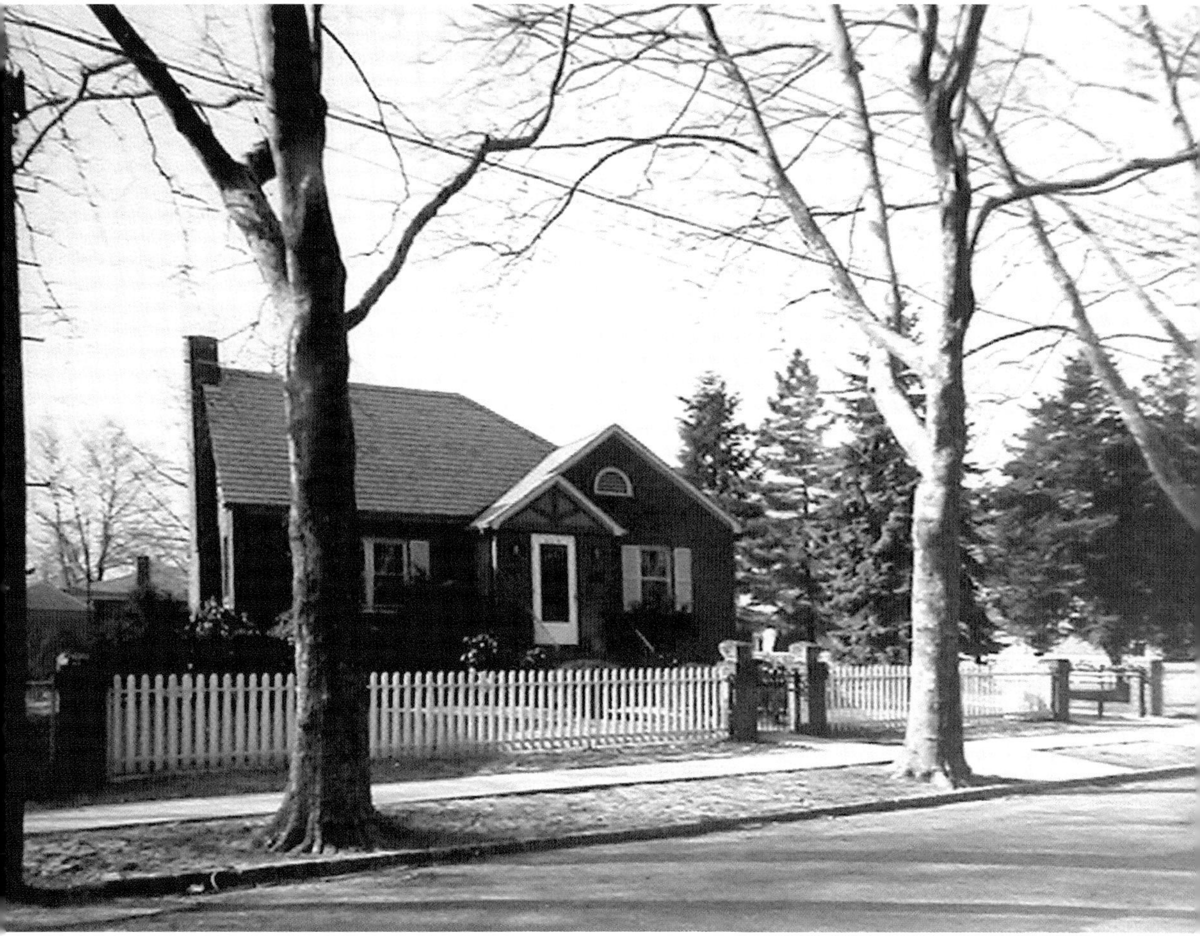

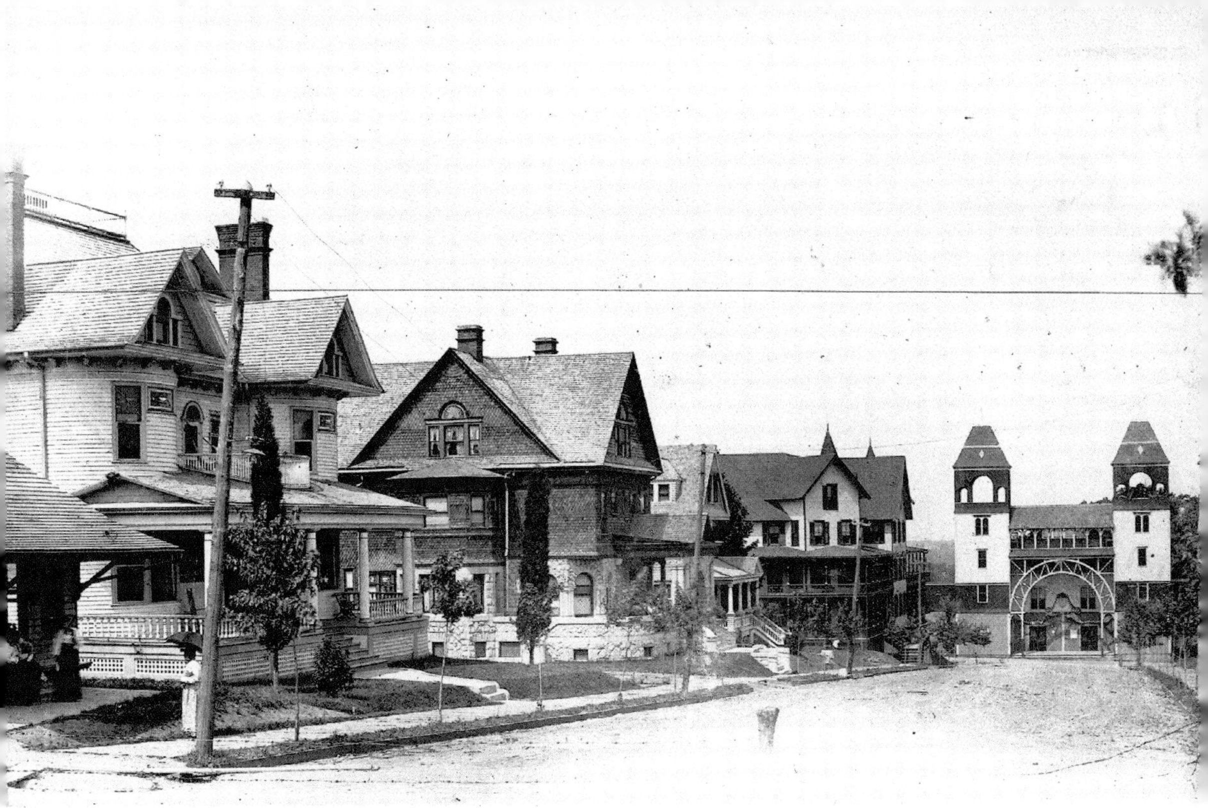

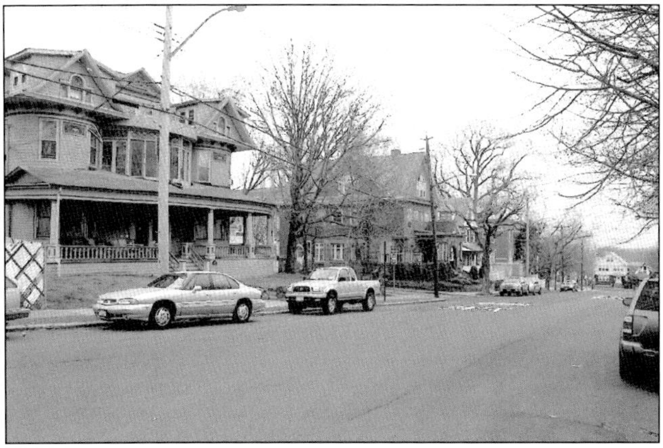

In this 1899 photograph is Prohibition Park, originally conceived as a summer community by the National Prohibition Party in 1887 by Dr. Rev. William H. Boole. Originally part of Gov. Thomas Dongan's 5,100-acre estate (1683), the organization only sold parcels to those supporting the Prohibition cause. The acreage was bound by Watchogue Road, Demorest, Maine, and Wardwell Avenues with its entrance at Maine and Jewett Avenues. The streets of the community were names for the dry states of the union (Maine, New York, Ohio, and Virginia) and for the party's candidates for president (Livermore, Bidwell, Fiske, and Woolley). Interest in the park waned after a fire destroyed part of the complex in 1904. The Park Company began to sell parcels to others than those supporting their cause, and the original community faded away.

Donald Trump honed his skills on Staten Island. As a young boy, he traveled with his father, Fred Trump, on the 69th Street ferry to help manage properties his father owned here, including the Grymes Hill Apartments. One of his jobs was to empty coins from laundry machines in the basements of his father's buildings. His decision to emblazon his name on everything he built was made when he attended the dedication of the Verrazano Bridge with his father. While everyone else was praised, the engineer (Othmar Ammann) responsible for building the bridge was not mentioned. He decided no one would ever forget who was responsible for the buildings he erected. After his father's death, the property remained in the Trump family until 2005, when it was sold.

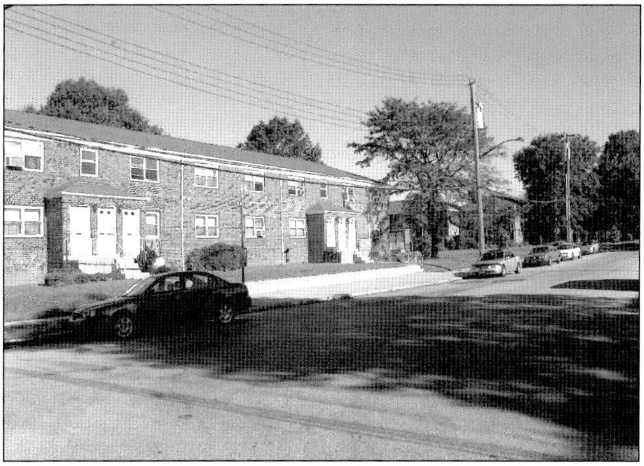

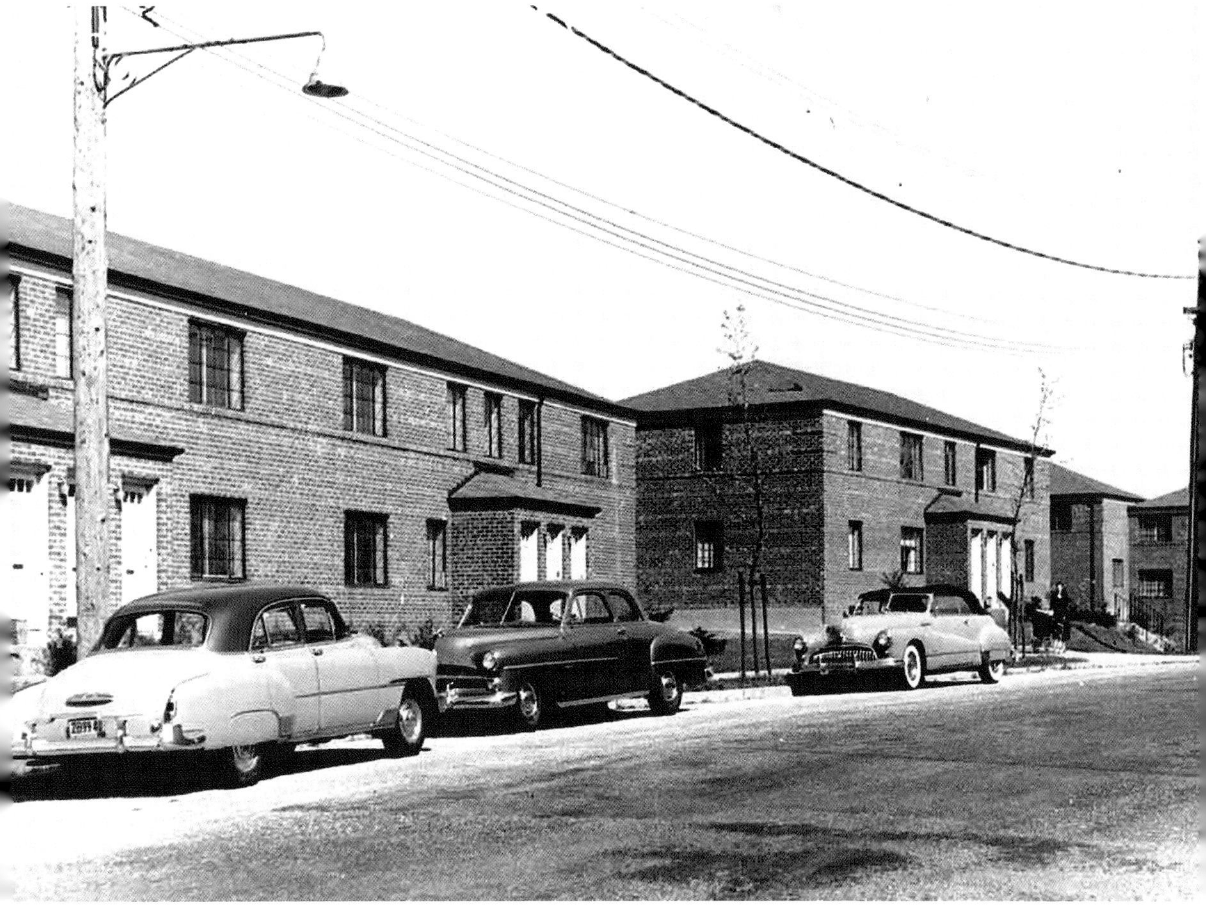

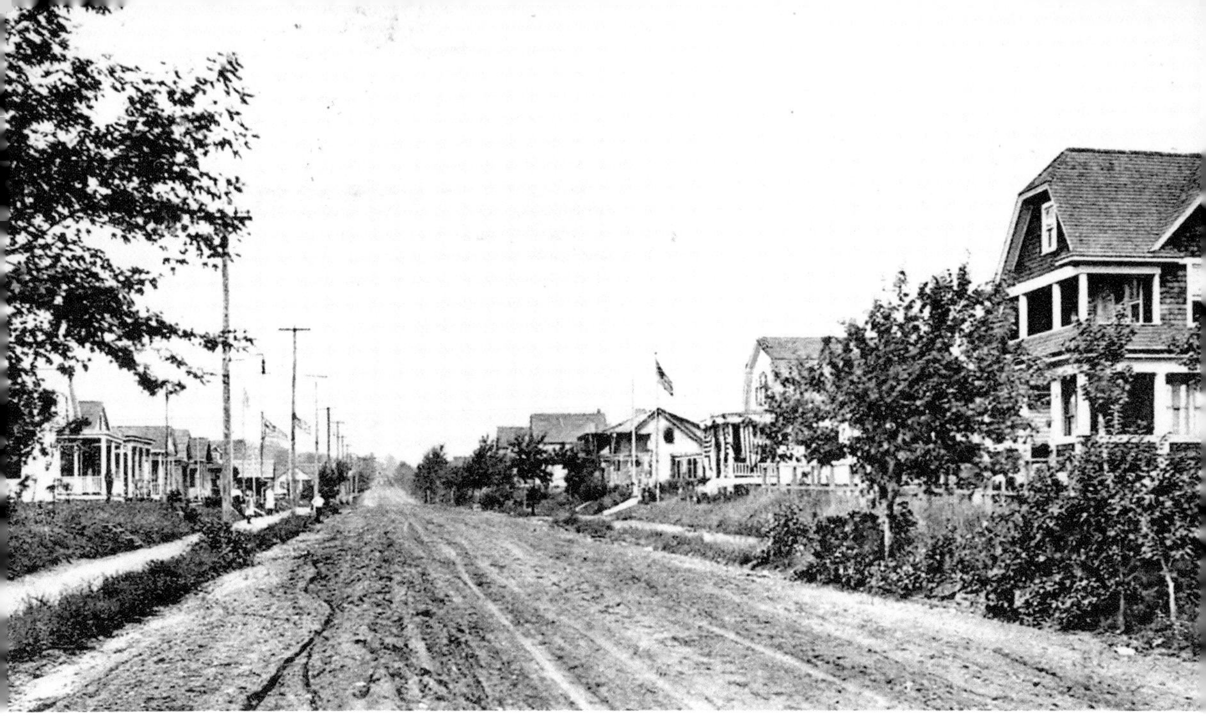

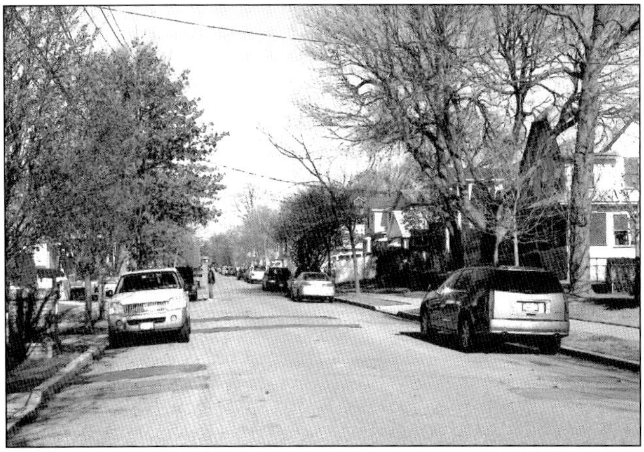

Although Tottenville is the southernmost part of New York State, it did not stop Manhattan and Brooklynites from seeking out the area's beautiful beaches and country setting for their vacations. Raritan Bay Park was established between Yetman Avenue and Loretta Street, from Hylan Boulevard to the Raritan Bay. At first, visitors used tents, which were later replaced with bungalows. As the area became more accessible, year-round homes replaced the bungalows. In this photograph of Rockaway Street looking north toward Hylan Boulevard, bungalows line the left side of the street while more permanent homes line the right. Today all the bungalows have been replaced by permanent housing.

Established in 1855, Masonic Lodge No. 381 held its first meeting at St. Paul's Methodist Episcopal Church on Amboy Road and Main Street in Tottenville. Under the direction of Master Ebert W. Hubbard, the lodge continued to grow, and after several moves, the lodge finally built its permanent temple at 236 Main Street in 1909. The United States Post Office maintained a branch in the temple until the early 1960s, when a separate building was erected two doors north on Main Street. Over the years, several other lodges moved their meetings to Main Street, including New Dorp Lodge No. 1092, Great Kills Lodge No. 912, Beacon Light Lodge No. 701, and the LaGuardia Lodge No. 1130.

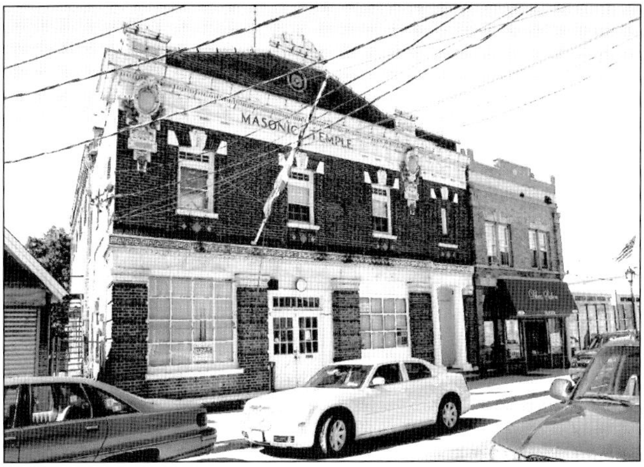

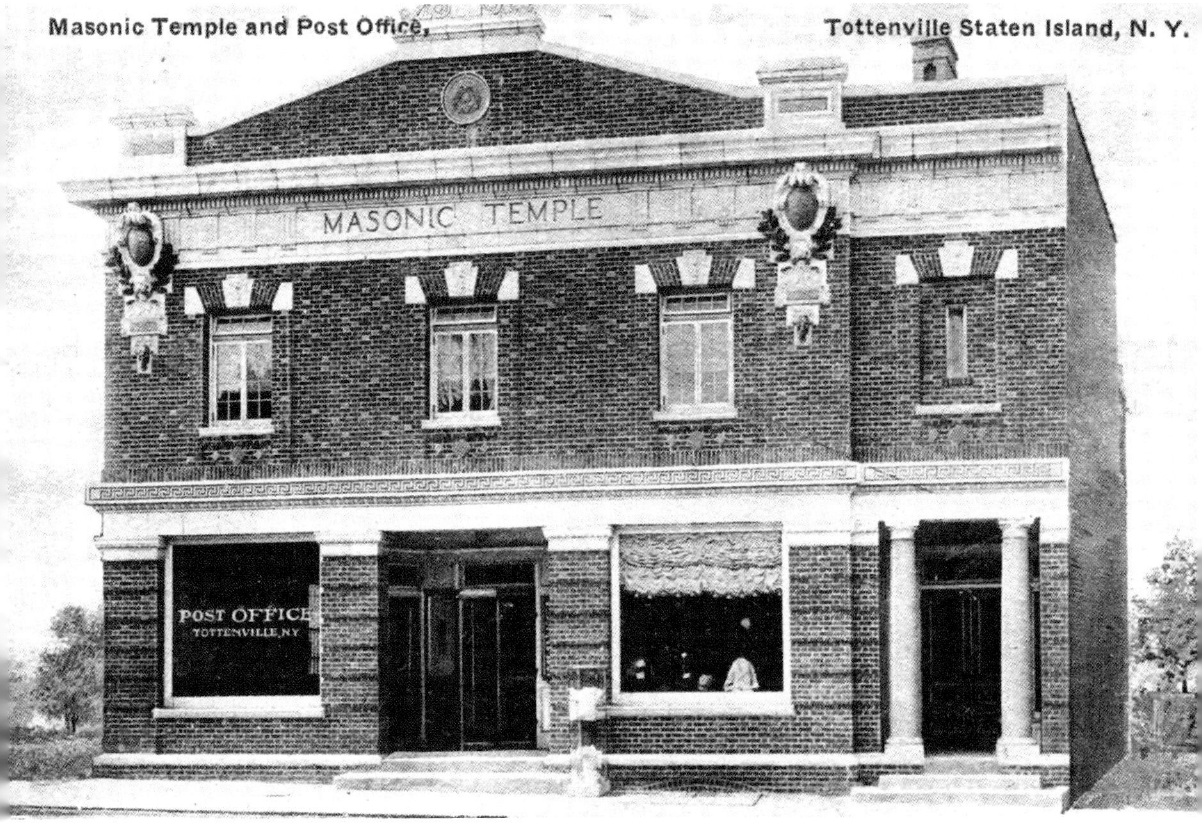

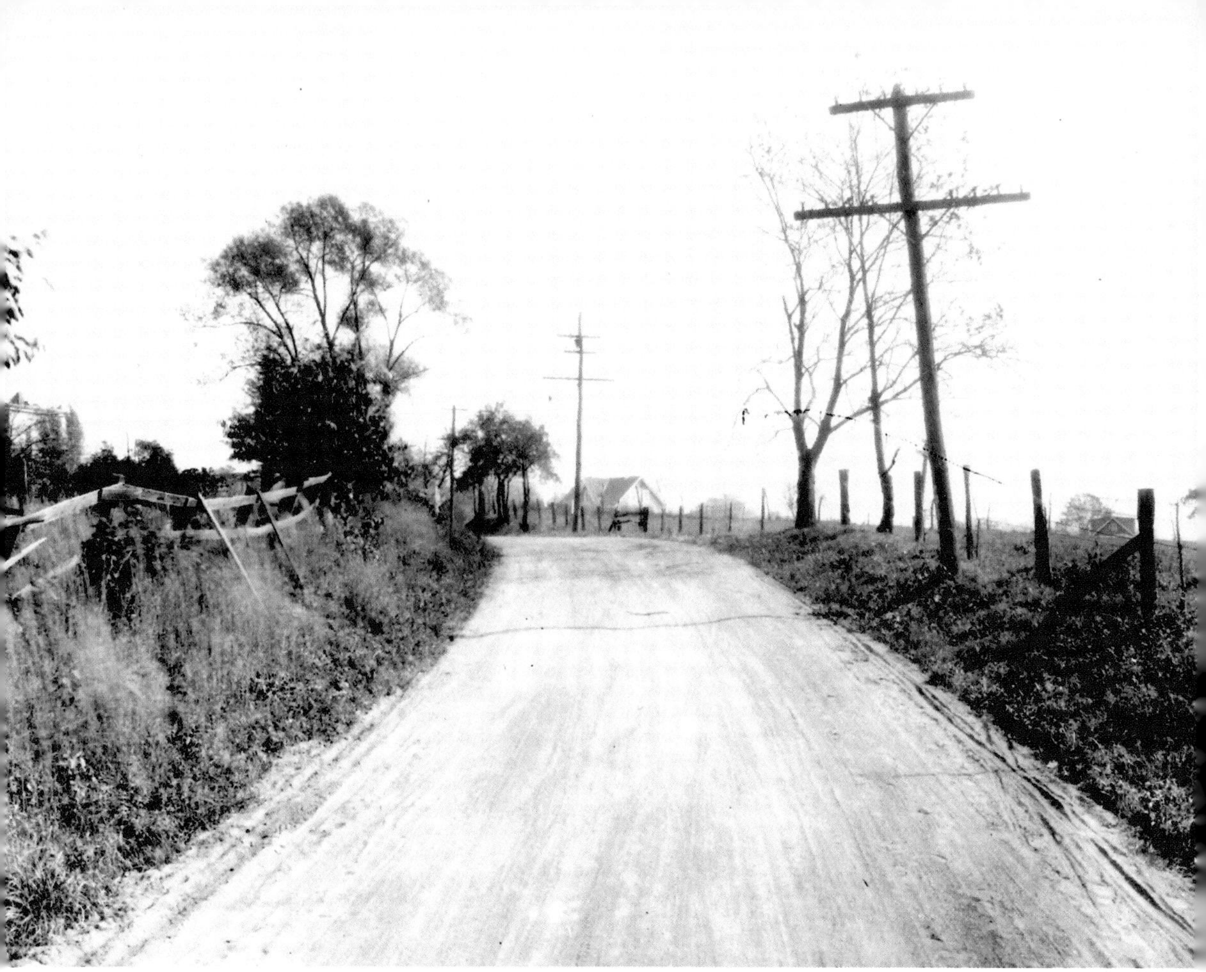

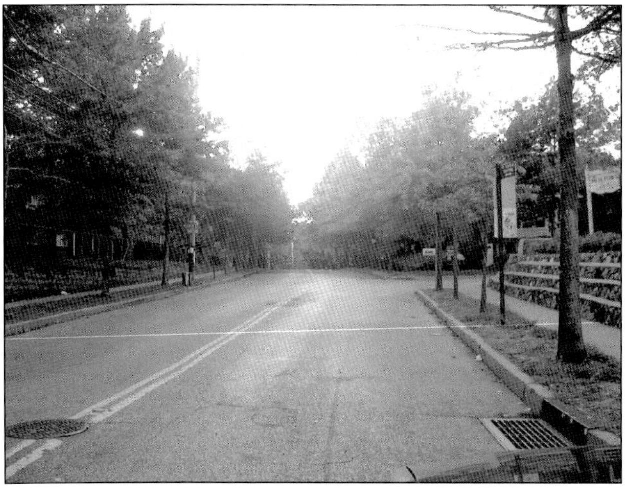

Old Town Road is one of the oldest roads in Staten Island and was first noted in 1677 documents. Like many Staten Island streets, Old Town Road does not follow traditional property lines and is believed originally to be an old Native American footpath. Dating back to about 1662, Oude Dorp was one of the first Dutch settlements on Staten Island. Together with Richmond Road, Old Town Road connected Oude Dorp (Old Town) with newer settlements in Kleine Kill (Fresh Kill) and New Dorp. The approximate location of the original town is near the bend in the road by St. Mary's Cemetery. (Historic photograph courtesy of the Staten Island Historical Society.)

Unlike many Staten Island roads that had to bend and twist to move around hills, streams, swamps, or other obstacles, New Dorp Lane did not have to contend with any of these obstructions. As a result, New Dorp Lane follows an almost straight line from Richmond Road to New Dorp Beach on the South Shore. Before the Richmond County Fair Grounds were built, this "straight run" was used for horse racing by many horsemen from the metropolitan area. The part on New Dorp Lane pictured here provides a view north from the shore toward Hylan Boulevard, with Bungalow Row on the left and Miller Field, originally owned by William H. Vanderbilt, on the right.

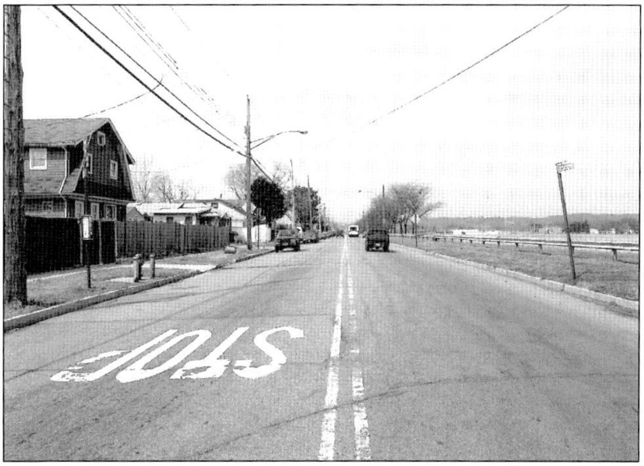

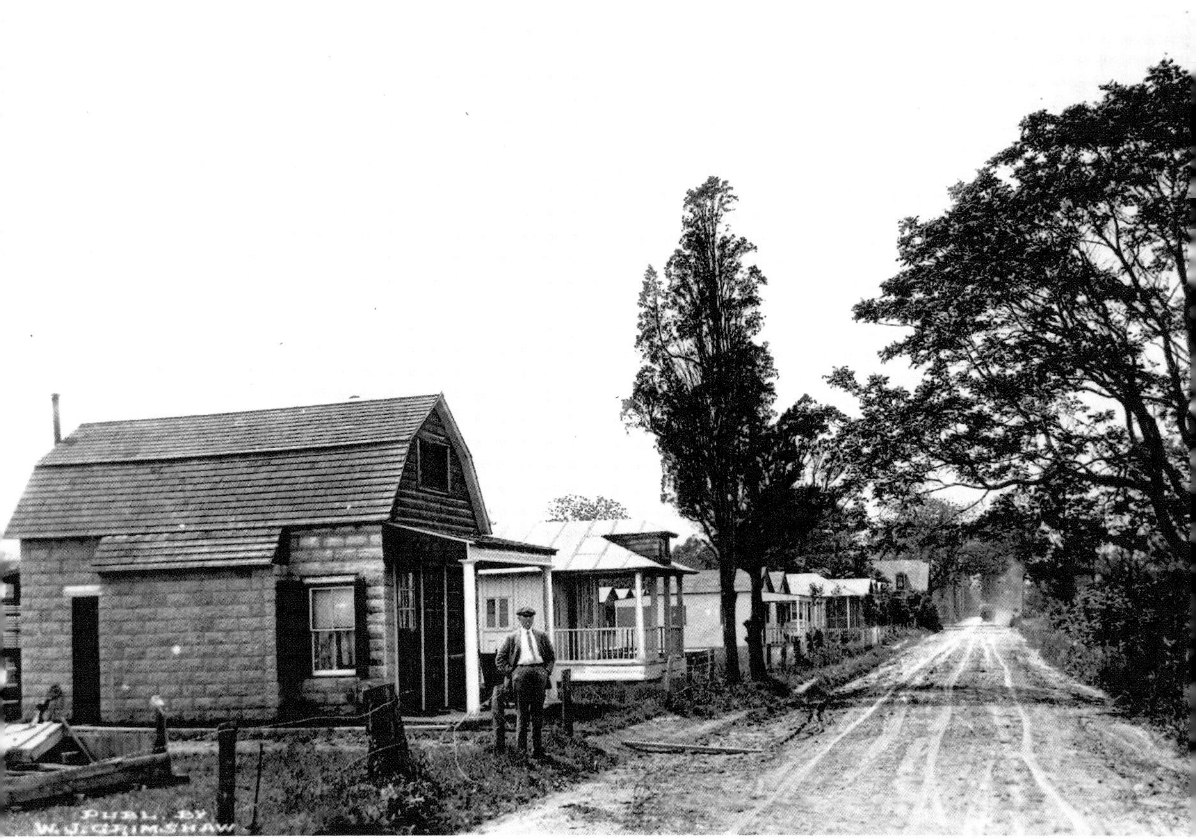

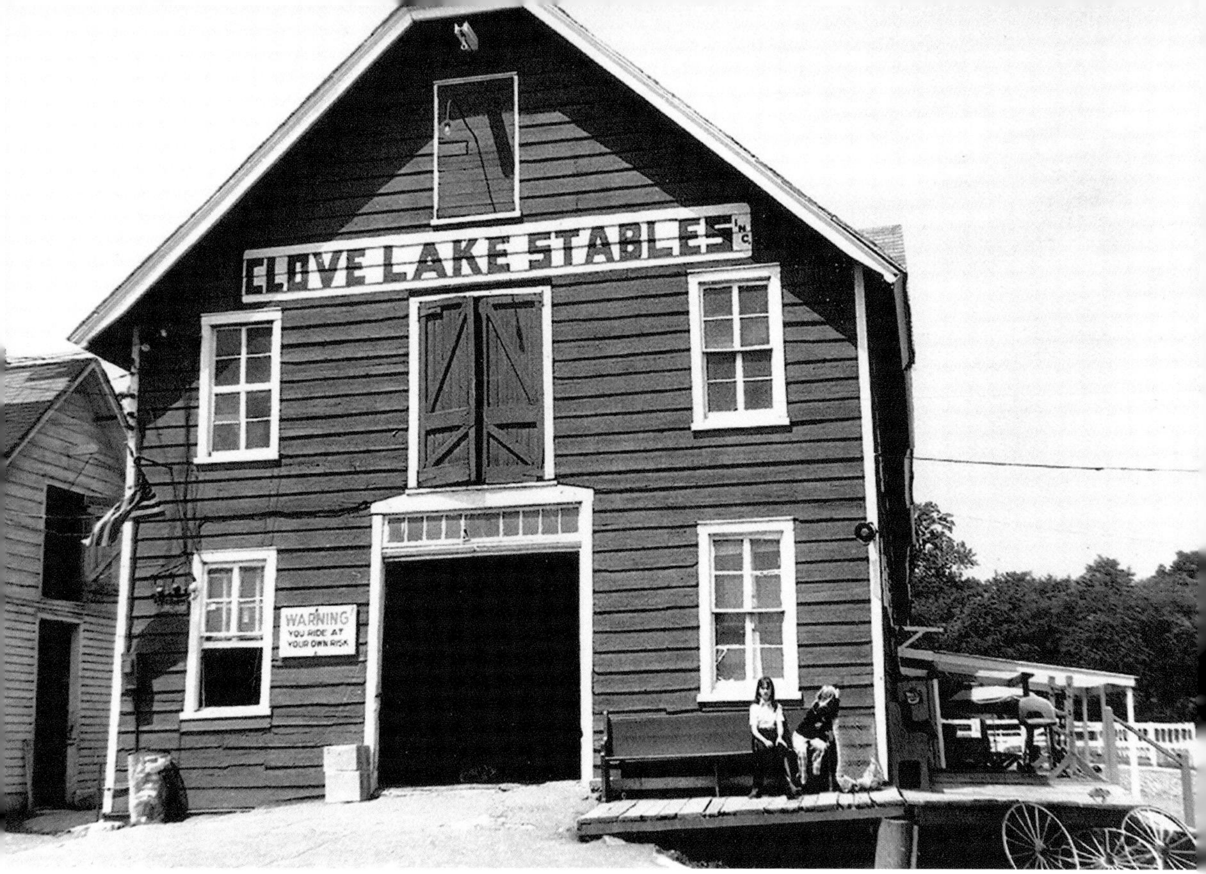

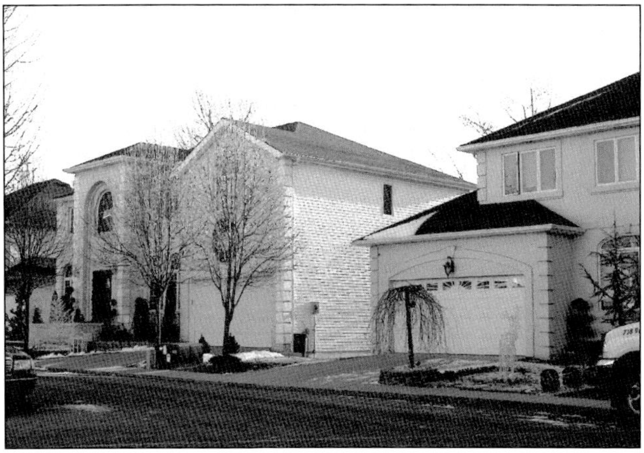

Built around 1840 in West New Brighton, the house and stables were owned by the Franzreb family. The Clove Lake Stables was one of the largest stables on Staten Island, and during the spring, summer, and fall, it offered hayrides and horseback riding over bridle paths in Clove Lakes Park. During the winter, it offered horse-drawn sleigh rides. With the value of property escalating, the stable and surrounding land was sold to a developer in 1983, and 66 homes were built on the eight-acre site.

Howard Avenue was named for Maj. George Howard, who built one of the first estates on Grymes Hill in 1830. Other notables that built estates on Grymes Hill were Suzette Grymes (for whom the hill was named) in 1836, Jacob Vanderbilt in 1847, and Sir Edward Cunard in 1850. Over the years, many of these estates and large houses were razed to build additional residential units. One such home was at 50 Howard Avenue, pictured in this 1922 real estate advertisement. Today the home has been replaced by garden apartments.

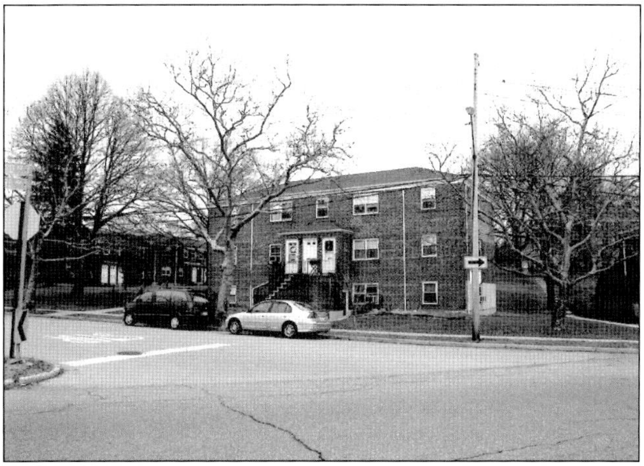

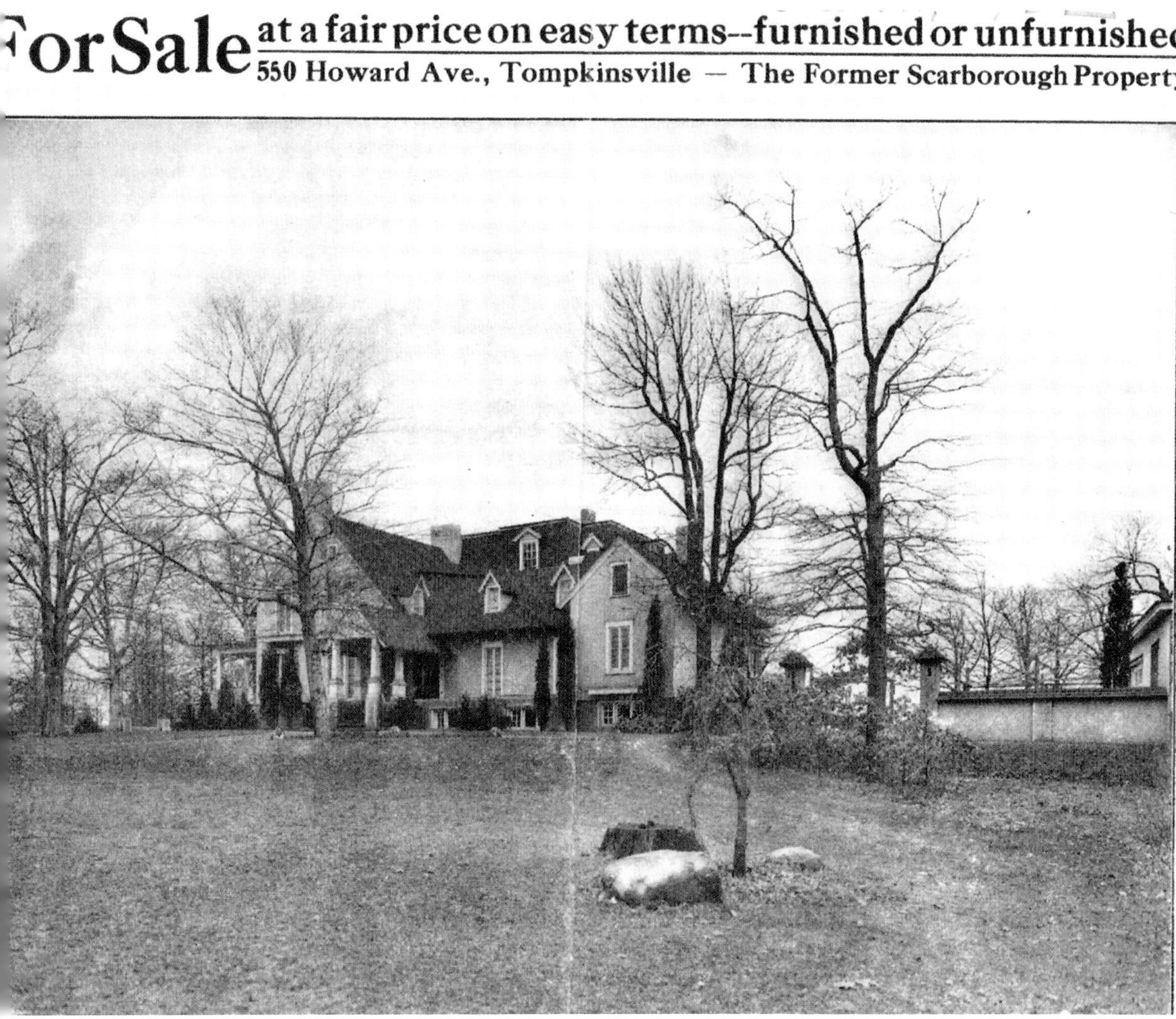

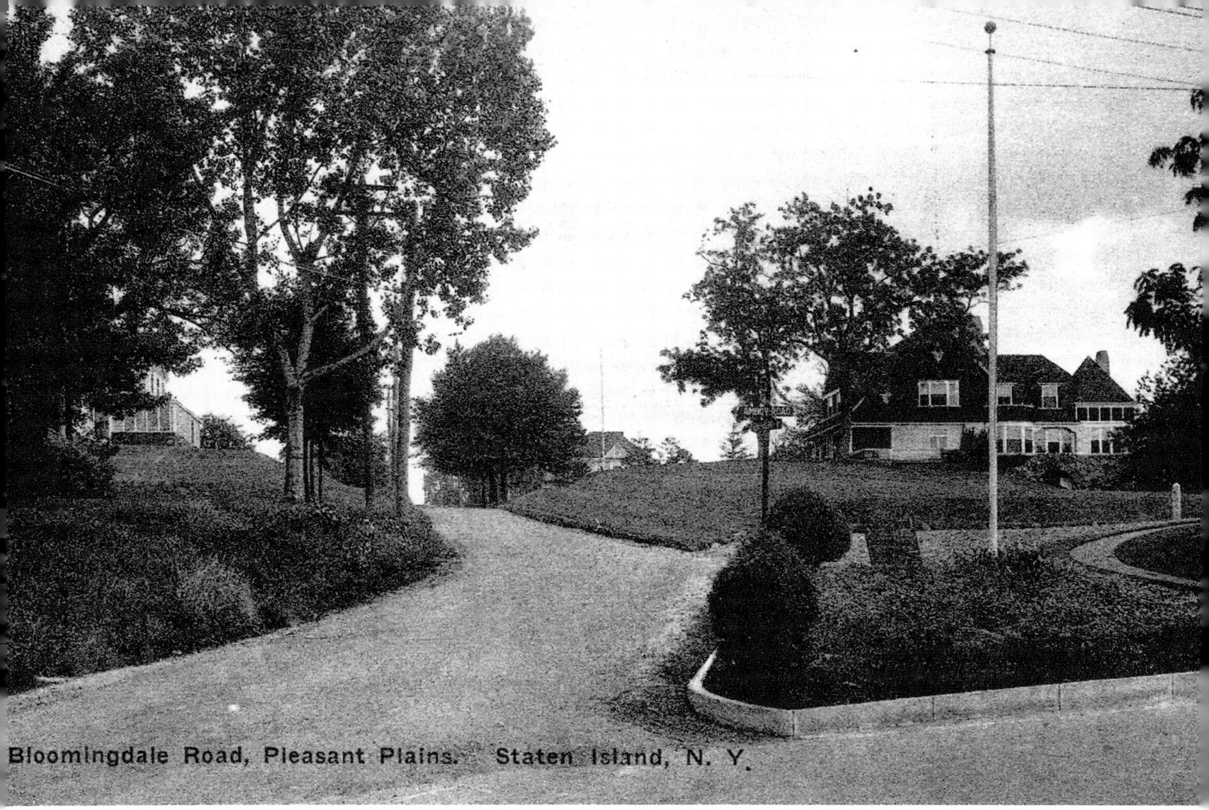

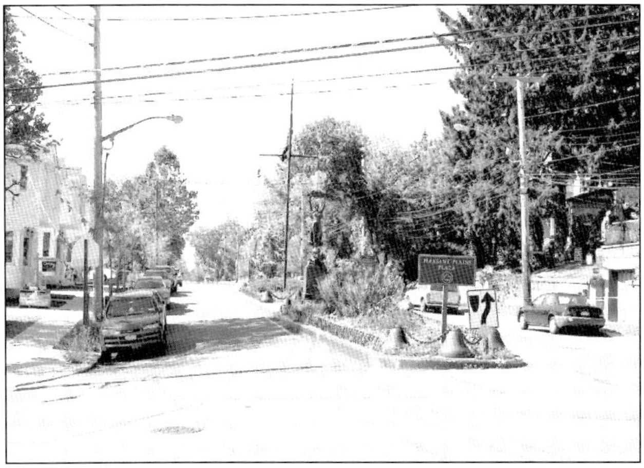

This Pleasant Plains "triangle" became the site for a World War I memorial called Winged Victory. The 10-and-a-half-foot statue, created by Tottenville resident George Brewster, sits on a five-and-a-half-foot marble base that holds the names of 493 World War I veterans from the South Shore. Originally erected in 1923, the statue was knocked off its base in 1974. Stored during repairs, it was stolen and not replaced until 1997, when a replica was erected at a cost of $270,000. To protect it from automobile accidents, a traffic island 160 feet long and 15 feet wide was created.

Chapter 2

SPORTS AND RECREATION

In 1905, the Tottenville Arrows team was formed and later evolved into the Staten Island Stapes and played in the National Football League from 1928 to 1932. The Stapes began as a semiprofessional team, playing their games in Stapleton Park, East Shore Oval, and finally in Thompson's Stadium and played against such teams as the Chicago Bears, the Green Bay Packers, and the New York Giants. The Giants traveled to Thompson Stadium by taking the ferry, a short train ride to Stapleton, and then walked up Canal Street. During their four seasons in the NFL, the Stapes never finished higher than sixth place and played their last games in 1932.

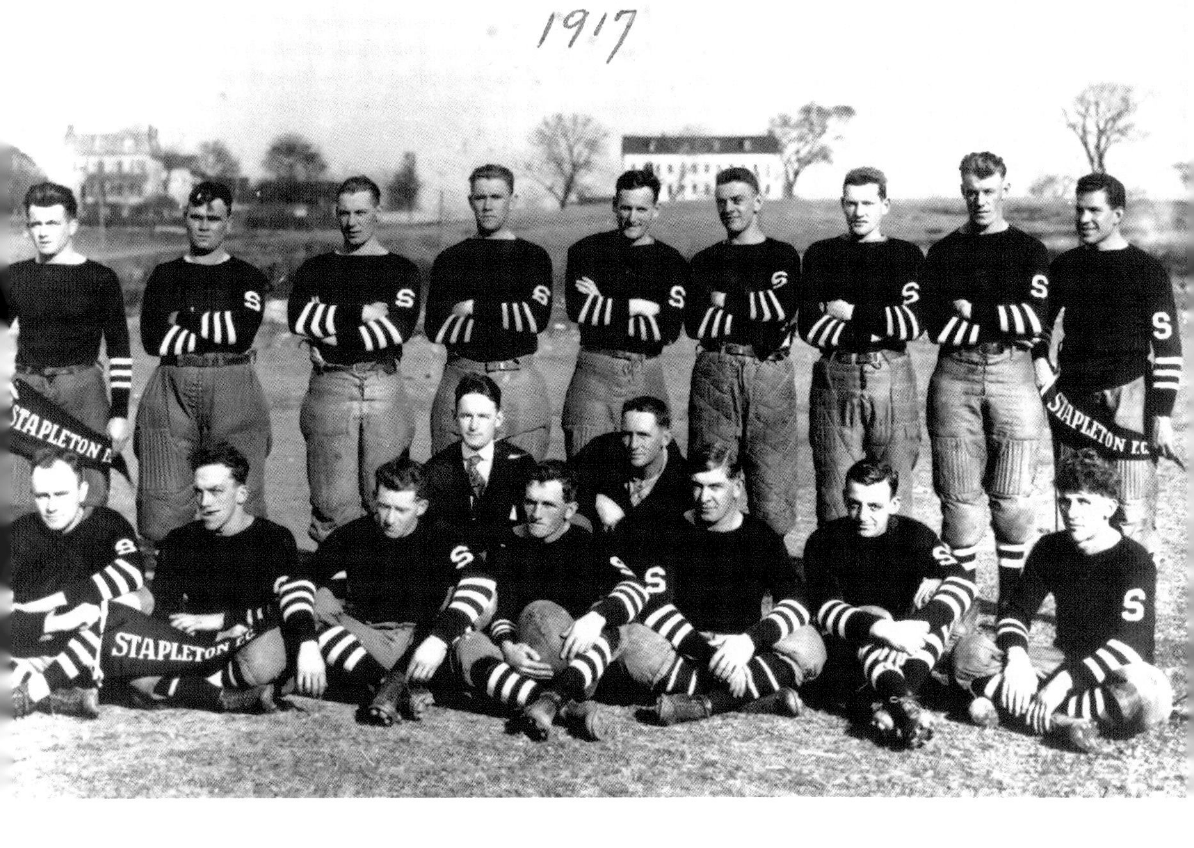

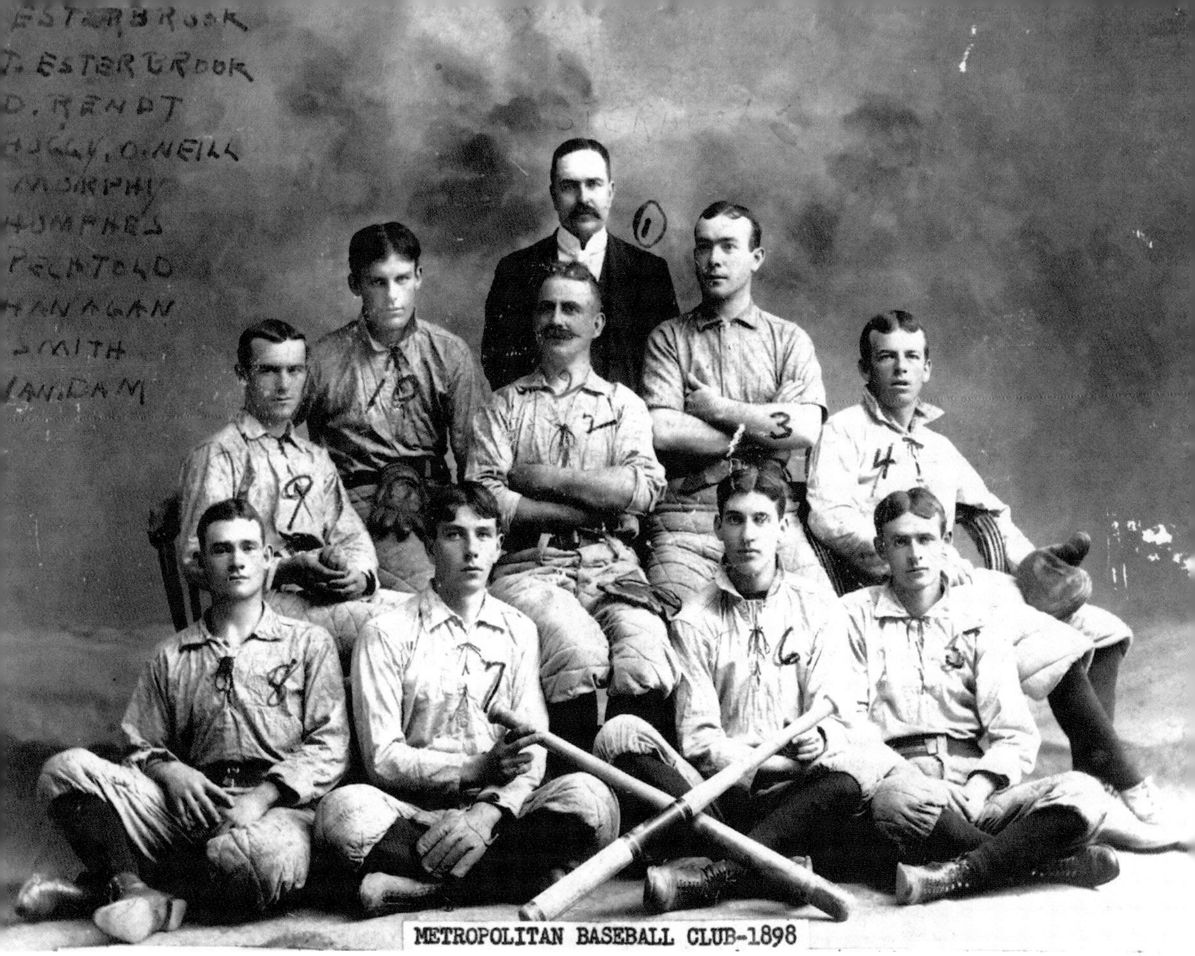

The Mets (Metropolitan Baseball Club), of the American Association, was founded in 1880 and won the association's championship in 1884 but lost to the Providence Grays in the first "World Series." They played in the original Polo Grounds and Metropolitan Park in Manhattan and were moved to a stadium built next to the St. George ferry terminal in 1885. The team was owned by Erastus Wiman, president of the Staten Island Rapid Transit Railroad Company, and in 1887, after two seventh-place finishes, the team was sold and moved to Kansas City. Today a Class A farm team of the Yankees plays in the Richmond County Bank Stadium built near the site of the original ballpark and won the New York–Penn League Championship in 2000, 2002, and 2005 (pictured below).

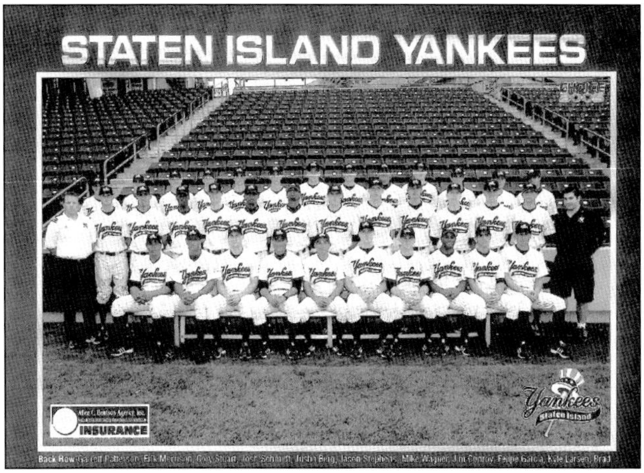

The East Shore Oval baseball field was a popular attraction in the early part of the 1900s. Located on Front Street, between Prospect and Water Streets in Stapleton, it offered spectators a view of the harbor as they enjoyed watching a game of baseball. In 1989, the navy opened a port for ships near the location on the East Shore Oval; however, in a cost-cutting measure just four years later, the base was closed. Until a permanent use is agreed upon, the site has been used by a variety of interests, including a movie studio, warehousing, and courtrooms for the city.

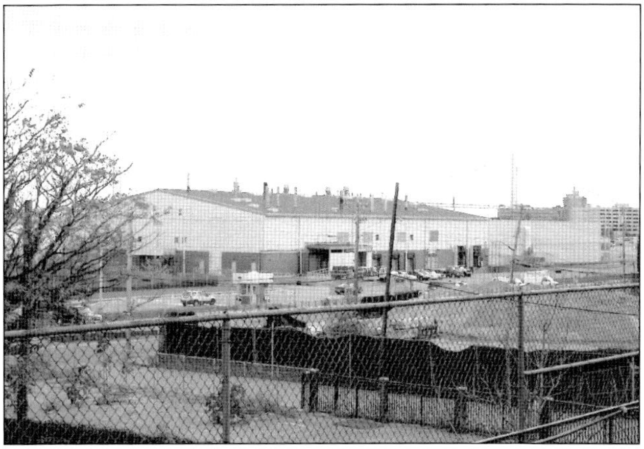

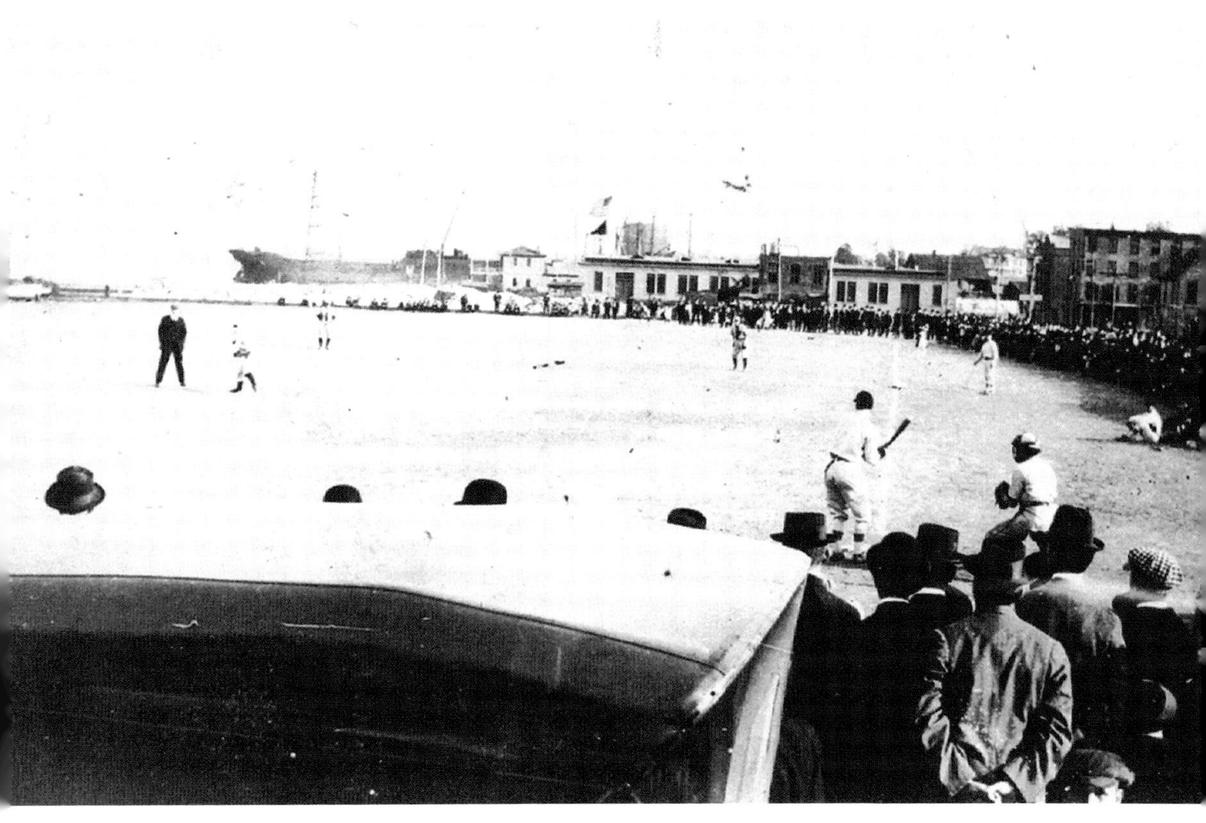

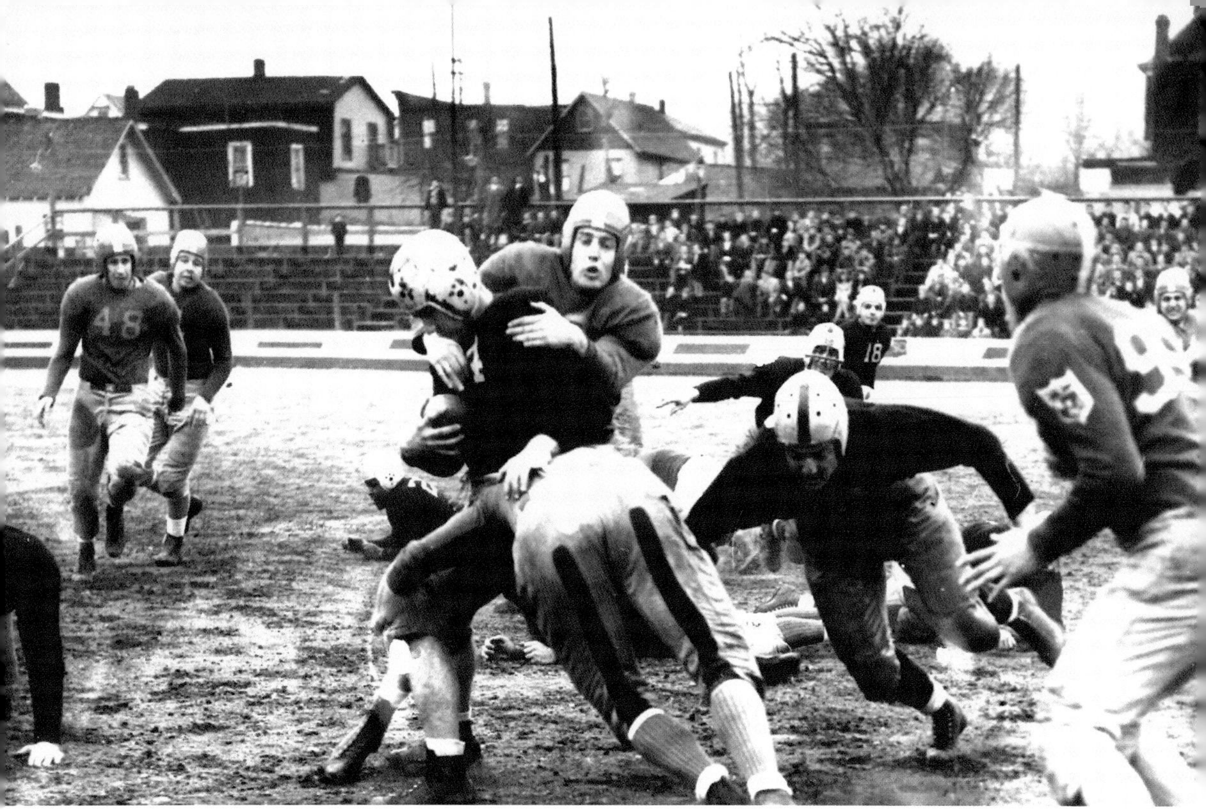

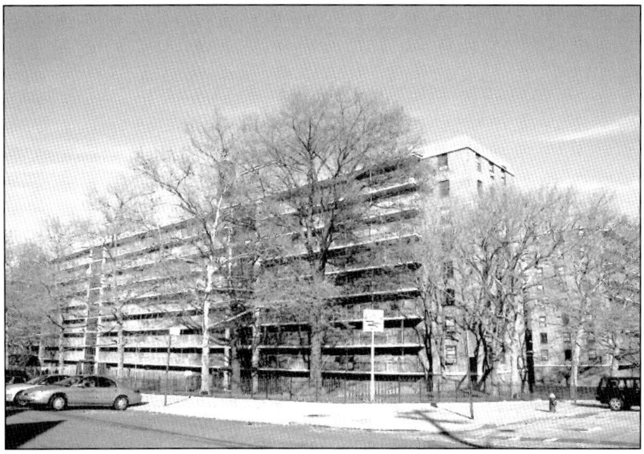

Col. Edward Thompson of Grymes Hill built the 9,000-seat Thompson Stadium because of his love for sports. The stadium, now the site of Stapleton Houses, was the home of the National Football League's Staten Island Stapes. The stadium hosted games against such teams as the Chicago Bears, the Green Bay Packers, and the New York Giants. During their four seasons in the NFL, the Stapes never finished higher than sixth place and played their last games in 1932. The stadium also hosted a wide variety of events in addition to professional football, including baseball, auto racing, and amateur and professional boxing.

Originally part of the estate of Henry P. Delafield in Livingston, five acres were purchased by the Staten Island Cricket and Tennis Club in 1886. The club is credited with bringing lawn tennis to North America and hosted the Eighth National Tennis Championships at its facility in Livingston in 1888. In 1930, the land was purchased by the New York City Parks Department. The city planned to name this new recreational park Livingston Park but were persuaded to name it after Randolph St. George Walker Jr., who was killed in action during World War I. In this 1895 photograph, the Staten Island Ladies Club is hosting an event at the park.

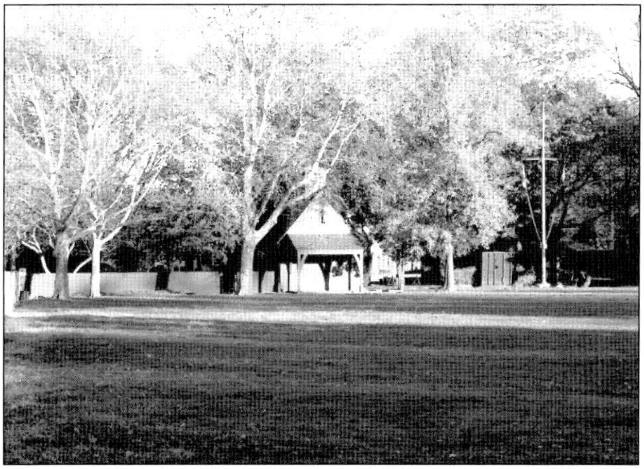

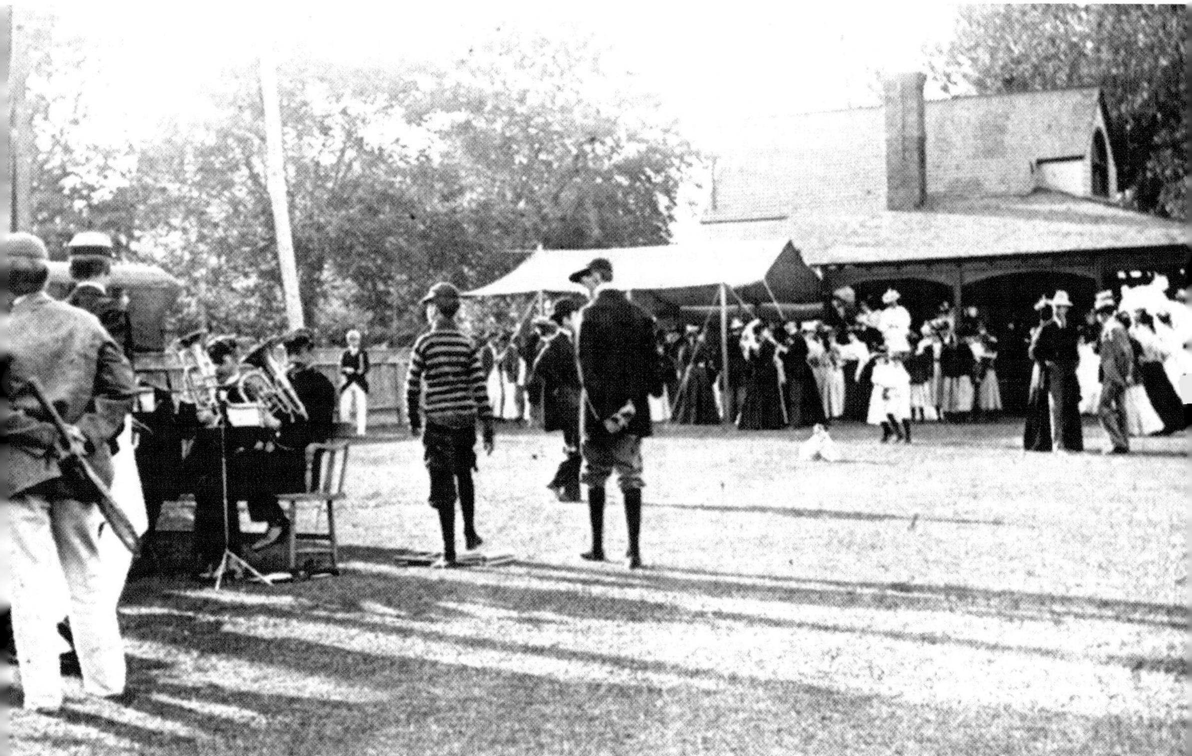

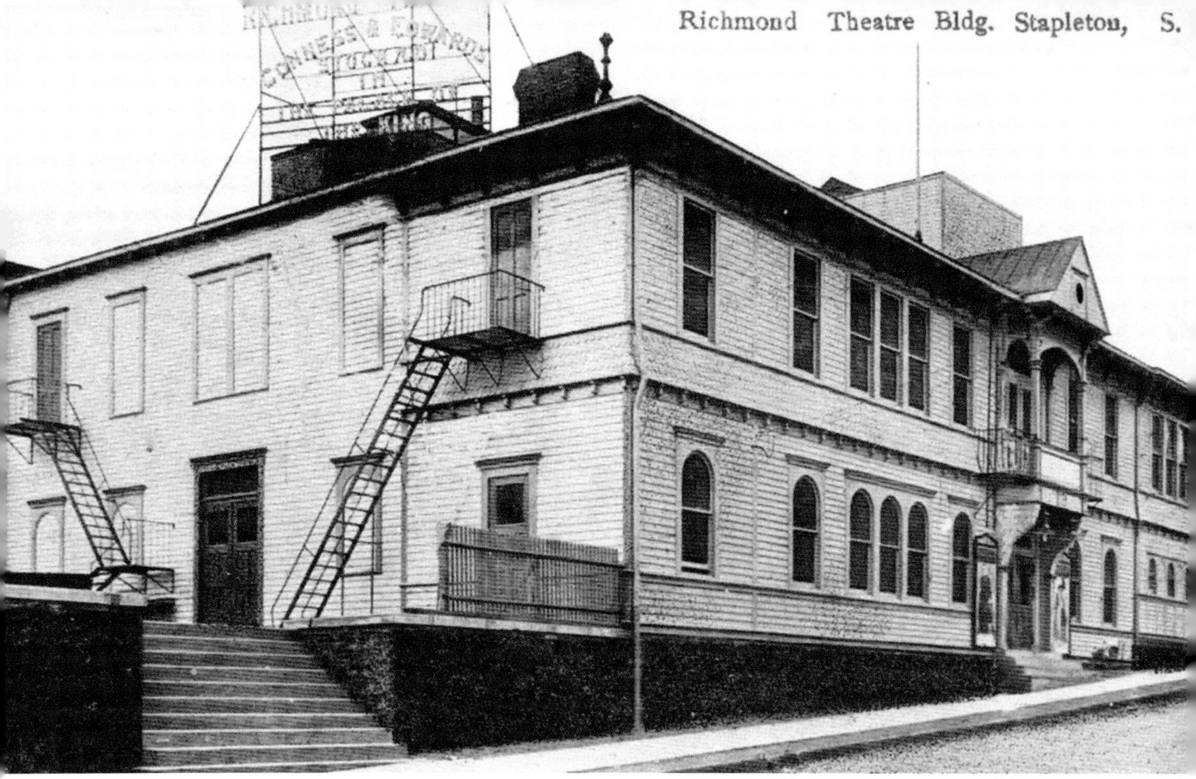

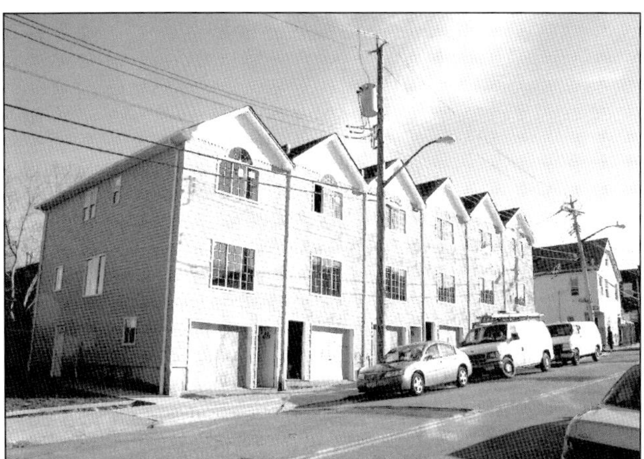

Built in 1890, the Richmond Theatre was known as Turn Hall, a German American gymnasium, located just around the corner from Washington Park (now Tappen Park). In 1906, it became the Richmond Theatre, offering live stage performances of stock companies and vaudevillians. With the advent of motion picture popularity, the theater was converted to a "moving picture house" in the 1920s and continued to provide entertainment for moviegoers until it was destroyed by fire in the 1950s. Recently a developer has constructed six new homes on the site.

In the early 1900s, motion pictures were all the rage, and Staten Island was no exception. In 1915, there were 24 theaters from St. George to Tottenville, with a seating capacity of 10,281. Pictured here is the Palace Theatre in Port Richmond. Built around 1915, opposite Bennett Street on Port Richmond Avenue, this theater was so popular that pictures were held over to accommodate additional crowds. Eventually theater attendance declined, and the building was torn down in 1951 to make way for other businesses.

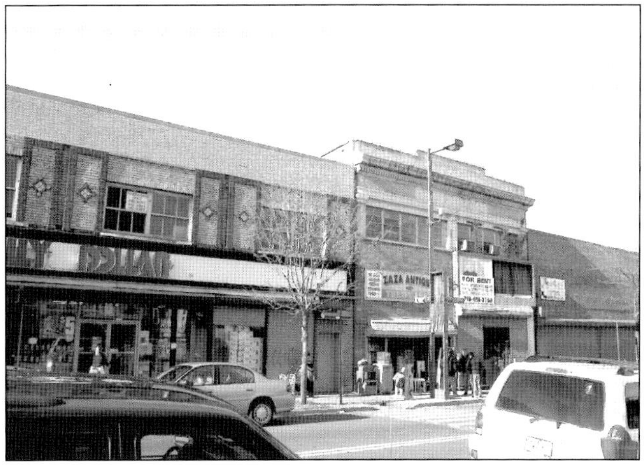

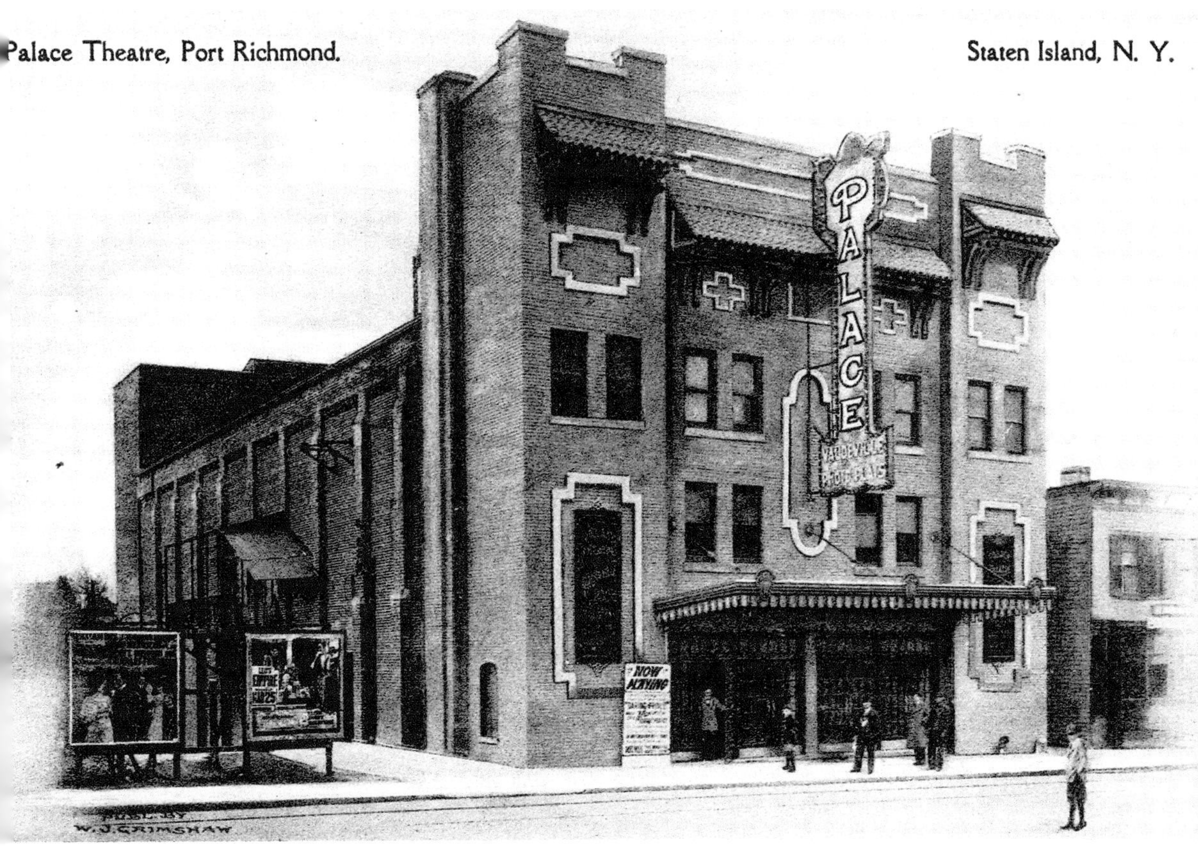

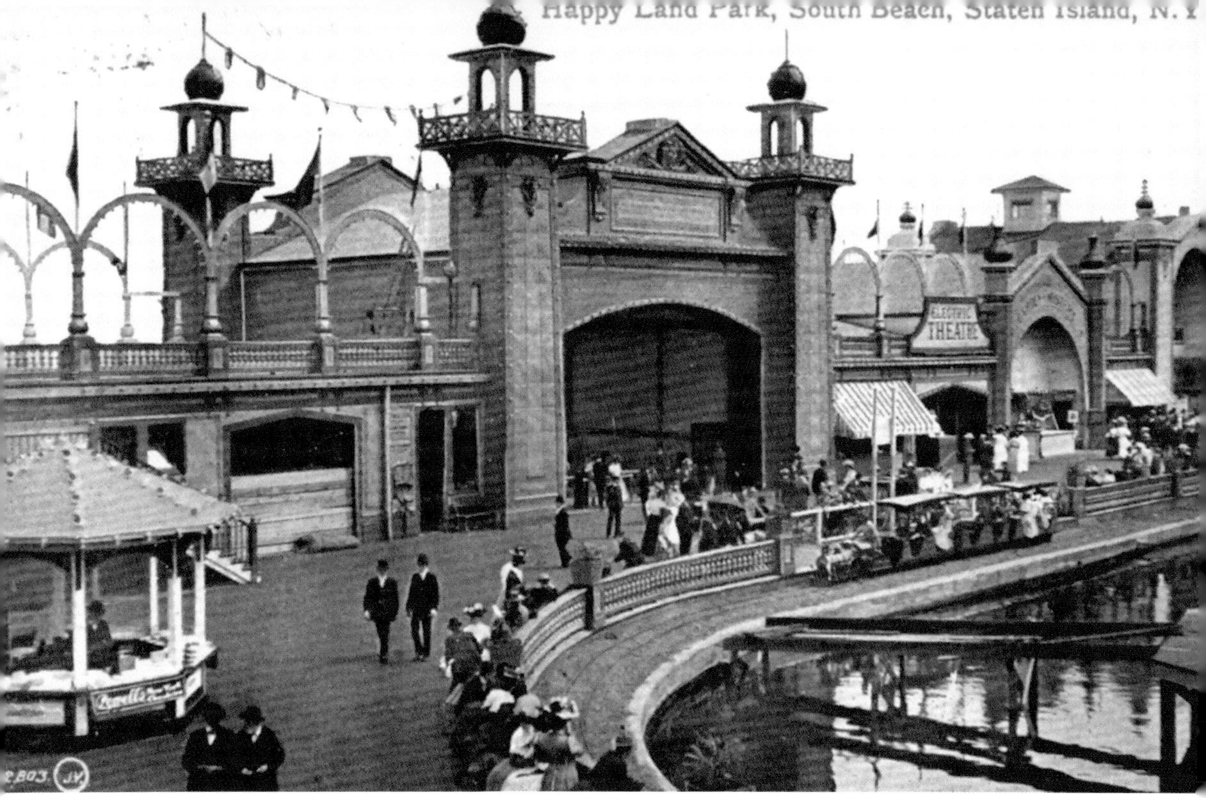

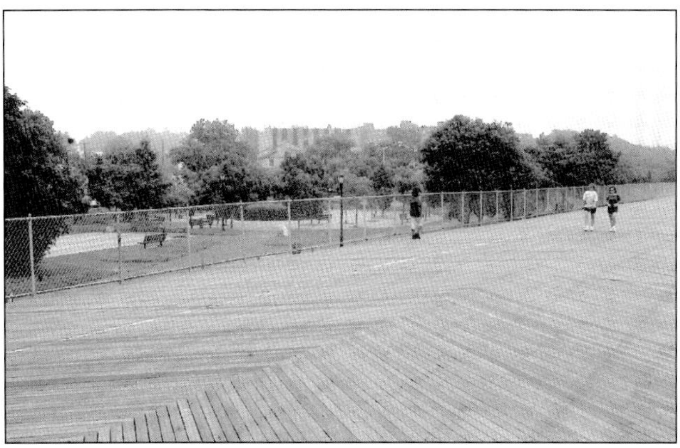

In the early 1900s, a resort and amusement park called Happyland was built, attracting over 30,000 people on opening day. It soon became one of the most popular amusement parks on the East Coast, rivaling Coney Island and Luna Park. The park offered amusement attractions, dance pavilions, shooting galleries, and a carousel. Happyland's large hotel and casinos, complete with vaudeville shows, drew tourists from all over the metropolitan area to come and stay for the weekend. A railroad line from St. George was constructed, and in 1890, boats started running to South Beach from Whitehall Street in Manhattan, and later lines came from Brooklyn. Hit by several fires and increasing pollution, the resort's appeal diminished over time, and the last amusement closed in the 1950s.

During the early 1900s, movies were all the craze, and theaters were popping up everywhere. In 1915, the Palace Theatre opened on Craig Avenue in Tottenville between Main Street and Bentley Avenue. During its 12 years of operation, the Palace was proud and often advertised that it only showed "First Class Motion Pictures." However, the theater was not designed for "talkies," and so after they were introduced, the Palace began losing its audiences. In 1927, the Stadium Theatre opened around the corner on Main Street, showing the "new movies," and in 1928, the Palace closed. Recently developers have built homes on the original site of the Palace.

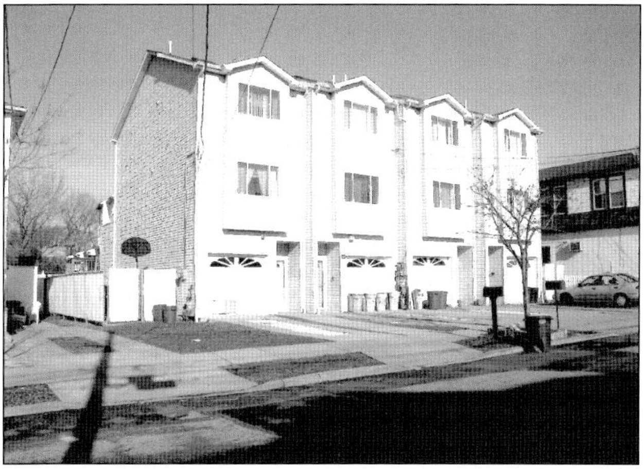

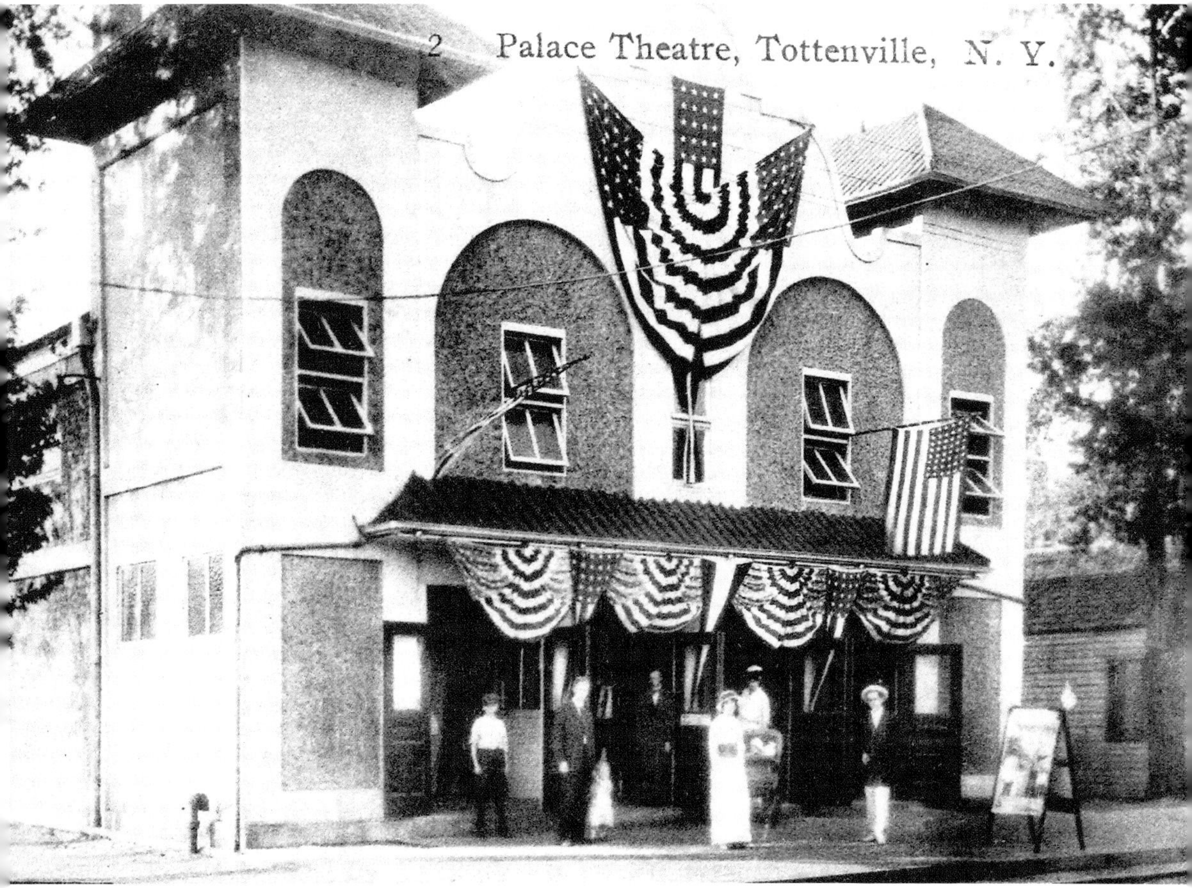

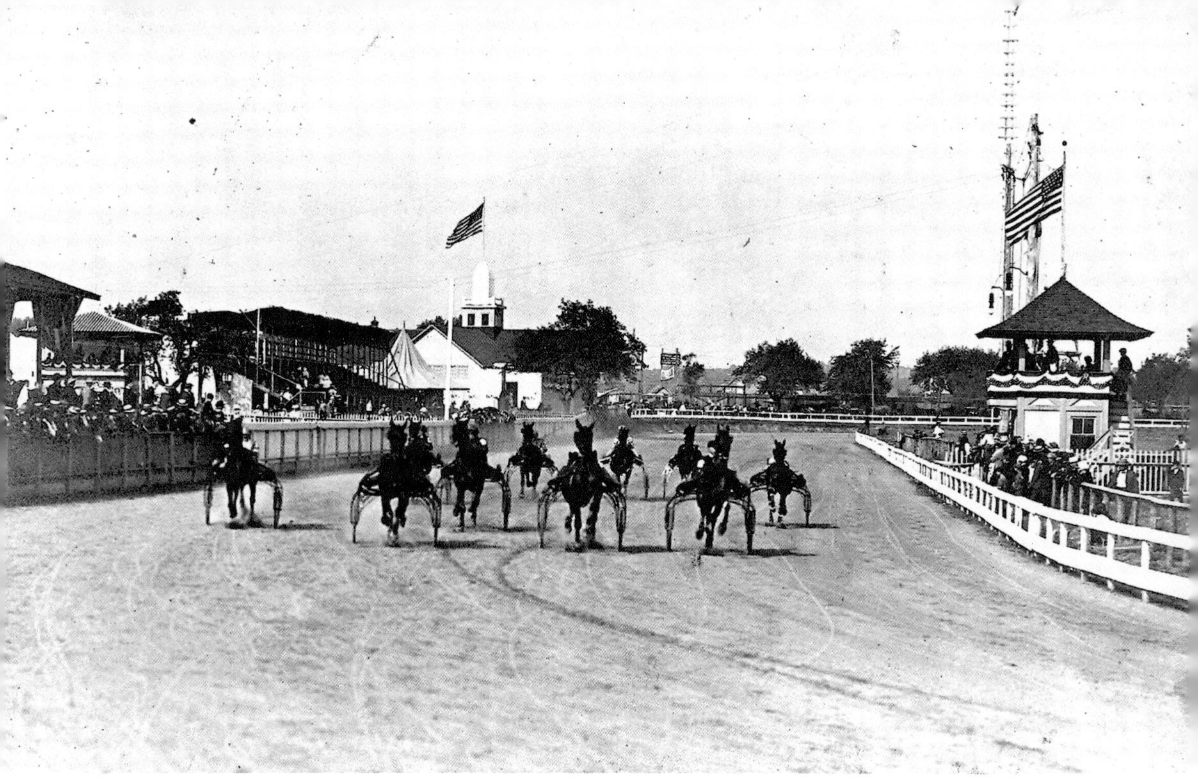

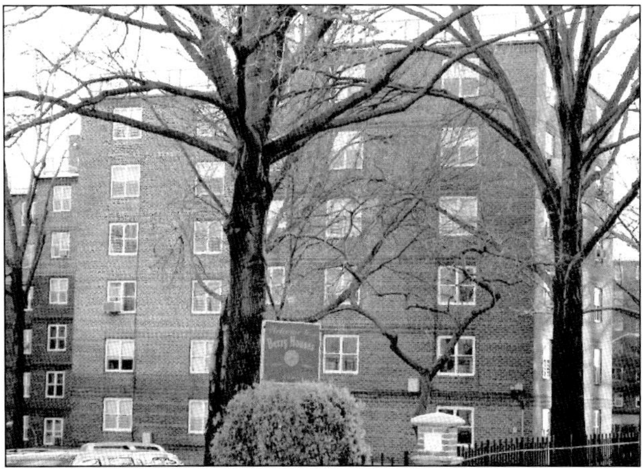

Staten Island was a farming community for most of its early years. Old-fashioned county fairs were a common occurrence. Fairs were held at several locations on the island, dating back to the early 1800s. In the 1860s, the Richmond County Agricultural Society held the annual events on their property along New Dorp Lane, now part of Miller Field. The fair was moved to Staten Island Athletic Club's grounds in West New Brighton after the club disbanded. In 1905, the festivities were moved once again, this time to the new Richmond County Fair Grounds in Dongan Hills. As farming began to disappear, other attractions such as automobile, trotter, and dog racing became more popular. In 1950, the site gave way to the Gen. Charles W. Berry Houses.

In 1896, Midland Beach began attracting residents and tourists alike. Many people traveled by trolley or excursion boats from Manhattan and Newark, New Jersey, on a summer Sunday to enjoy the beaches and boardwalk businesses. Resorts, complete with hotels and amusement attractions, were drawing thousands of people daily. In addition to its hotels and amusement park, Midland Beach had bandstands offering concerts and a long fishing pier. There also was a casino, which, along with gambling, provided vaudeville entertainment for the public. Originally owned by the Midland Railroad Company and later sold to the Hincliffe family, the area began to decline after many attractions were destroyed by fire in the 1920s. Although attempts were made to rebuild, water pollution and the Depression contributed to its final demise.

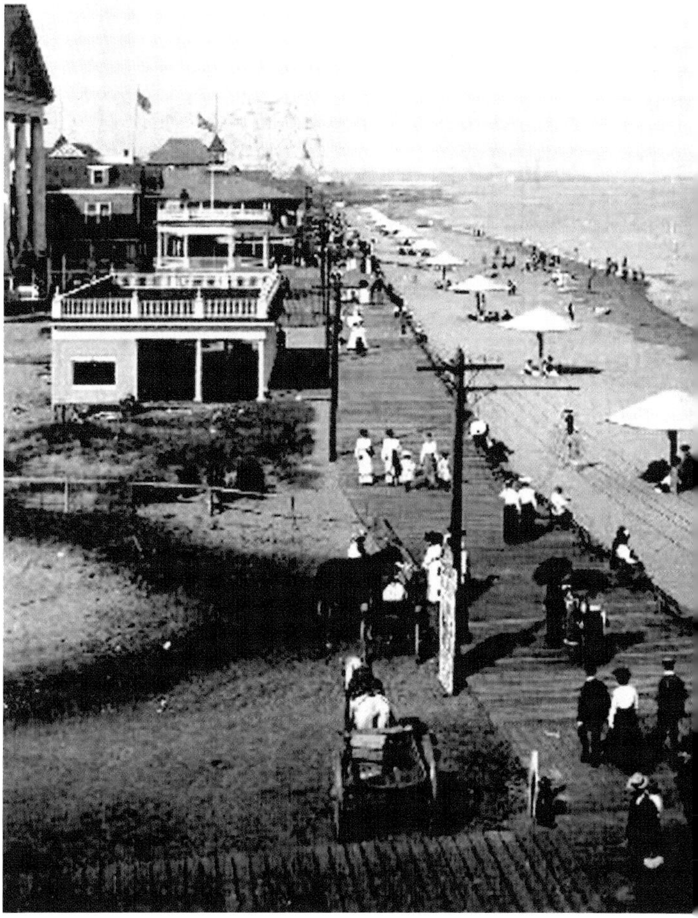

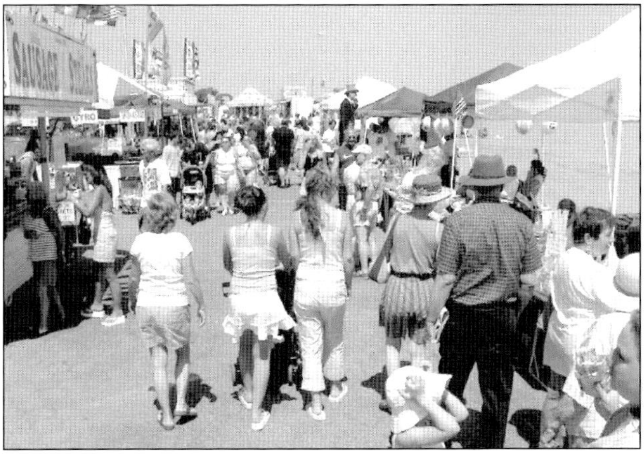

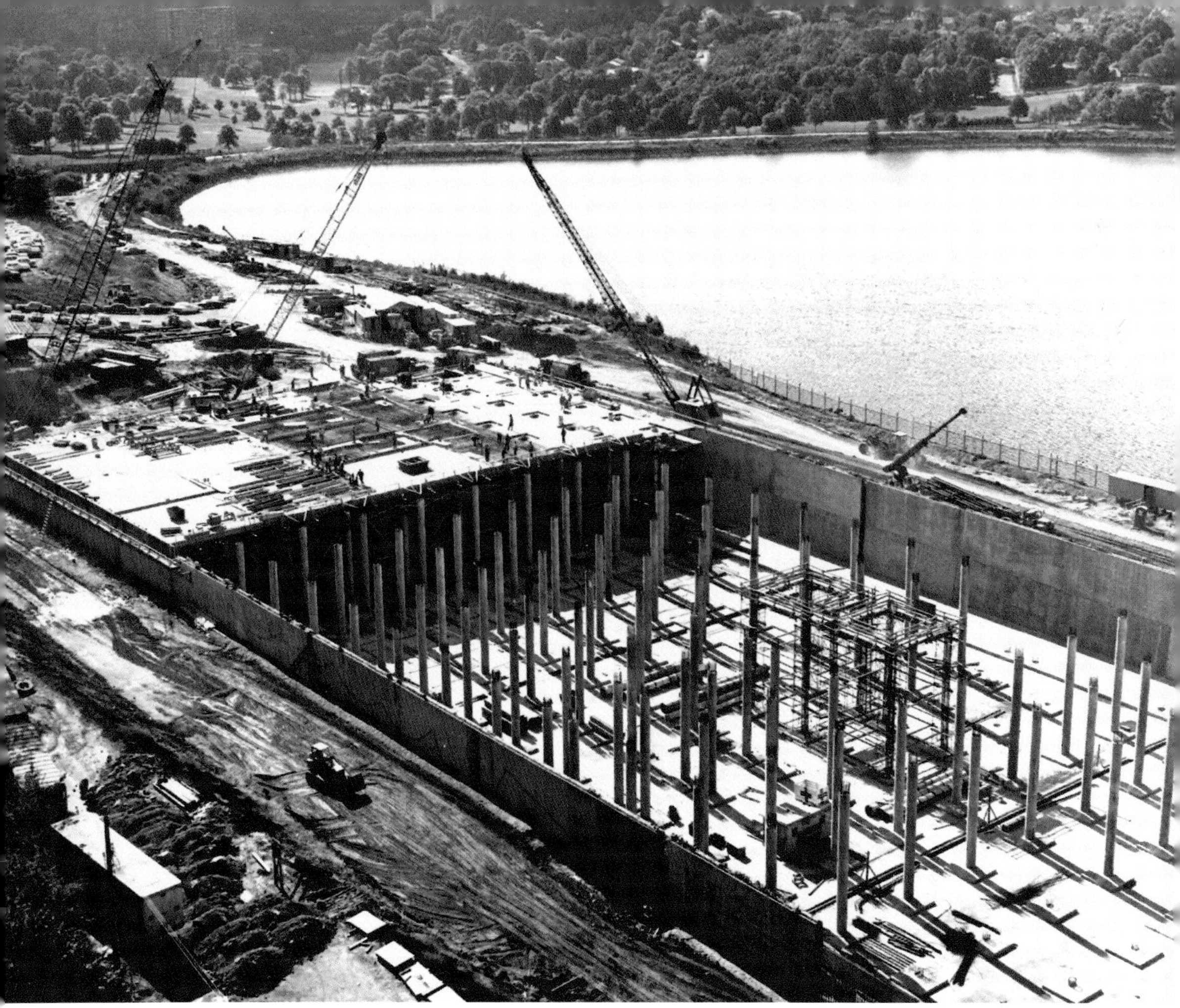

Silver Lake was a popular spot for many Staten Islanders during the summer. In the winter, the lake was used to harvest ice until 1917, when the lake was converted into a reservoir for the growing population. The continued encroachment of a developing island and pollution from seagulls forced the city to build underground storage tanks to protect Staten Island's water supply. Construction on the tanks was completed in 1971, and the 100-million-gallon storage tanks were connected to a new water tunnel the city constructed, providing a safe water supply for Staten Island. The old reservoir was returned to recreational use.

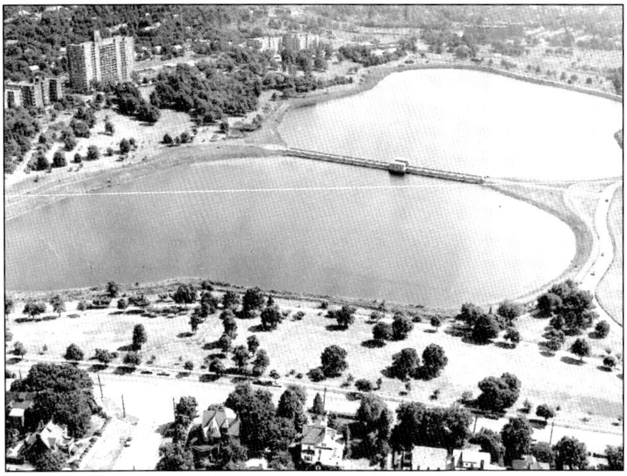

Chapter 3
PLACES OF WORSHIP

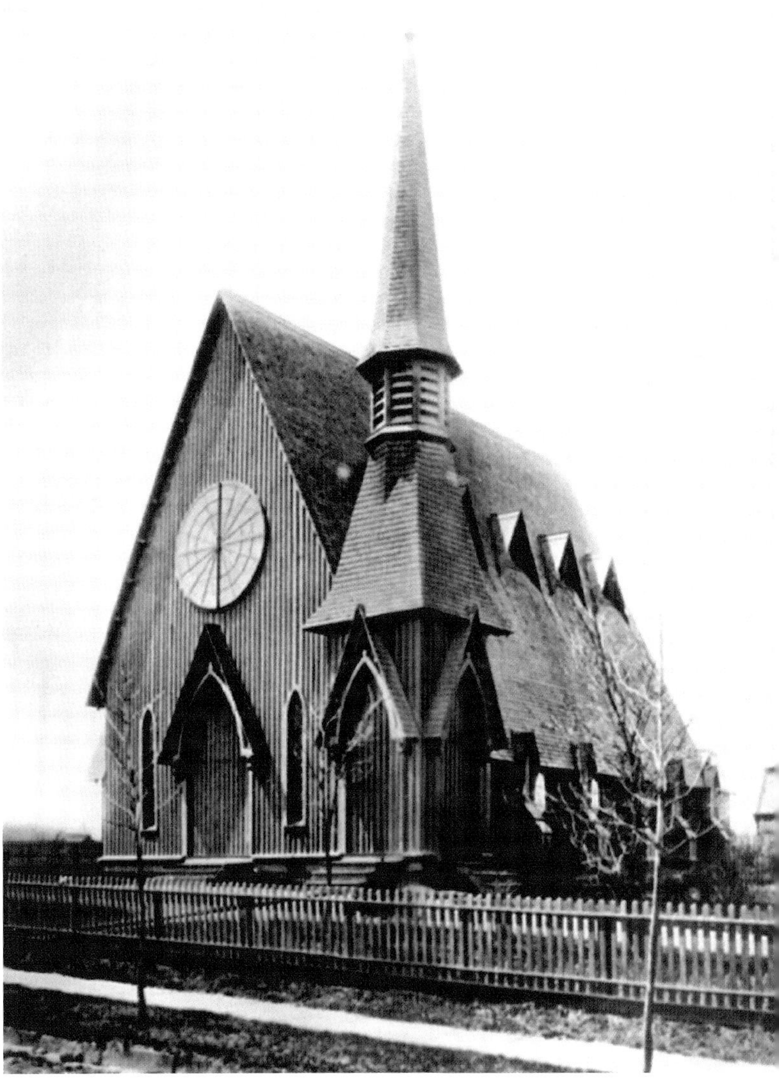

The first Unitarian church was built in 1853 on Cebra Avenue. The building was sold in 1865, and a new one was built three years later on Clinton Avenue. Members of the congregation included the Shaw, Goodhue, Jewett, and Curtis families. George William Curtis would often conduct services for the congregation when a minister was not available. The church collapsed during the Great Blizzard of 1888, and a new church was built on the same site.

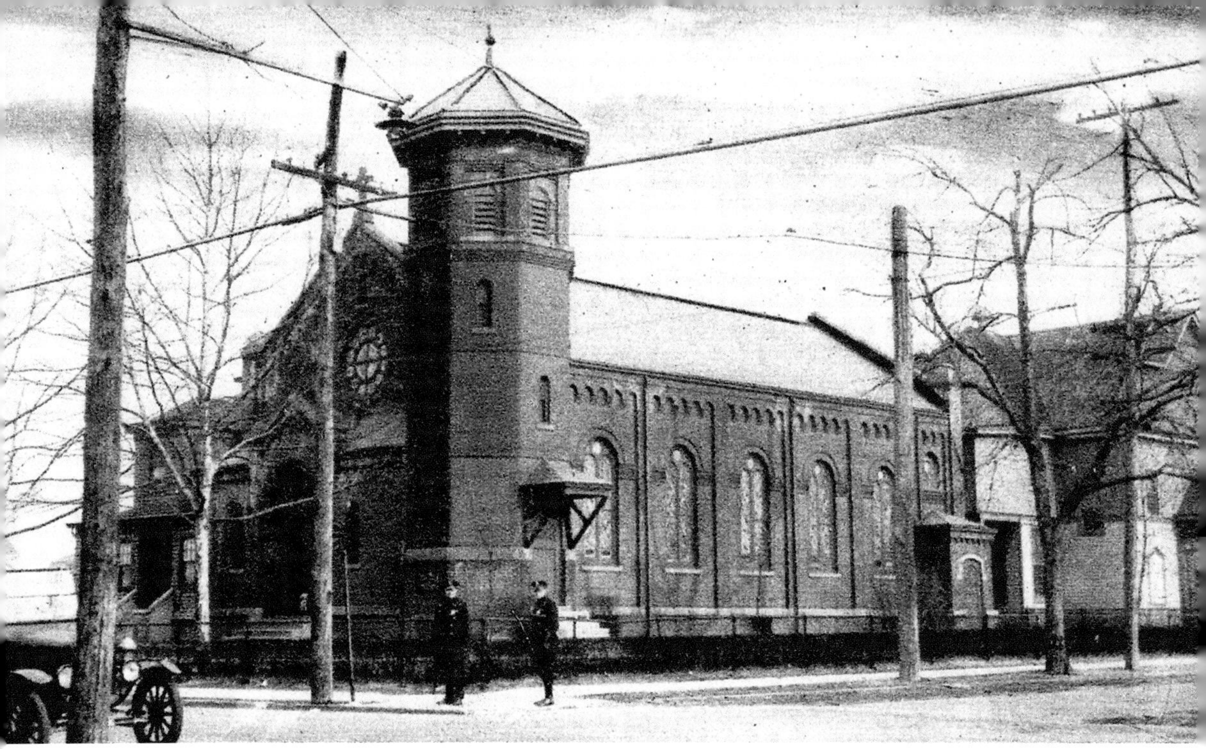

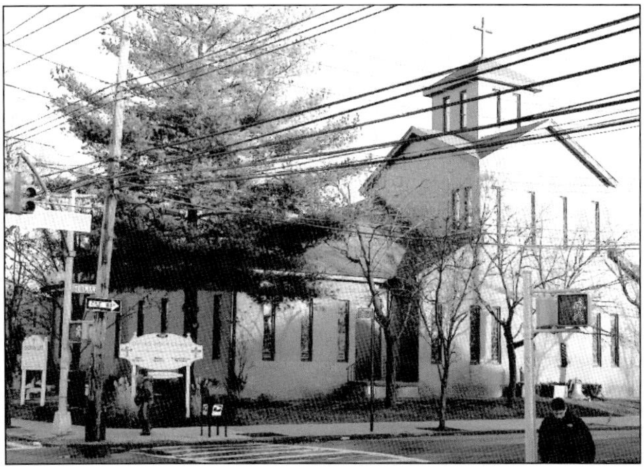

Our Lady Help of Christians (Tottenville) was built in 1898. Until 1916, it was the only Catholic church along the South Shore, with its parish extending all the way to Eltingville when Our Lady Star of the Sea was established. Prior to 1890, Catholics would travel often by walking to St. Joseph's Church in Rossville. The church's basketball team gained prominence when it won the city, state, and national Catholic Youth Organization Championships in 1945. Two members of this team were drafted by the NBA: John Brown (Clemson University) and John Snee (Georgetown University), but both played in the National Industrial Basketball League (NIBL) instead. The present church was built around 1985, after the original was destroyed by fire.

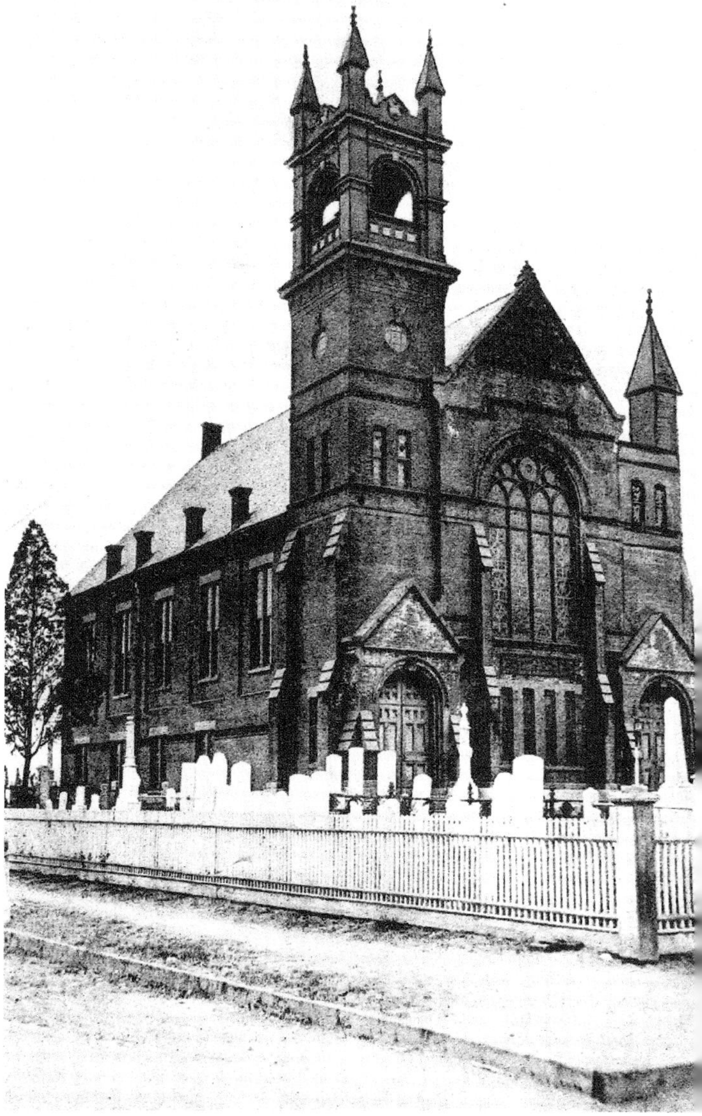

As the Methodist population in Westfield continued to grow, a larger meeting place was needed. In 1841, they built the Bethel Methodist Episcopal Church in Tottenville at the intersection of Amboy Road and present-day Bethel Avenue. Until that time, they met in the Tabernacle on Amboy Road near Richmond Valley. The Tottenville church was rebuilt twice, the last time was in 1886 after a fire. Eventually the congregation outgrew the church, which led to the construction of St. Paul's Methodist Episcopal Church in Tottenville. Although dedicated in 1856, St. Paul's Methodist Episcopal was not built until 1883.

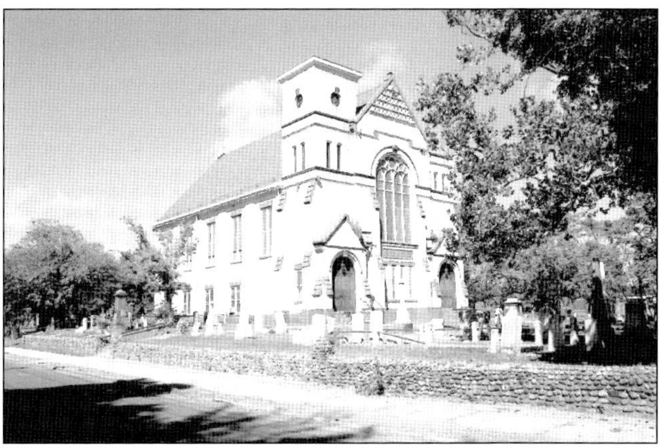

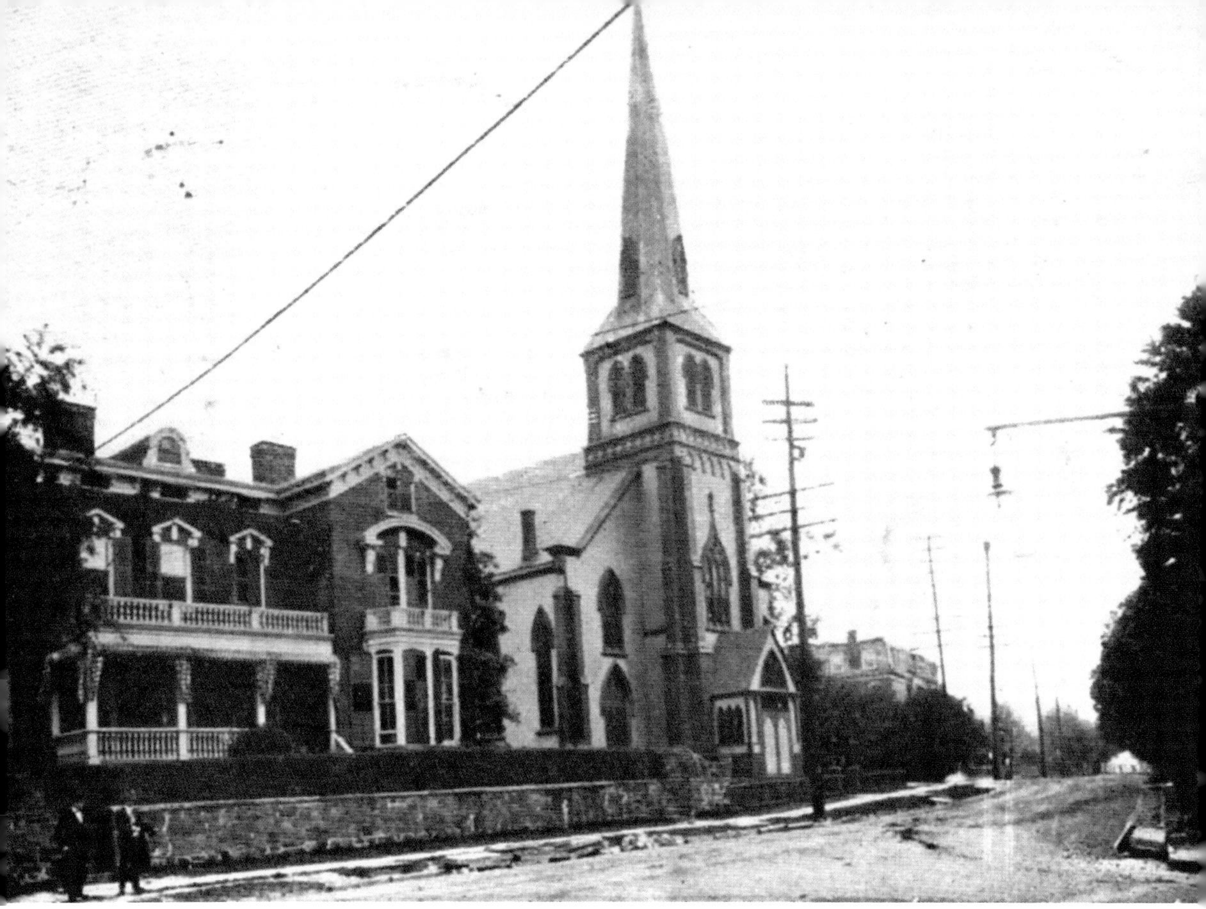

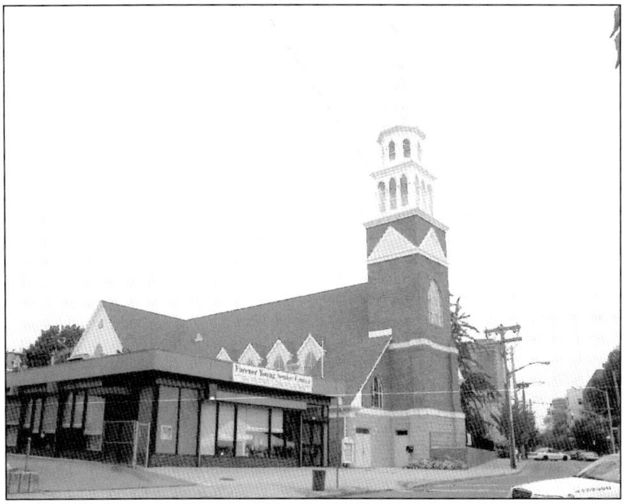

The Reformed Dutch Church of Tompkinsville was originally built in 1823 on a tract of land donated by Daniel Tompkins. In 1864, a new church was built at St. Mark's Place, and from this commanding point, its steeple could be seen by boats entering the upper bay of New York's harbor. Now known as the Brighton Heights Reformed Church, the building was destroyed by fire during a restoration project in 1996. Four years later, in March 2000, the rebuilt church was opened for services.

The first Catholic church on Staten Island opened in New Brighton in 1839 in a remodeled factory on Richmond Terrace. By the early 1840s, the present church was built at 53 St. Mark's Place, land that had been donated by the New Brighton Association. The "Cardinal's Tower," to the rear of the church, was named for John Murphy Cardinal Farley, who spent time at St. Peter's during the early 1870s. He had gone on to be named archbishop of New York in 1902 (the year the tower was built) and elevated to cardinal by Pope Pius X in 1922. The tower quickly became a familiar site to passengers on the ferry crossing the bay from Manhattan.

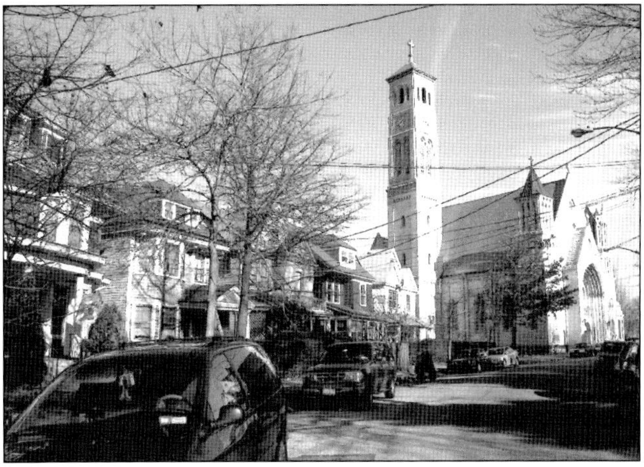

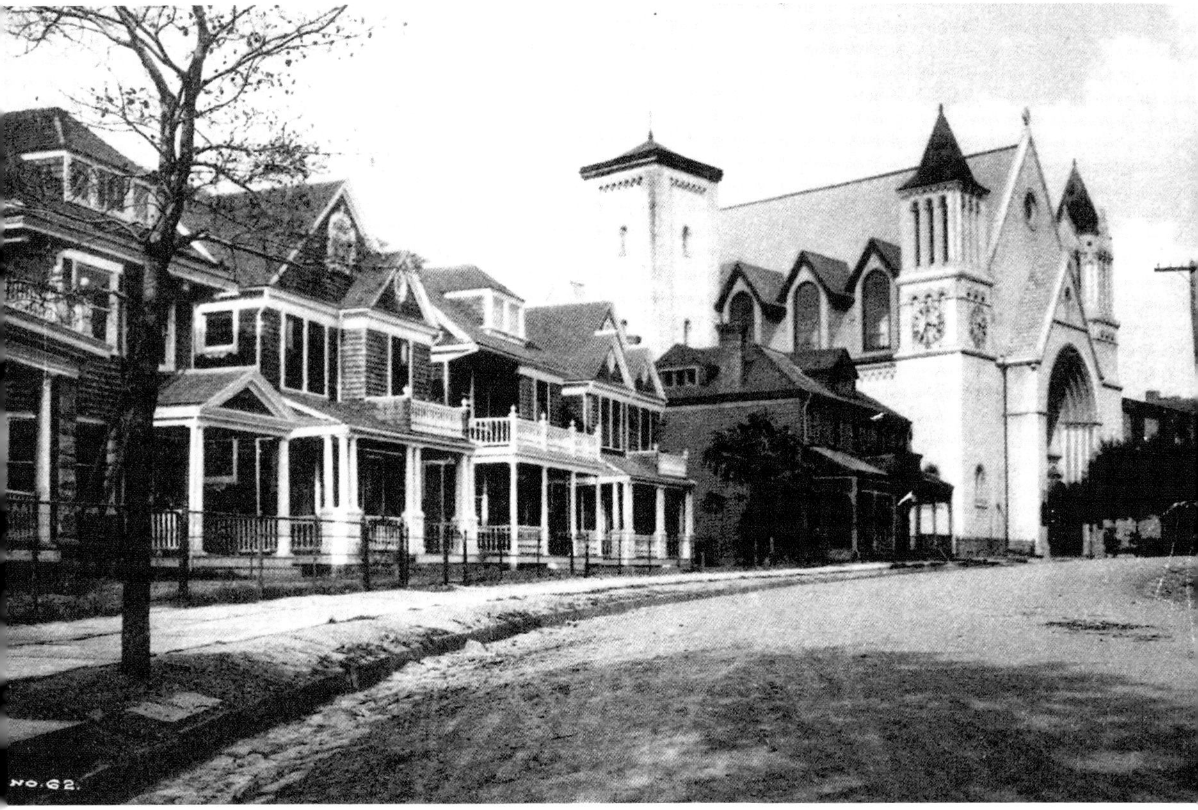

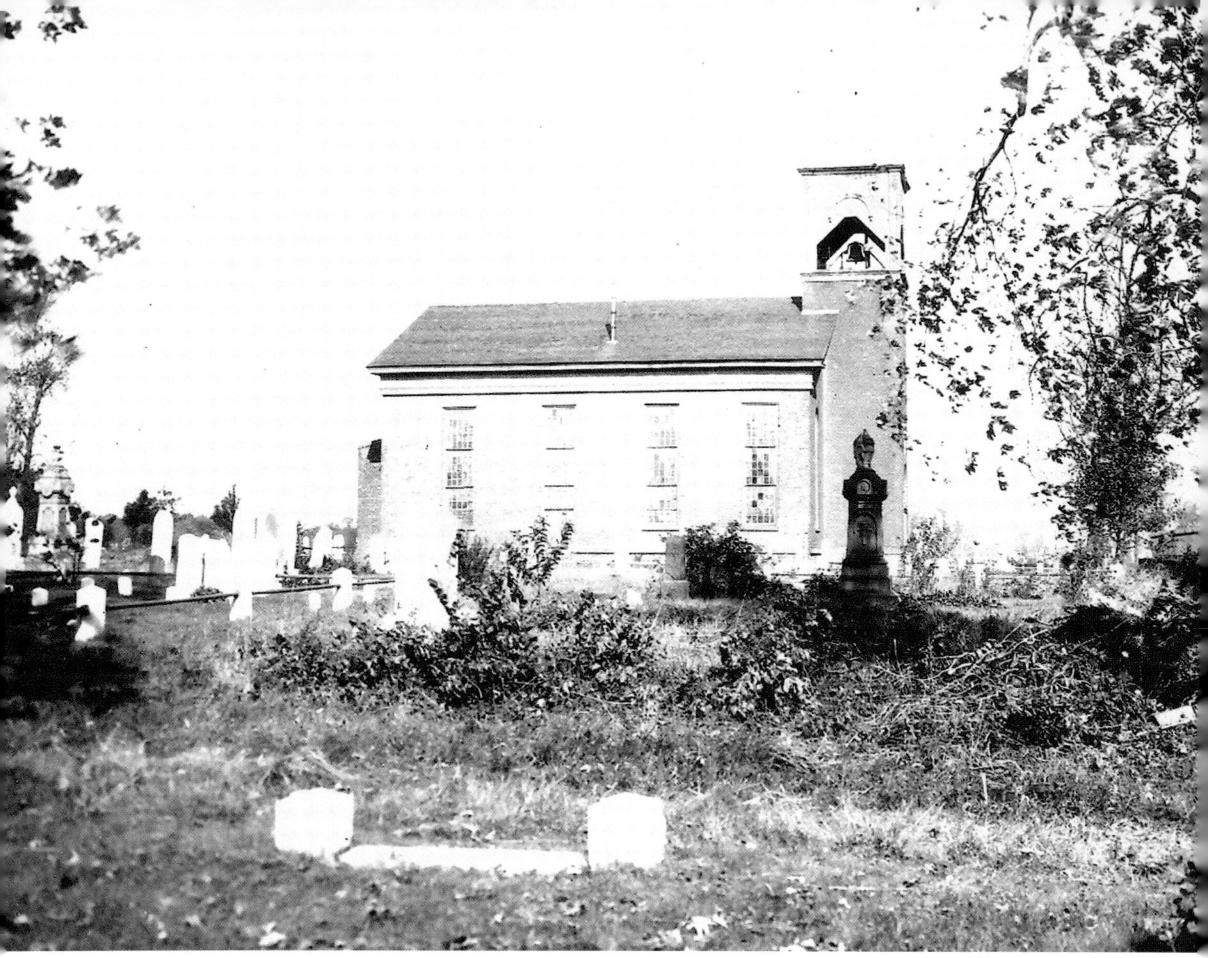

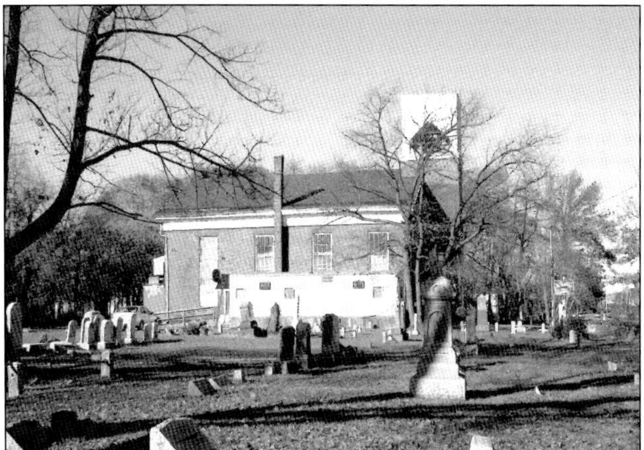

The Asbury Methodist Church (1970 Richmond Avenue) was constructed in 1802 as the Methodist Episcopal Church of Northfield. In 1849, it was renamed for Bishop Francis Asbury, the first missionary sent to America by John Wesley. His first sermon was given on Staten Island at the home of Peter Van Pelt in 1771, and he went on to become the founder of American Methodism. Although he did not live on Staten Island, he visited here frequently to preach. The front of the church was rebuilt in 1878, the same year the tower was added. The church became a city landmark in 1967 and today is home to Son-Rise Interfaith Charismatic Church.

The Moravian Church, constructed at the intersection of Richmond and Todt Hill Roads at New Dorp in 1763, was the first Moravian church built on Staten Island and the last house of worship built before the Revolution. The structure functioned as the meeting place for worshipers as well as home for the minister. After a new church was built in 1845, the original church was moved to its present location behind the new church and became the cemetery's offices. It was not until the late 1800s that other Moravian churches were built on Staten Island. In 1873, the Moravian Castleton Hill was built on Victory Boulevard, and in 1896, a third Moravian church was built in Great Kills.

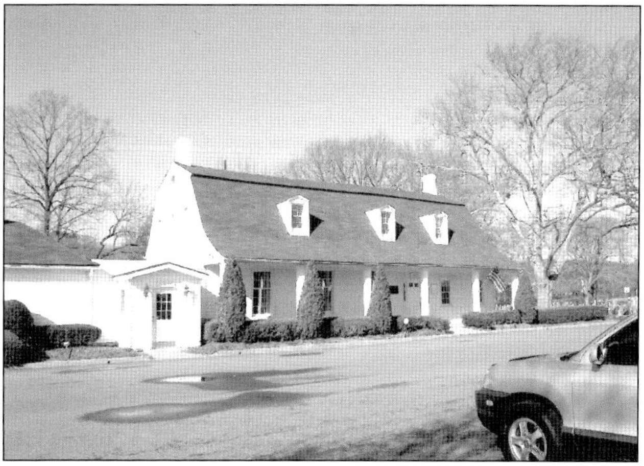

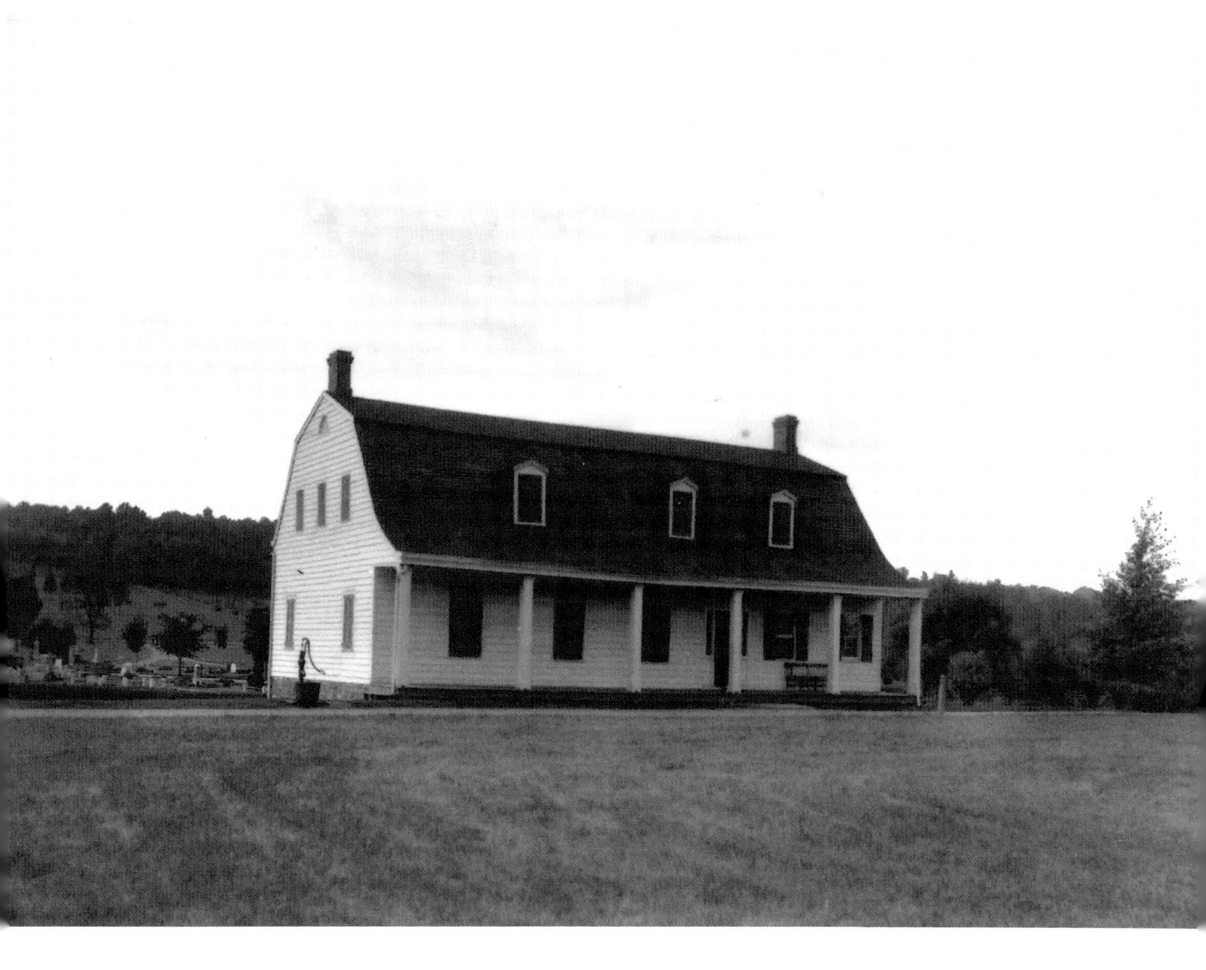

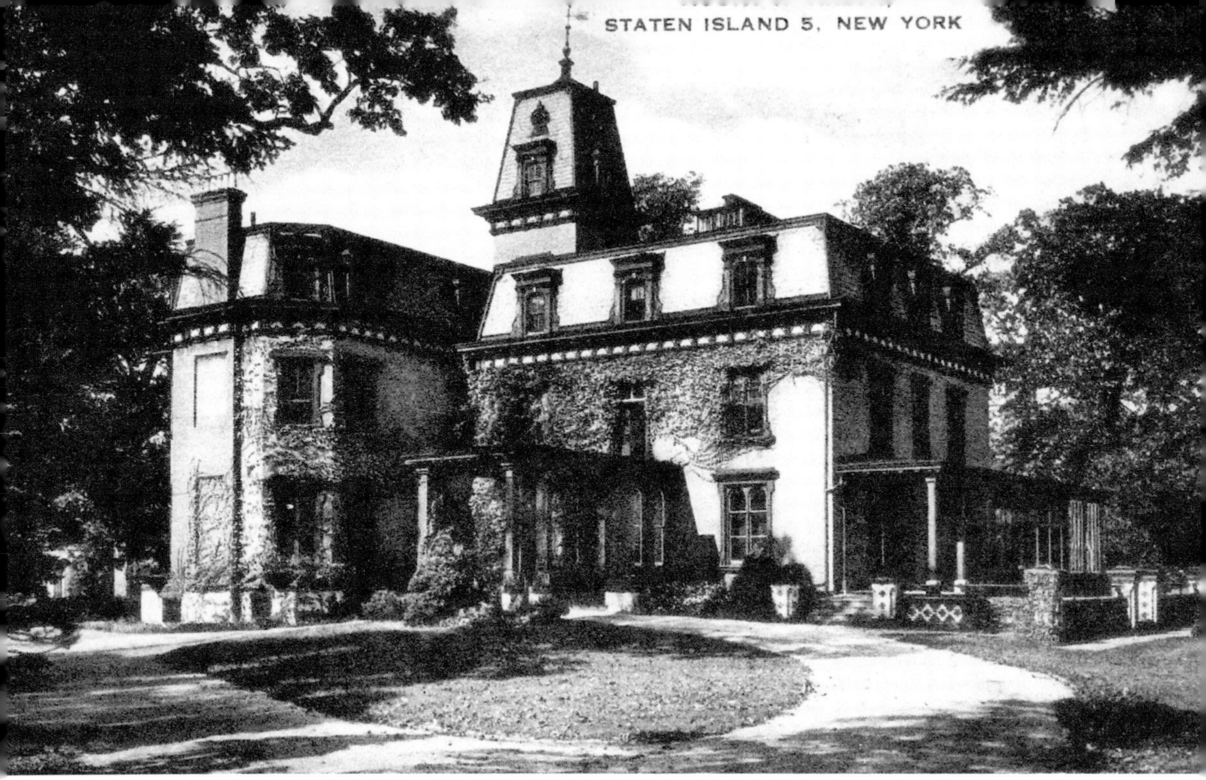

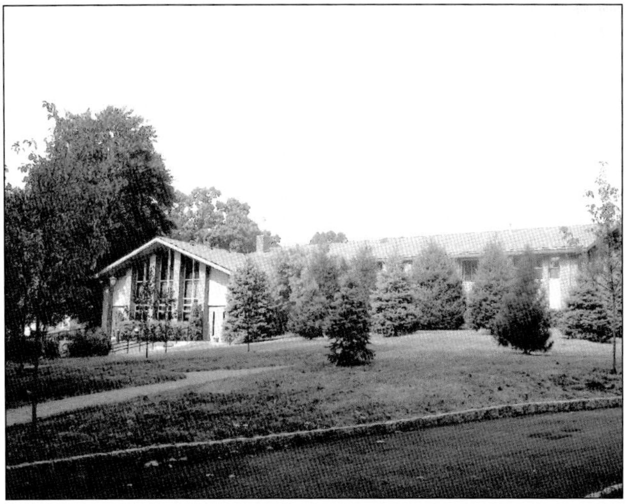

Mount Manresa, located on Fingerboard Road, is the birthplace of the laymen's retreat movement in the United States. The retreat house was opened in 1911 by Rev. Terrance Shealy on the grounds of the former Mayer Estate, also known as Fox Hill Manor, built by Henry Lewis Mayer in 1840. Reverend Shealy, a Jesuit, was the "father" of the retreat movement in America. Part of the original 18-acre estate was used to build the Staten Island Expressway. Mount Manresa is still operated by the Jesuits and is open to all denominations.

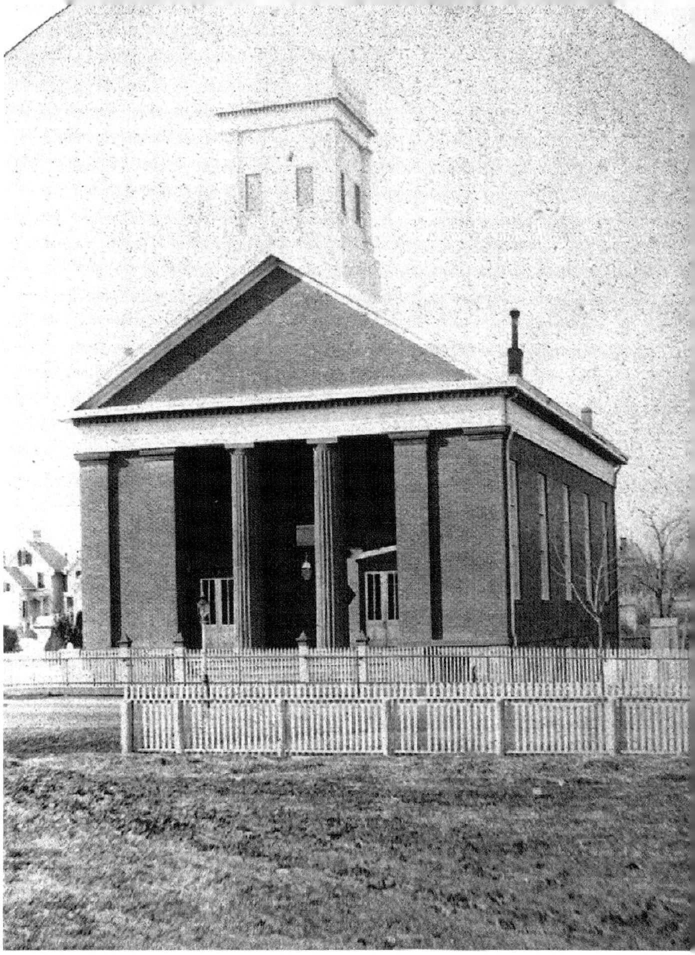

In the early 1700s, Dutch migration to Staten Island was concentrated on the island's north shore in Port Richmond. In 1715, the growing congregation erected the Reformed Dutch Church of the North Shore at 54 Port Richmond Avenue. Left in ruins after the Revolutionary War, the church was rebuilt in 1786, and again in 1844. The original church was built without seating, so worshipers brought their own chairs and benches to sit. Men and women did not sit together; women sat in the middle of the church while the men sat along the walls. The first Dutch Reformed church built on Staten Island was about 15 years earlier in Greenridge on Arthur Kill Road just north of Richmond Avenue.

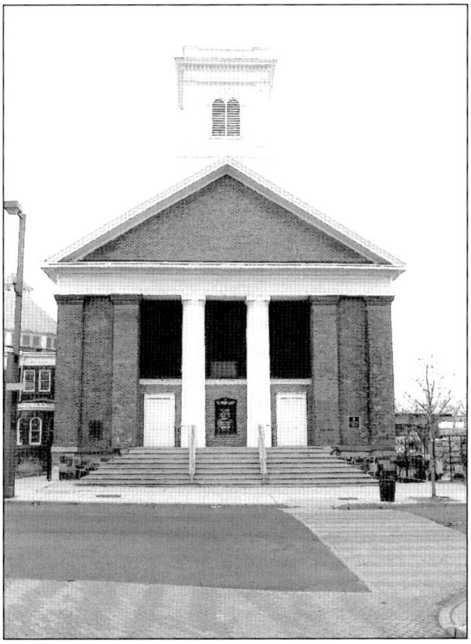

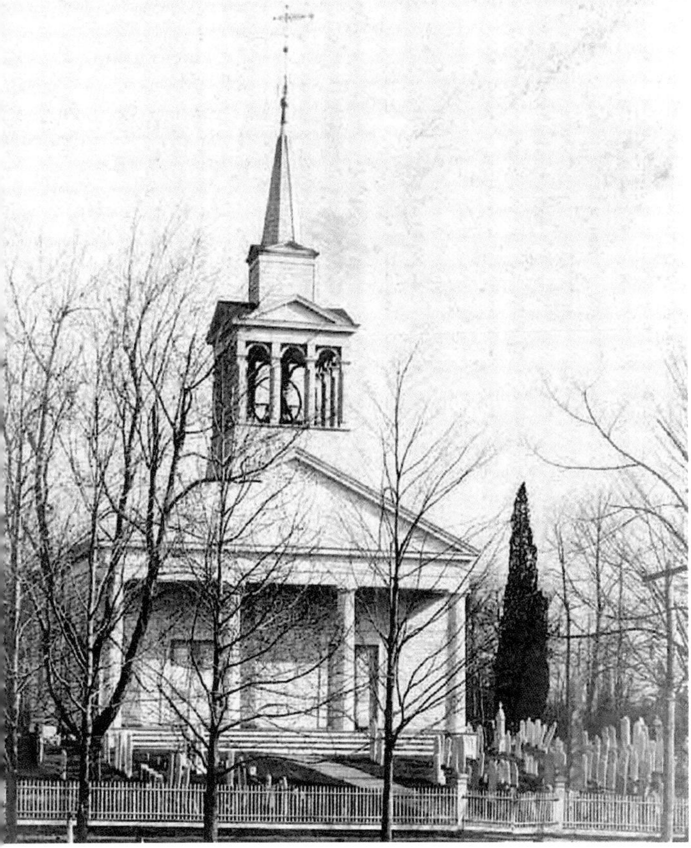

Organized in 1787, the Woodrow United Methodist Church is the oldest Methodist Episcopal church on Staten Island. Located at 1109 Woodrow Road, the present church was rebuilt in 1842 after the original structure was struck by lightning, and the bell tower was added in 1876. Many prominent families were members of the congregation, including Bedell, Seguine, Sleight, Totten, and Winant. Before the church was built, the congregation was served by Bishop Francis Asbury and other ministers from New Jersey. In those early days, men and women did not worship together (men sat to the right of the minister and women to the left), and the only heat was provided by heated bricks and foot warmers. In 1969, the building was designated a New York City landmark.

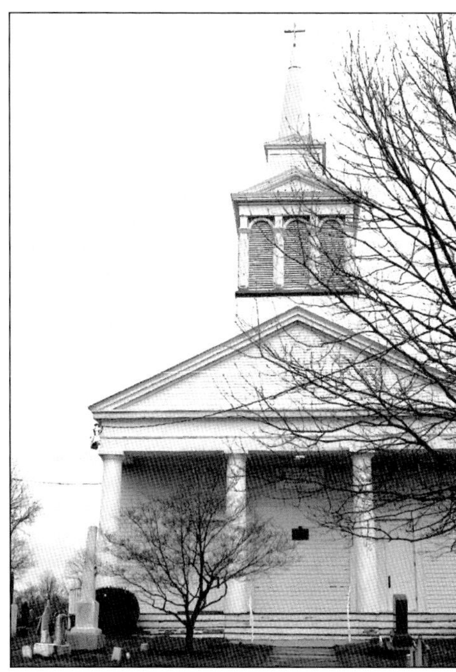

Huguenots on Staten Island can be traced back to Pierre Billiou, who led one of the first settlements in 1661. Over the years, they flourished and built several churches. In 1851, the Church of the Huguenots was built in Bloomingview. Referred to as the little "Brown Church," the structure stood until 1918, when it was destroyed by fire. It was not until six years later, in 1924, that another church was built at its present location on Huguenot Avenue, and it is known today as the Huguenot Reformed Church.

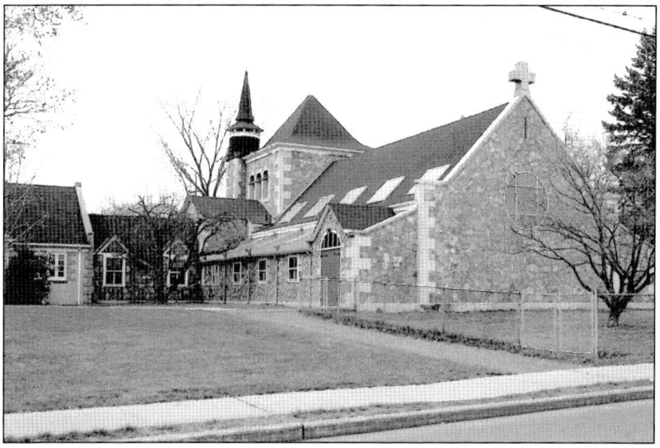

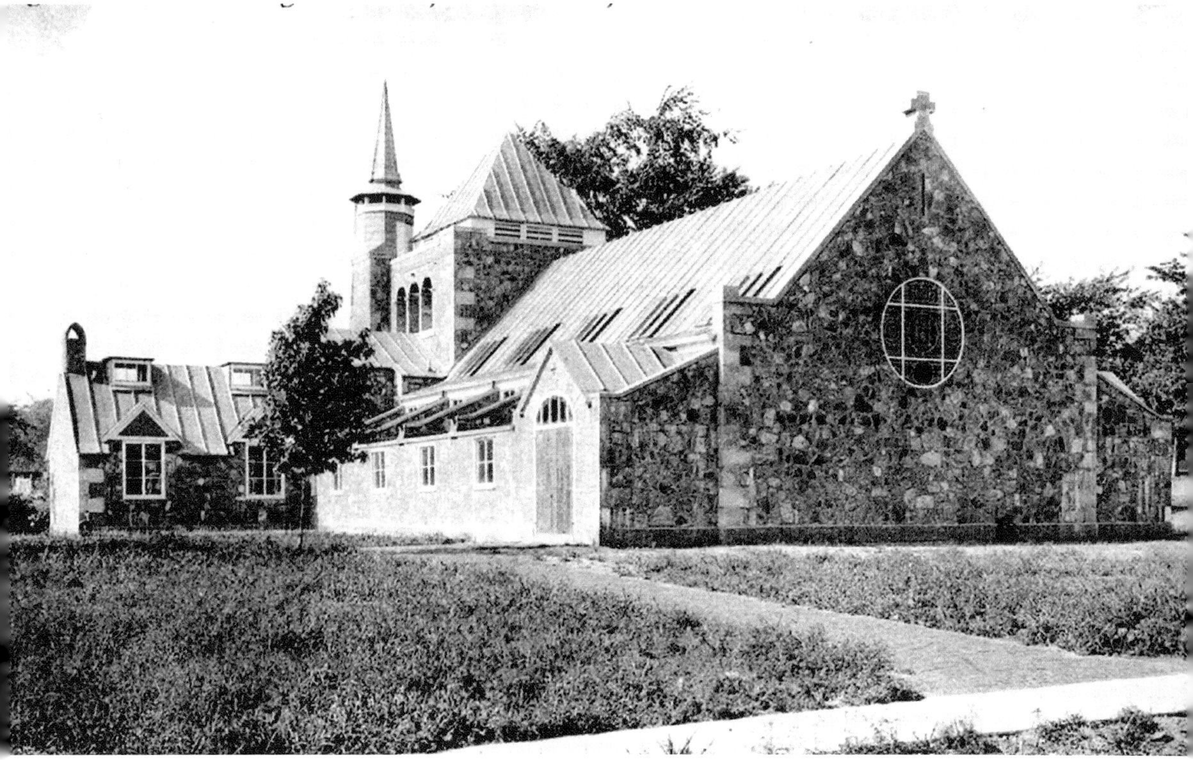

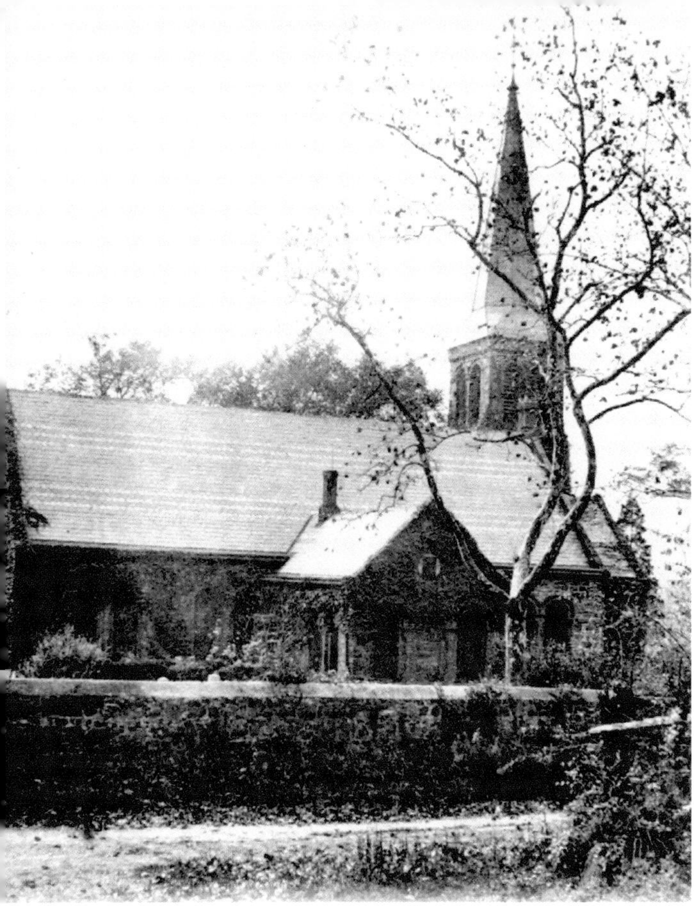

St. Andrew's Episcopal Church, located at 50 Old Mill Road just outside Historic Richmond Town, is the oldest Episcopal church on Staten Island. Construction on the original church began in 1709; however, successive fires in 1867 and 1872 required significant rebuilding of the structure, incorporating part of the original church walls into the final structure. During the Revolutionary War, several skirmishes took place at the church. Once in 1776 and again in 1777, the British retreated to the church to fight off the "rebel" attacks. During these skirmishes, the church was used as a hospital by the British for casualties. Each time, the "rebels" were driven off but not before every window in the church had been destroyed by gunfire. The church was designated a New York City landmark in 1967.

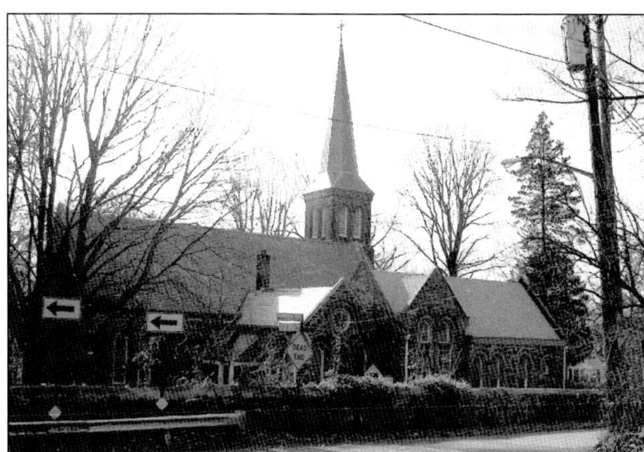

The Hotel Castleton was one of Staten Island's grandest hotels. It was built in 1889 on St. Mark's Place in St. George across from Curtis High School. It was destroyed by fire in 1907 and never rebuilt. A mural in Borough Hall depicts the fire that destroyed the hotel. Castleton Park Apartments now occupy the former site.

Chapter 4

HOTELS, INNS, AND TAVERNS

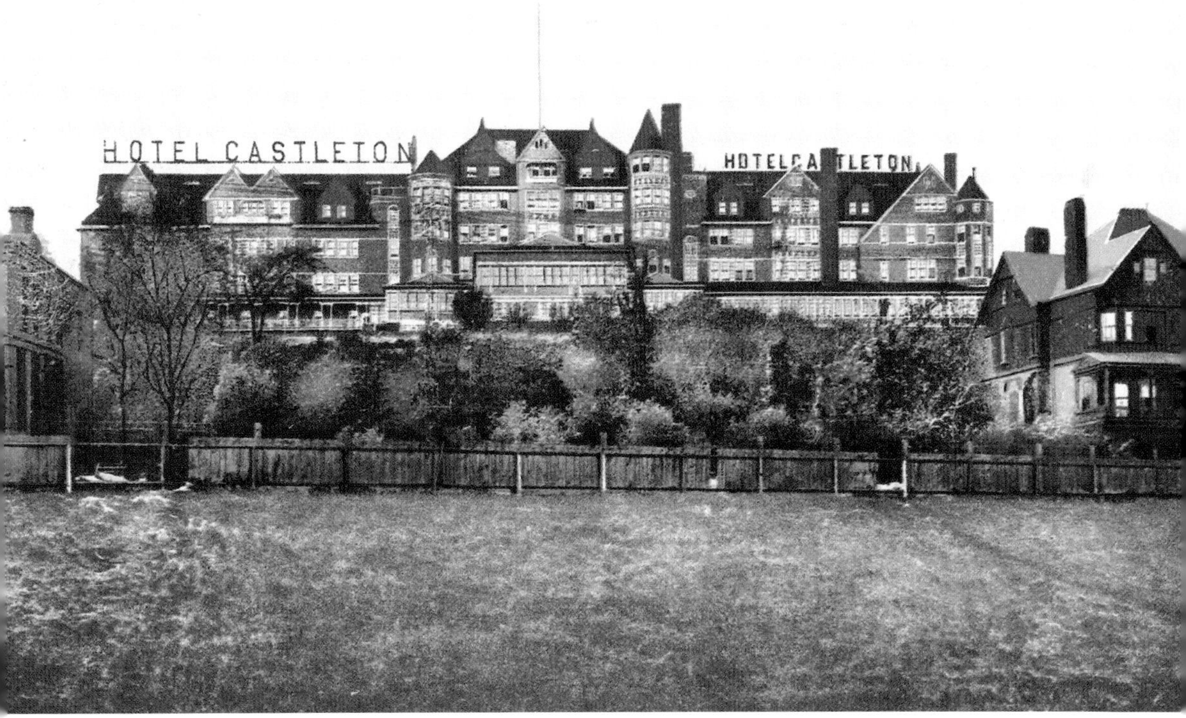

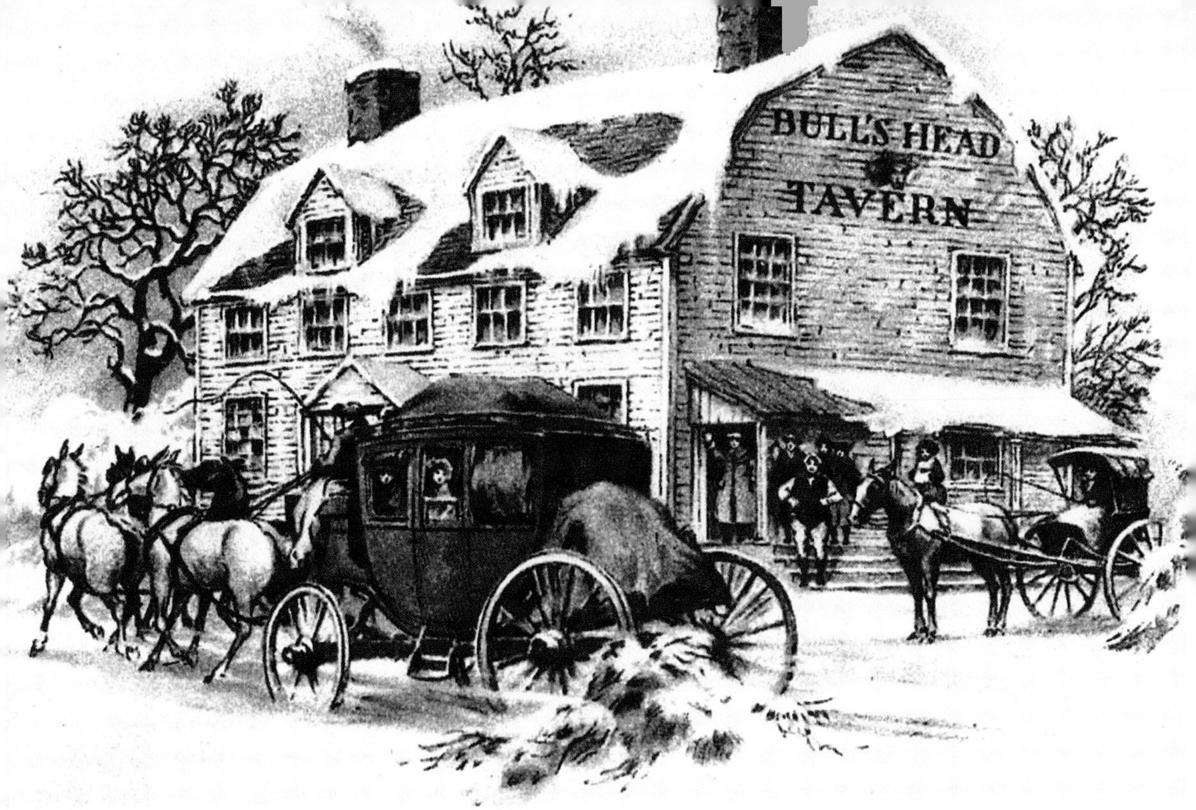

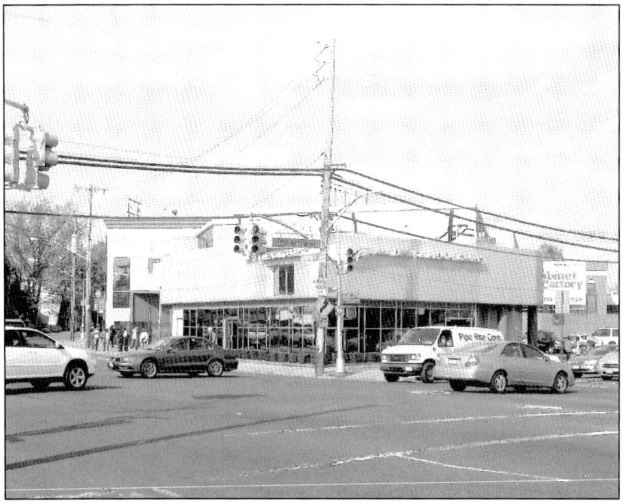

During the Revolutionary War, the British landed 30,000 troops on Staten Island in preparation for the Battle of Long Island. While some islanders were sympathetic to the revolutionary cause, many remained loyal to the crown. The Bull's Head Tavern, located at the intersection of Richmond Turnpike (Victory Boulevard) and Old Stone Road (Richmond Avenue), became a notorious Tory headquarters. While early names for this area were London Bridge and Phoenixville, the tavern's reputation resulted in the entire area being referred to as "Bulls Head." Today this intersection is one of the busiest in the entire city.

After the War of 1812, the nation experienced unprecedented growth. Staten Island grew as well and became a resort for those living in Manhattan from the pressures of a growing city. Many hotels and resorts were built on Staten Island to accommodate those seeking its serene setting. Built around 1838, originally as the residence for Thomas Davis, the Pavilion Hotel expanded over the years and at one time was able to accommodate between 300 and 400 guests. During its heyday, the hotel was host to such notables as Pres. Martin Van Buren, Henry Clay, and Jenny Lind. The hotel became a safe haven for the wives and children of Confederate officers during the Civil War. Eventually the popularity faded, and in 1904, the building was demolished.

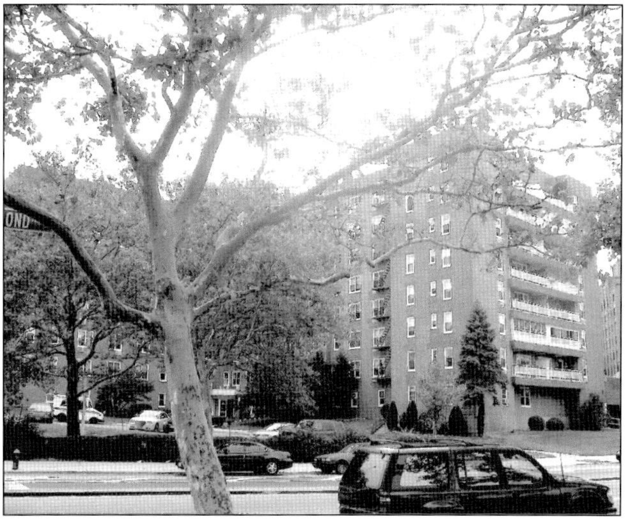

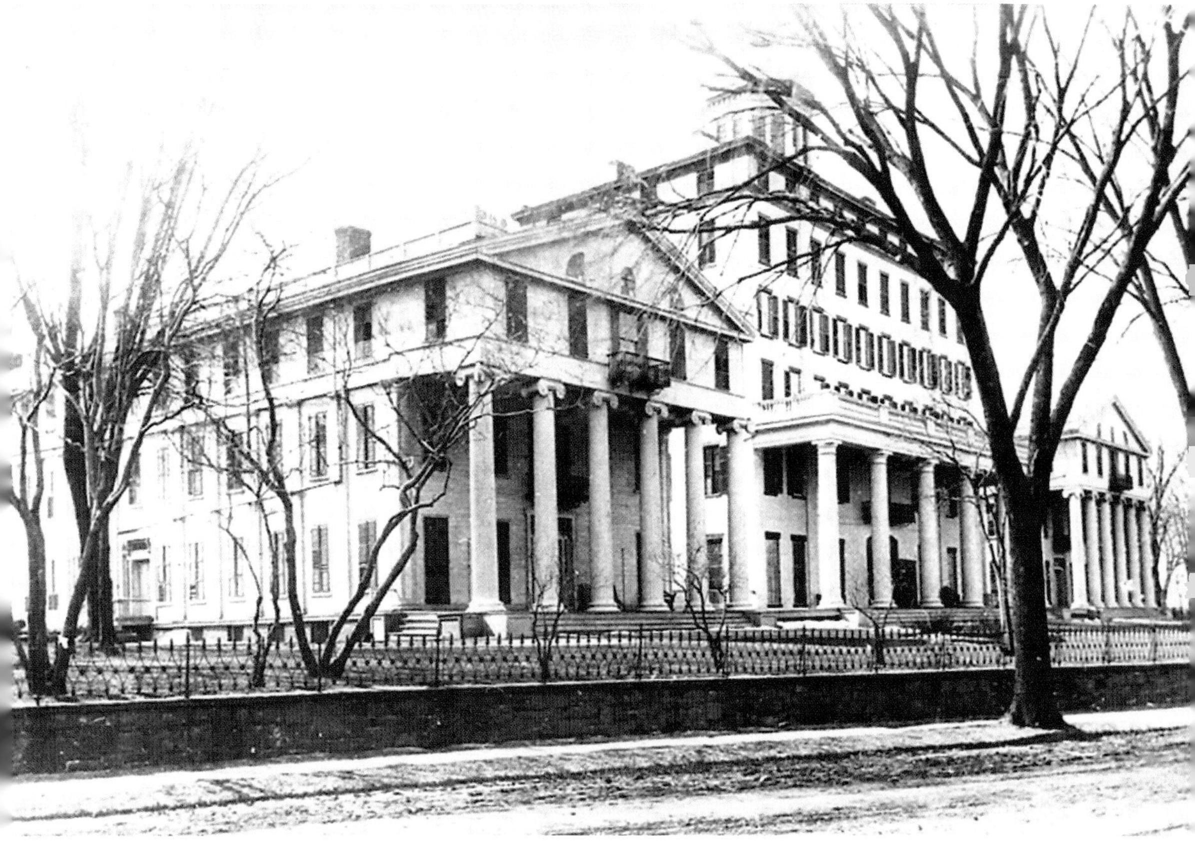

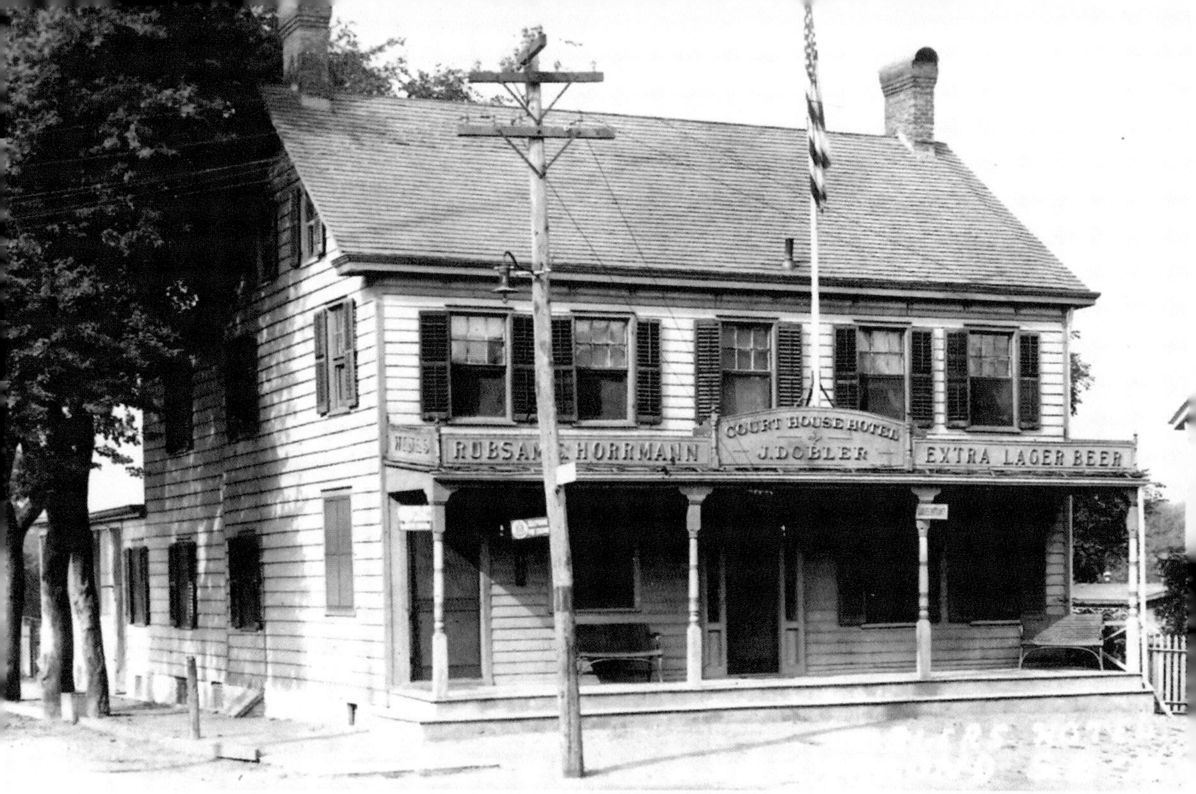

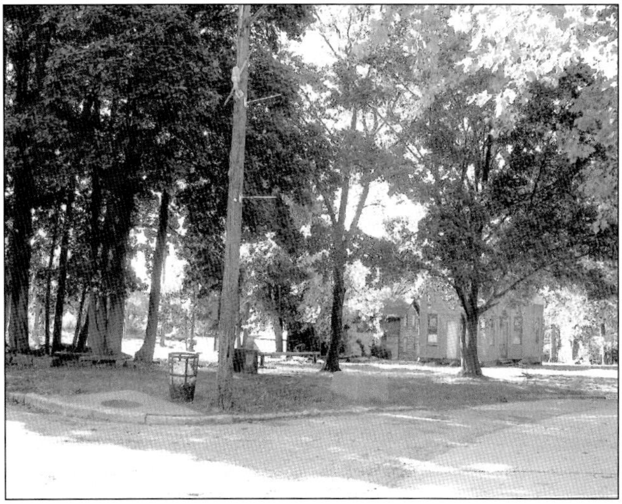

The courts and other government functions brought several developers to Richmondtown, including Joseph Lytle. In about 1858, he built an 11–guest room hotel on the corner opposite the Third County Courthouse on Center Street. Across the street from the Third County Courthouse, his business prospered until the court was relocated to St. George in 1919. The real deathblow, however, came during Prohibition, when in 1932, the hotel was forced to close its doors for good. The building was torn down around 1942 and is today used as a picnic ground for visitors to Historic Richmond Town.

In 1910, Albert P. Semler built a hotel near his park and picnic grounds in Grant City. Like many other hotels of its time, the hotel was built near the railroad station on Lincoln and North Railroad Avenues (the New Dorp Station). The park and picnic grounds were built in the 1890s and offered athletic fields for softball, baseball, and football and even included a dance hall for patrons' entertainment. Many businesses and families enjoyed picnics at the park until it closed. Today an apartment building on the northeast corner of Lincoln and Railroad Avenues stands on the site of the hotel and park.

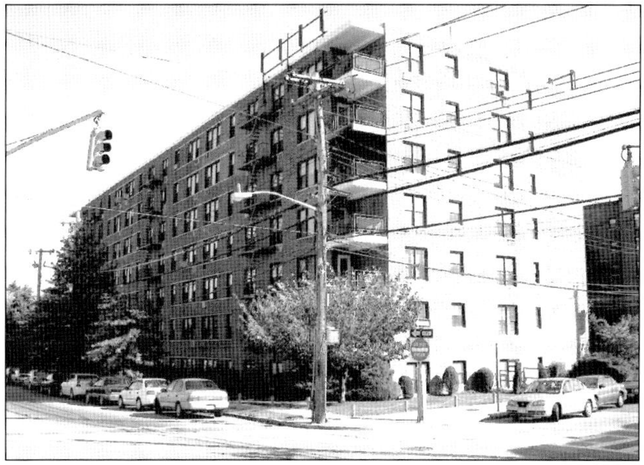

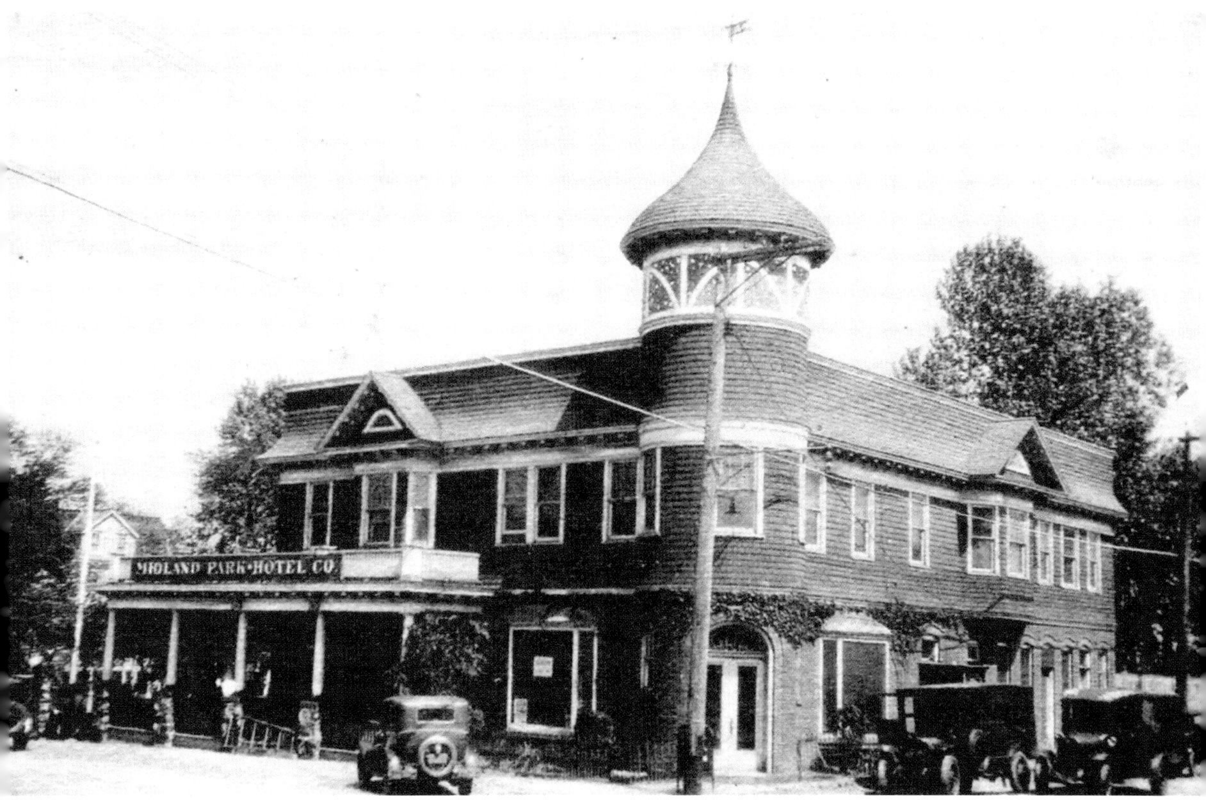

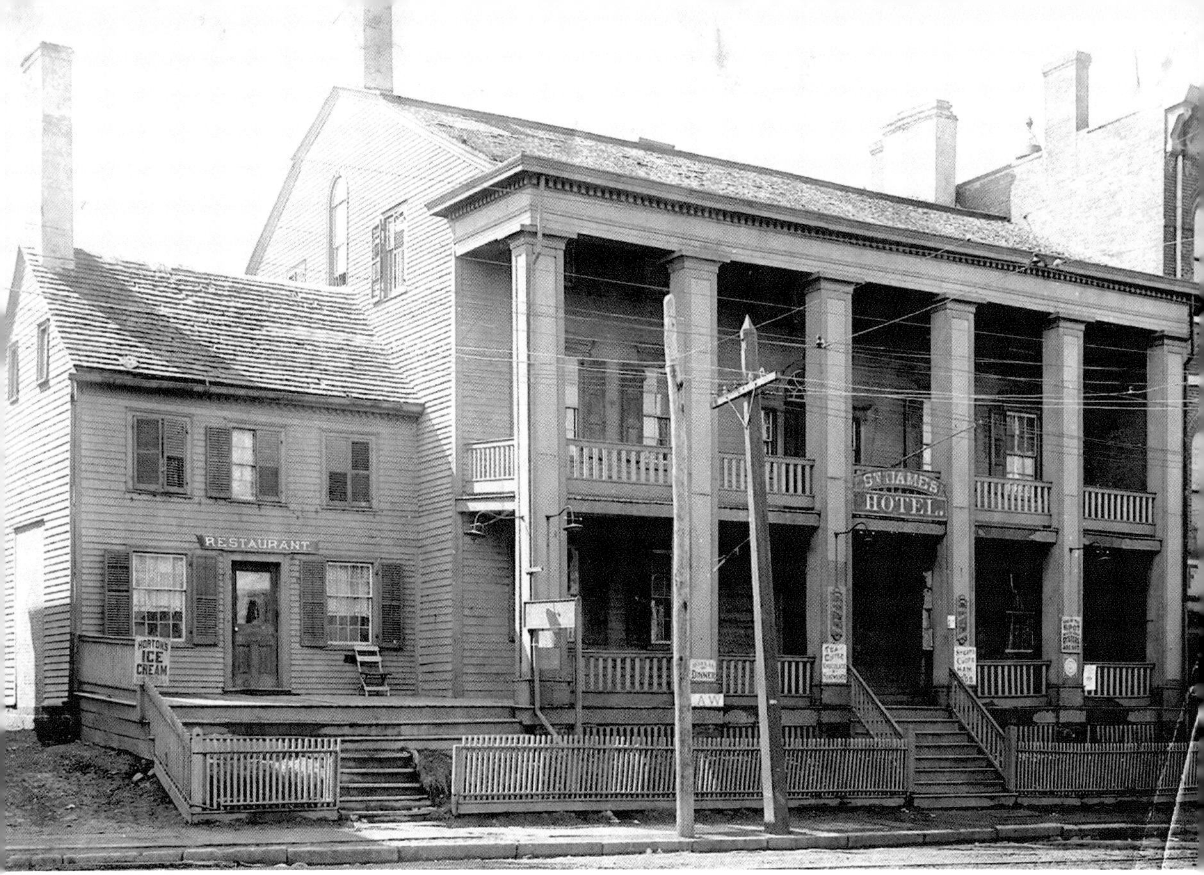

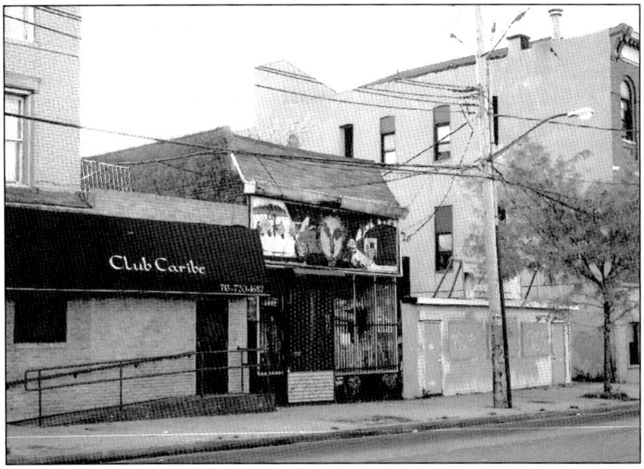

Built at 2040 Richmond Terrace in 1795, this was the private home of Gozen Ryers, a judge of the county. After Ryers's death in 1802, the house was used as a private residence by several families until 1820, when it was sold and converted into the Port Richmond Hotel. During the intervening years, the hotel had several owners and name changes. In 1870, it was known as the Continental Hotel; in 1893, the St. James Hotel; and in 1920, the Danner's Hotel. After a series of failed businesses, the building fell into disrepair and was torn down around 1945. Its most famous guest was Aaron Burr, who made it his home for a year before his death on September 14, 1836.

The Black Horse Tavern was built in 1754 at the intersection of Richmond and Amboy Roads. During the Revolutionary War, British officers lived there during their occupation of Staten Island. After the war, the tavern stayed open until the 1870s, when it fell on hard times and was forced to close. However, it was later enlarged and reopened only to close for good during Prohibition like so many other establishments of its kind. In 1935, it was torn down to widen Richmond Road to accommodate the increase in traffic.

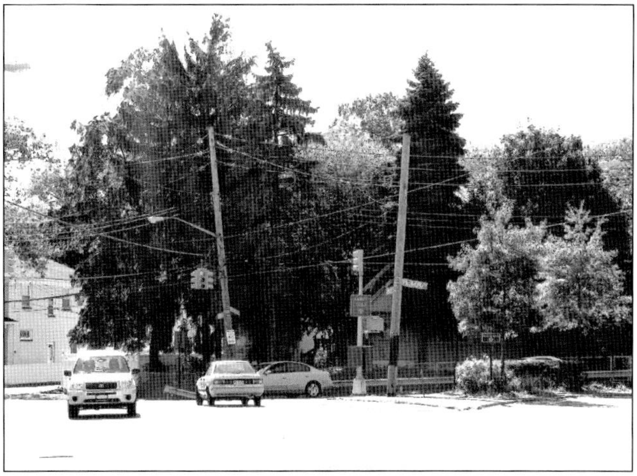

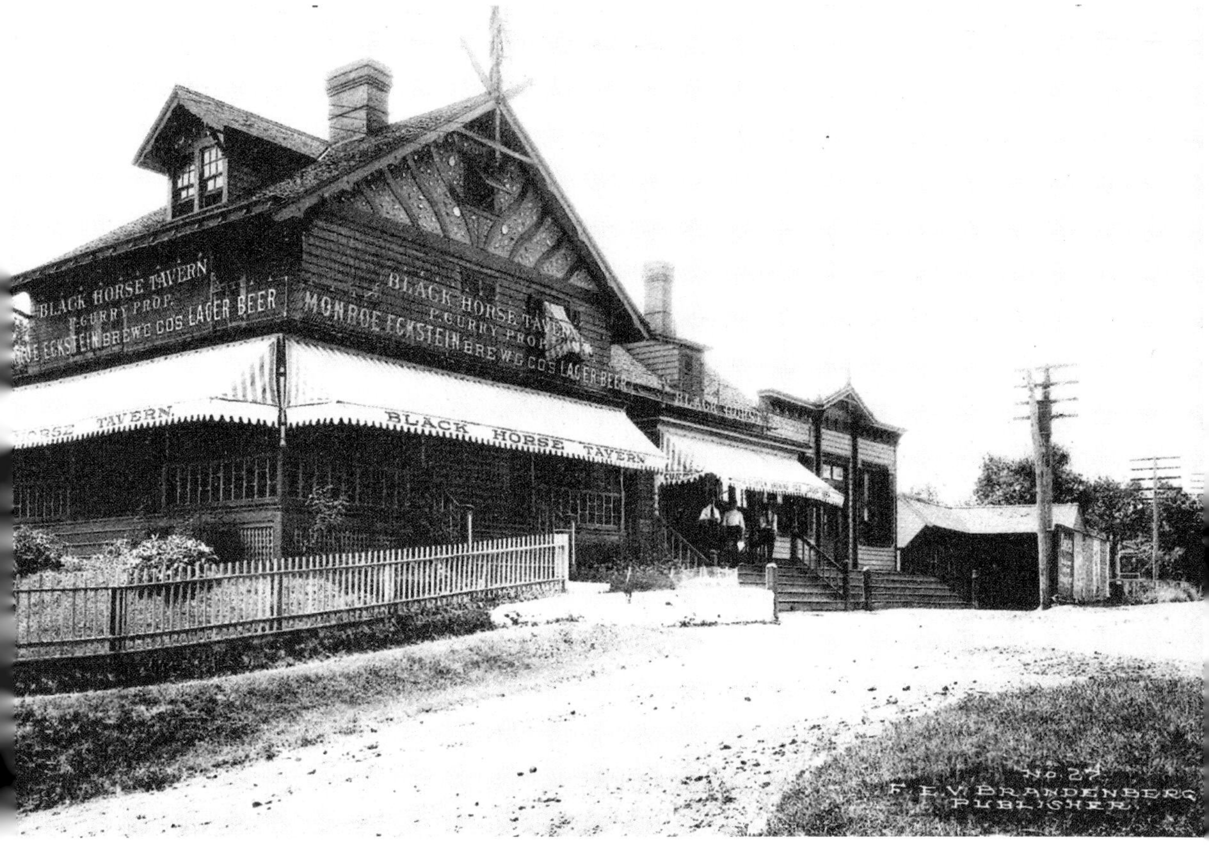

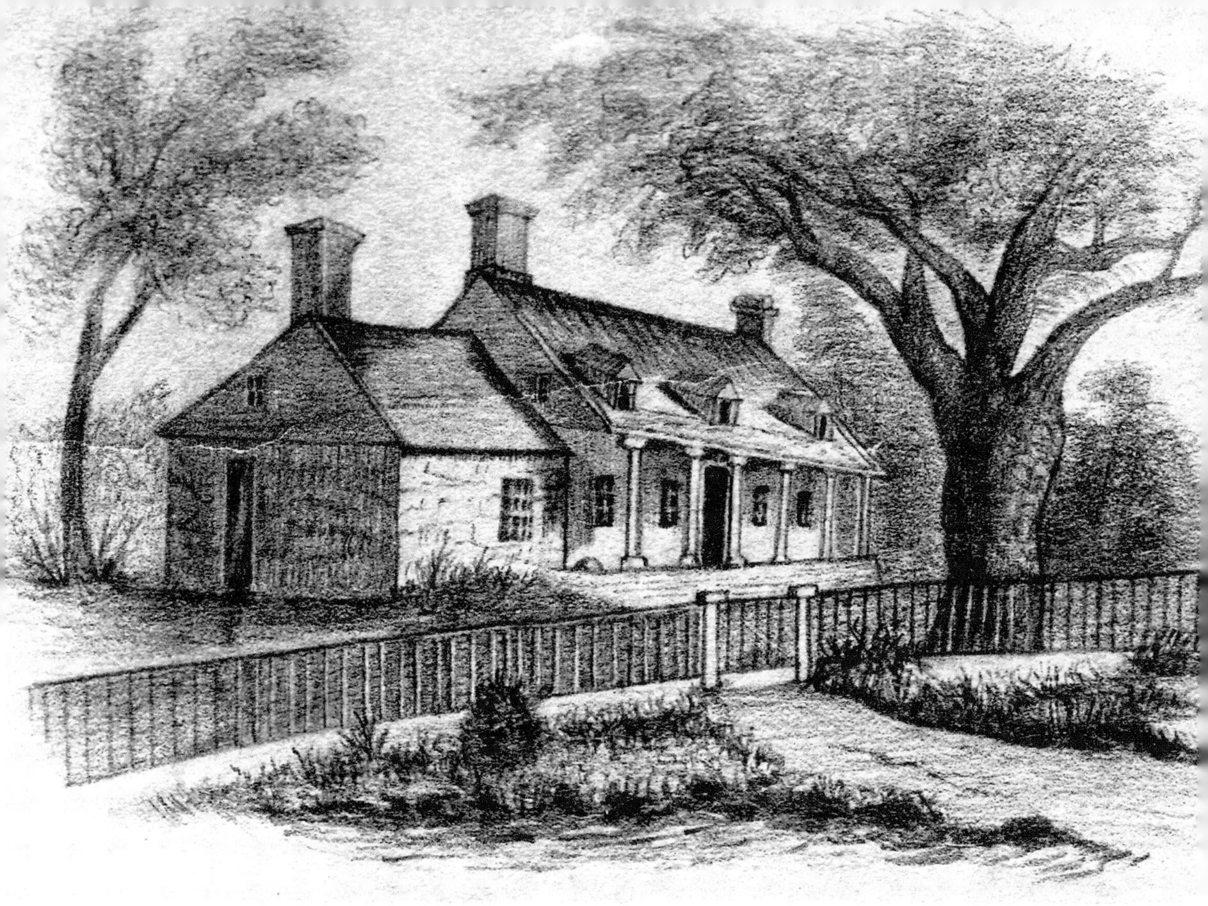

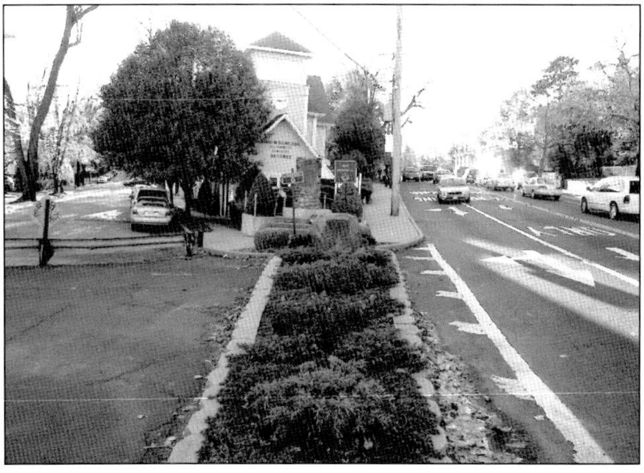

One of Staten Island's many taverns and inns was the Rose and Crown, built on King's Road (Richmond Road) in New Dorp in 1665. The tavern became Gen. William Howe's headquarters after the British landed more than 20,000 troops on Staten Island in the summer of 1776. On July 9, 1776, British officers first read the rebels' Declaration of Independence in this tavern. A marker can be found at the intersection of New Dorp Lane and Richmond Road that marks the approximate location of the tavern.

The Planter's Hotel became a favorite destination of wealthy Southerners. The two-story brick building was erected in 1820 at the corner of Bay and Grant Streets in Tompkinsville. In 1859, Charles Hoyer opened a photographer's studio in the hotel, and a year later, it was taken over by John Loeffler. During the Civil War, patronage continued to decline, and the hotel ceased operations. Loeffler and his son August continued to run a very successful business there for over 50 years. The building, located at 368 Bay Street, was later used as a school for boys and then became an office for a lumberyard until it was demolished. Today the lot remains vacant and part of the Canal Lumber yards.

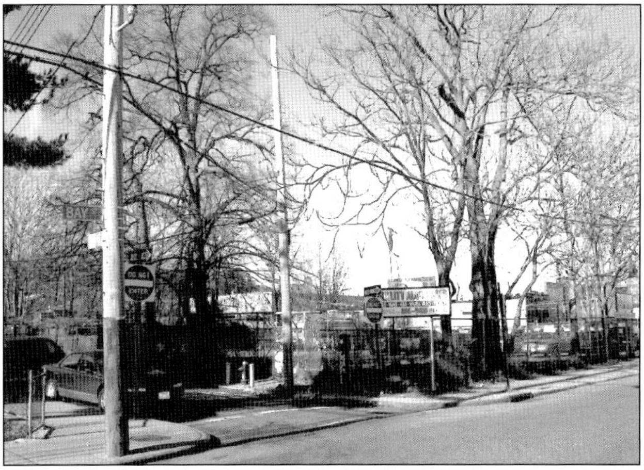

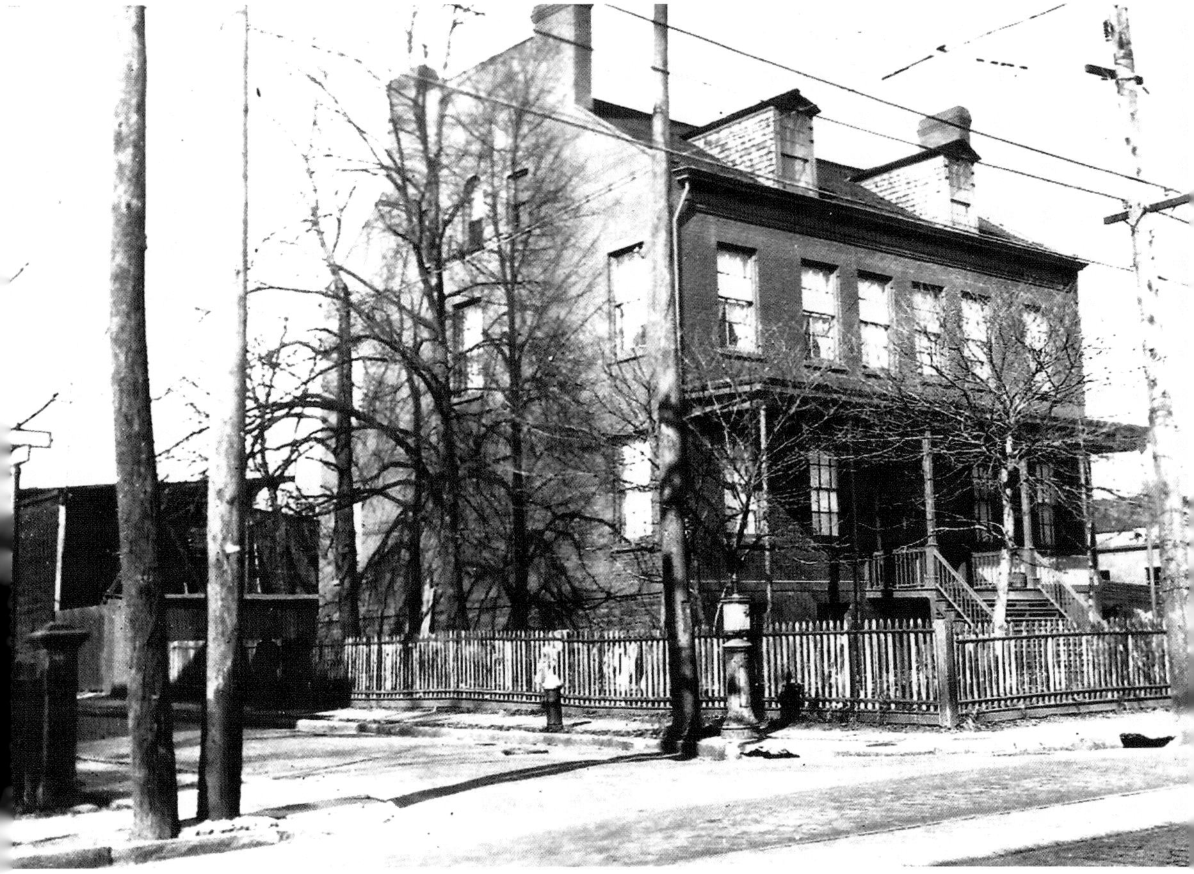

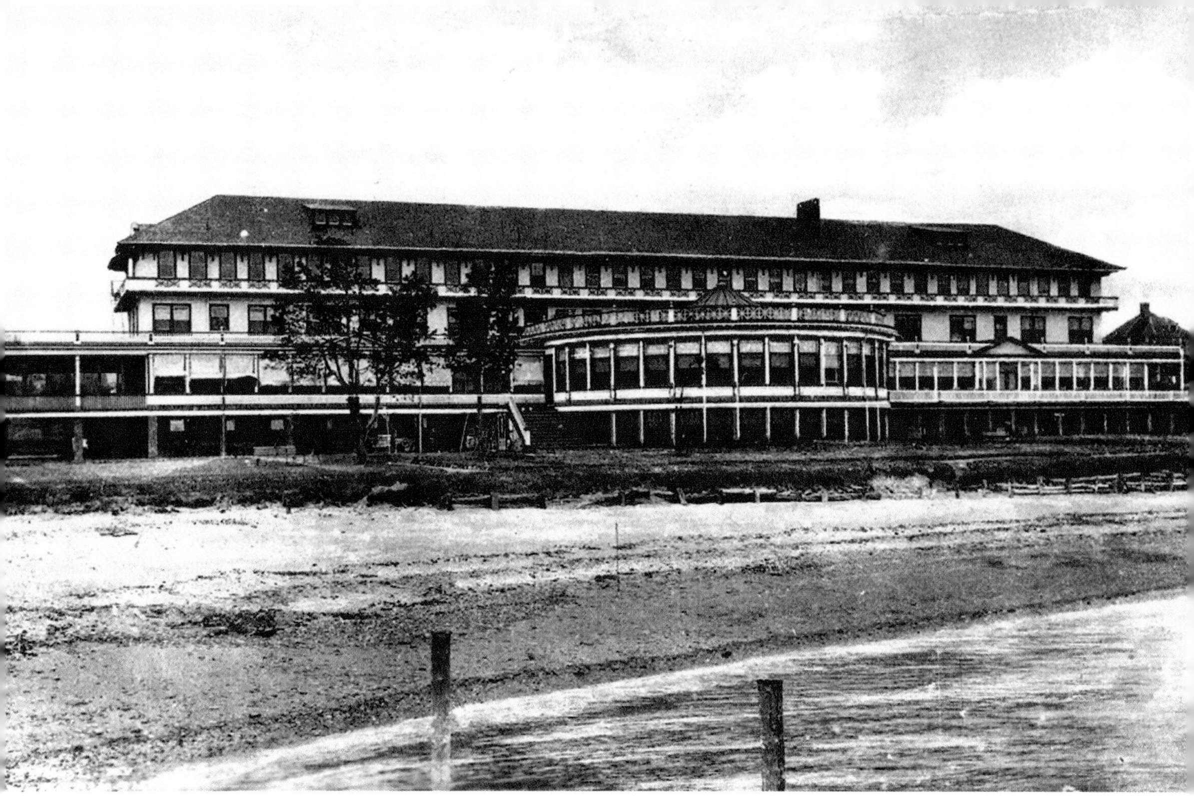

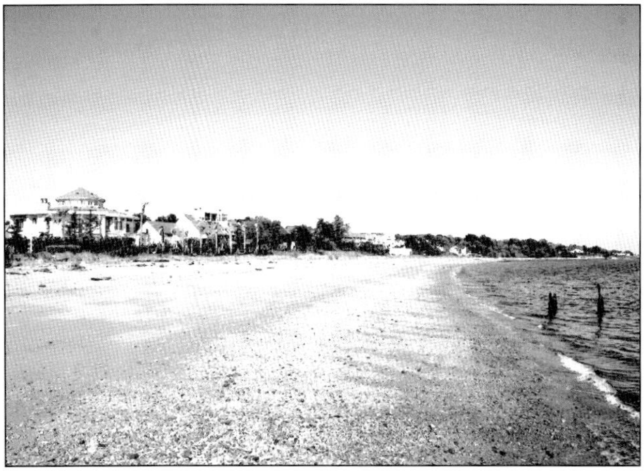

As the city entered the 20th century, people continued to seek out Staten Island's tranquil settings. In 1908, the Terra Marine Inn was opened at Huguenot Beach. This 150-room, three-story hotel boasted of "broad, shady, breeze-swept verandas, suites with a private bath . . . the best of food, choicest wines and painstaking service." Among the facilities available were a huge rotunda dining room overlooking the ocean, a rathskeller, a café, billiard rooms, and sun parlors. In 1911, the owners went bankrupt; however, the facility continued to operate under different owners until it was finally closed and demolished in 1948. Today houses along Nicolosi Drive were built on the site of the hotel.

The original structure was erected in 1859 on Arthur Kill and Sharrotts Roads in Charleston. Nicholas Killmeyer operated a general store there until the 1880s, when they enlarged the original two-story frame house to include a dining room and an upstairs hotel. The new operation was renamed Killmeyer's Union Hotel and survived well into the 20th century. In the 1930s, it was operated by the Poillon family and in the 1940s by the Simonson family, who renamed it the Century Inn. It was closed in 1977 and was not reopened until the 1990s when it was purchased by Ken Tirado, Ray Chrampanis, and Jim Stayoch. They renamed it Killmeyer's Old Bavaria Inn, and it continues operations today.

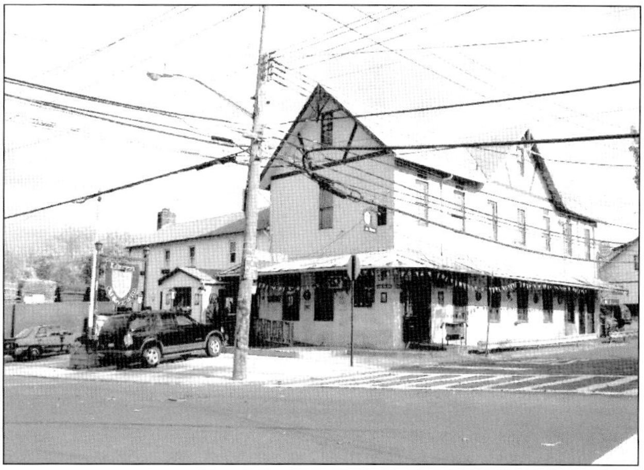

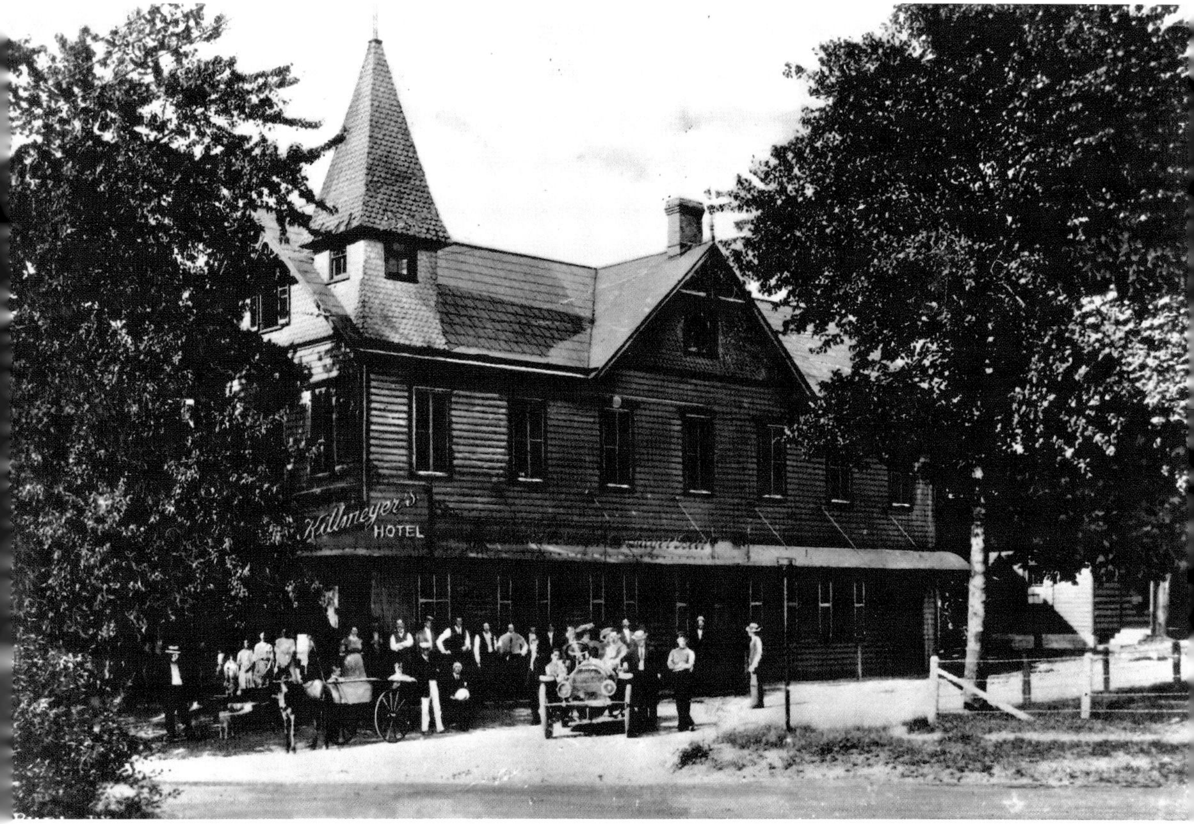

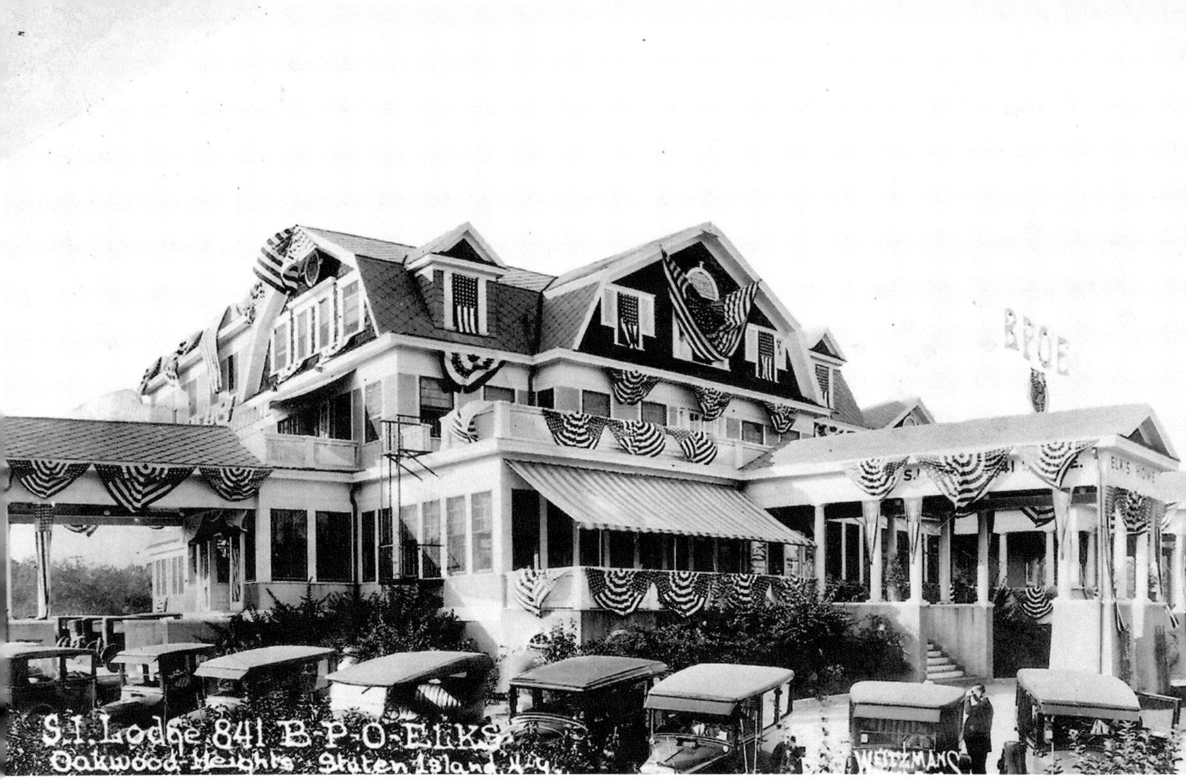

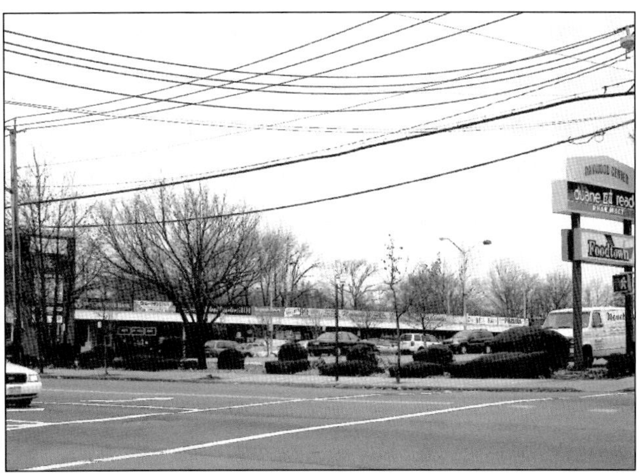

In the 1890s, a number of hotels were built throughout Staten Island to accommodate the many people seeking refuge from the hectic city life. In 1896, the Oakwood Park Hotel was built at the corner of Amboy Road and Clarke Avenue. Later known as the Oakwood Arms, it was considered a very fashionable spot until the 1920s, but after Prohibition became the law of the land, it closed. It became the home of the Oakwood Elks until 1943. After moving several times, they moved to their present location at 3250 Richmond Avenue in 1958. The once trendy hotel was torn down in 1947, and the six-acre parcel has become a popular shopping center.

A quarantine station was established on a 30-acre tract in Rosebank by the state of New York in 1799. The station was the destination of anyone coming into the harbor suspected of having a serious communicable disease. When yellow fever spread to the community, the station was burned down by a mob in 1858. Quarantine operations were moved to two man-made islands off South Beach.

Chapter 5
LANDMARKS AND HISTORIC PLACES

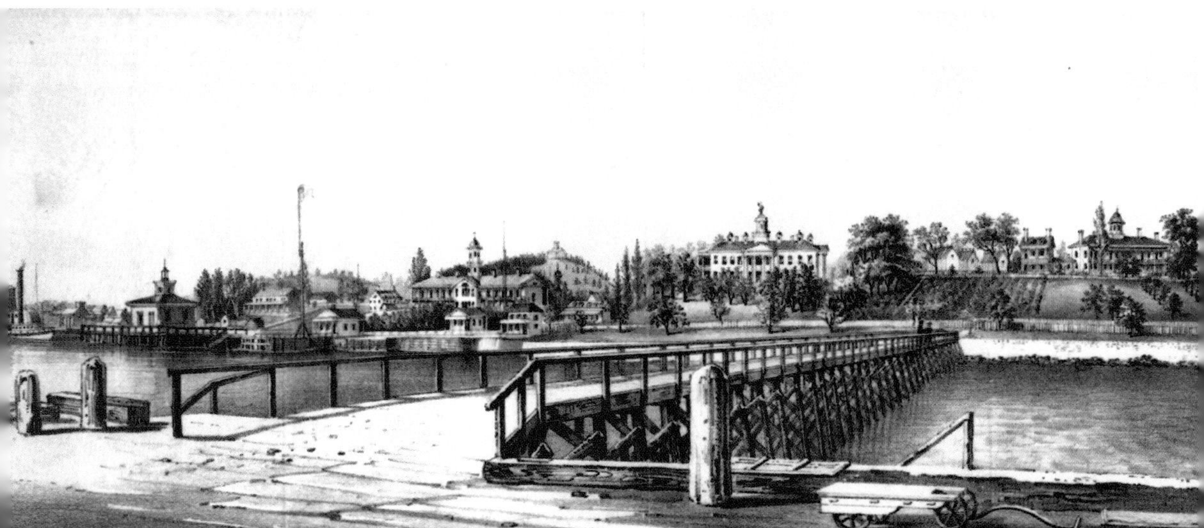

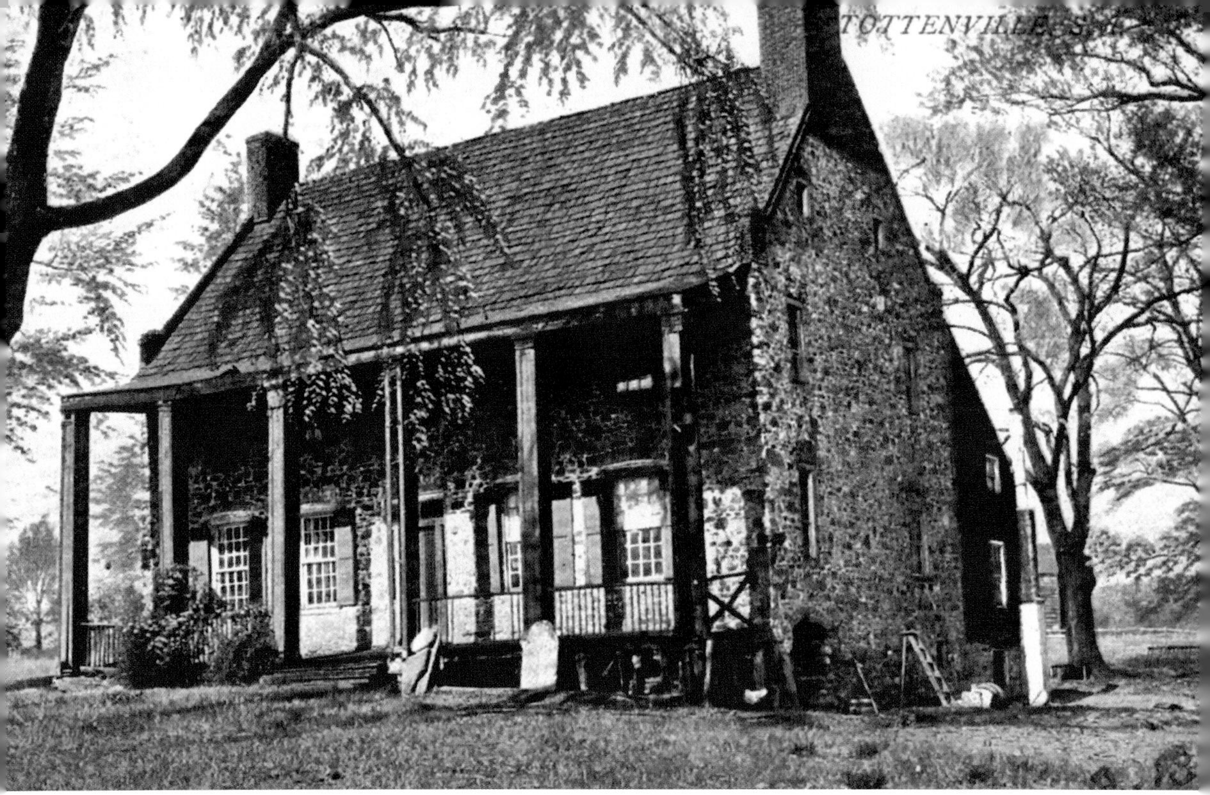

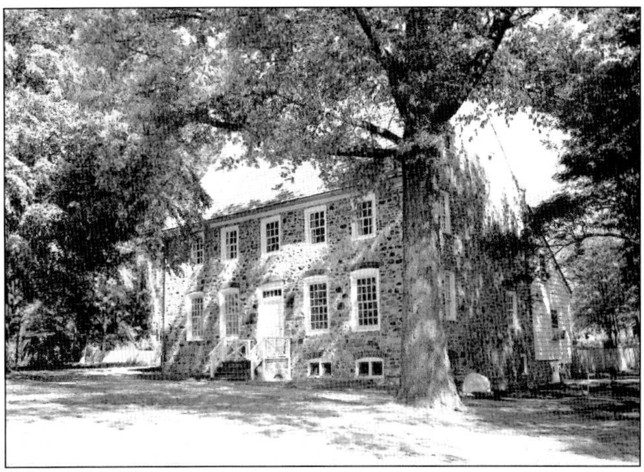

In the fall of 1776, the British were in control of New York. Adm. Lord Richard Howe sought an early end to the war and arranged a secret meeting with John Adams, Benjamin Franklin, and Edward Rutledge at the home of a British loyalist, Christopher Billopp. The meeting took place on September 11, 1776; however, the Americans refused to give up George Washington and their fight for independence, so the meeting failed to bring an early end to the war. Since that meeting, the house has been called the Conference House. In 1929, it was purchased by the city, restored, and opened to the public at 7455 Hylan Boulevard. In 1965, the house was granted landmark status by the City of New York.

This house was built in the 1840s and became home to Antonio Meucci and his wife, Ester, in 1850. There he continued his work on what he called a "telletrofone." Giuseppe Garibaldi lived with the Meuccis in their Rosebank home from 1851 to 1853, while in exile from his home in Italy. In 1907, on the centennial anniversary of Garibaldi's birth, the house was moved from its original location (just a few blocks away) to its present location at 420 Tompkins Avenue. A pantheon, pictured below, was built of wood over the house as a memorial to Garibaldi; however, it became infested with termites and was taken down around 1919. Today this landmarked building is home to the Garibaldi-Meucci Museum and is open to the public.

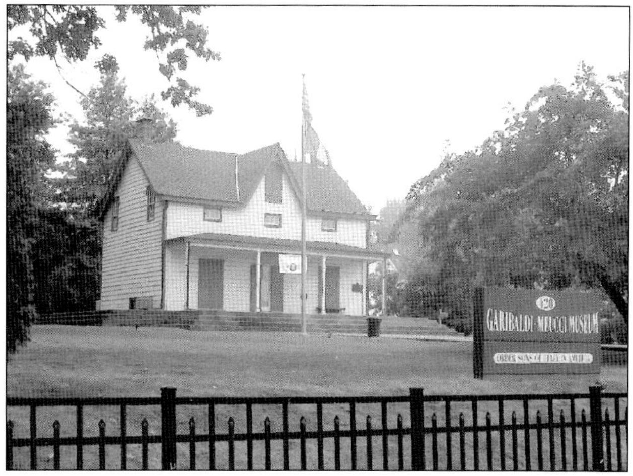

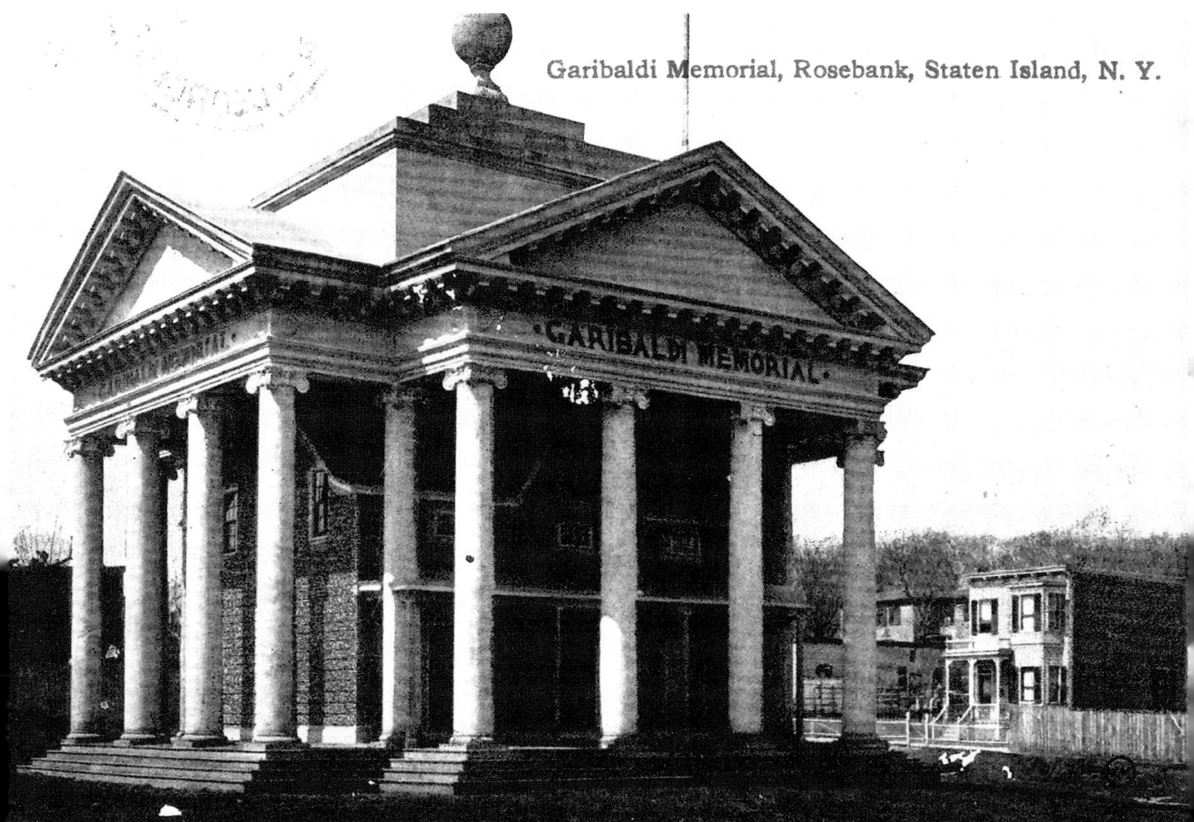

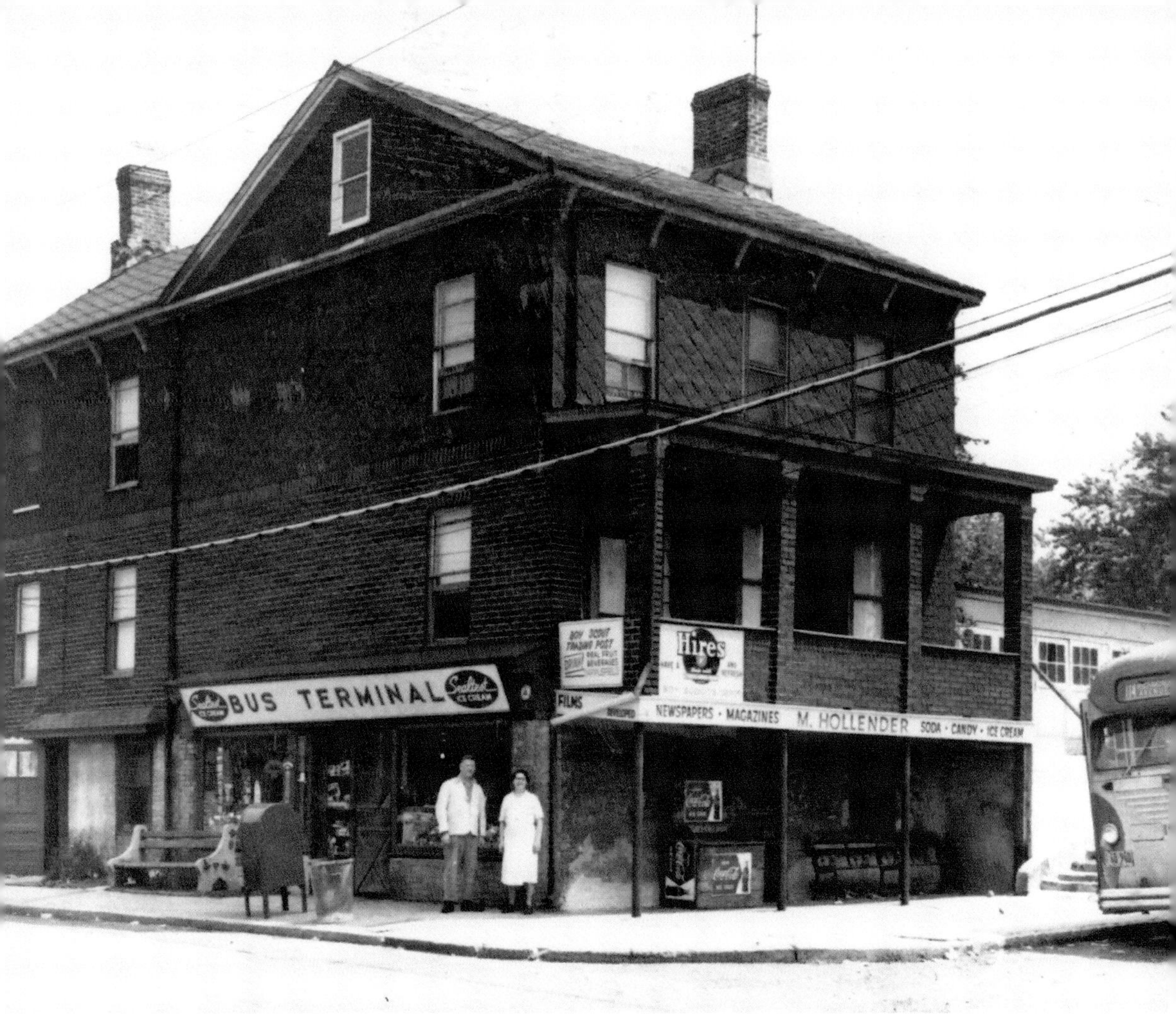

Prior to consolidation, Richmondtown was the civic center of Staten Island. The activity in and around the area drew many people, including developers, who provided housing, lodging, and business opportunities. Around 1839, as part of a real estate development, John Bennett built this house for his family. The Bennett family lived there from 1848 until around 1917. The house's proximity to the Third County Courthouse (across the street) allowed subsequent owners to use the building for other purposes, such as a restaurant, bus terminal, and seasonal snack bar. Today the house is part of the Historic Richmond Town Restoration and is open to the public.

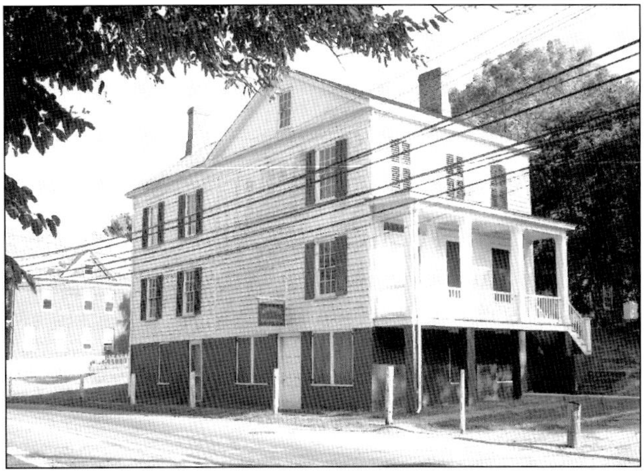

Constructed in 1889, the Edgewater Village Hall was one of only two village halls built on Staten Island before consolidation and served the village of Edgewater (Stapleton). The Edgewater Village Hall housed the village's supervisor and trustees, the local board of health, and village police courts. The building was restored in 1998 and is used as a community center and health clinic. The park surrounding the Edgewater Village Hall was originally called Washington Park. In 1934, it was renamed for James J. Tappen, a Stapleton resident killed in the Battle of Argonne, France, during World War I. Located at 111 Canal Street, the Edgewater Village Hall is a New York City landmark and is also listed on the National Register of Historic Places.

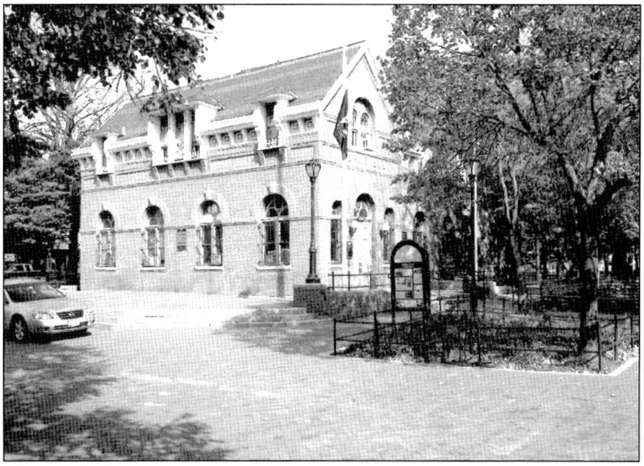

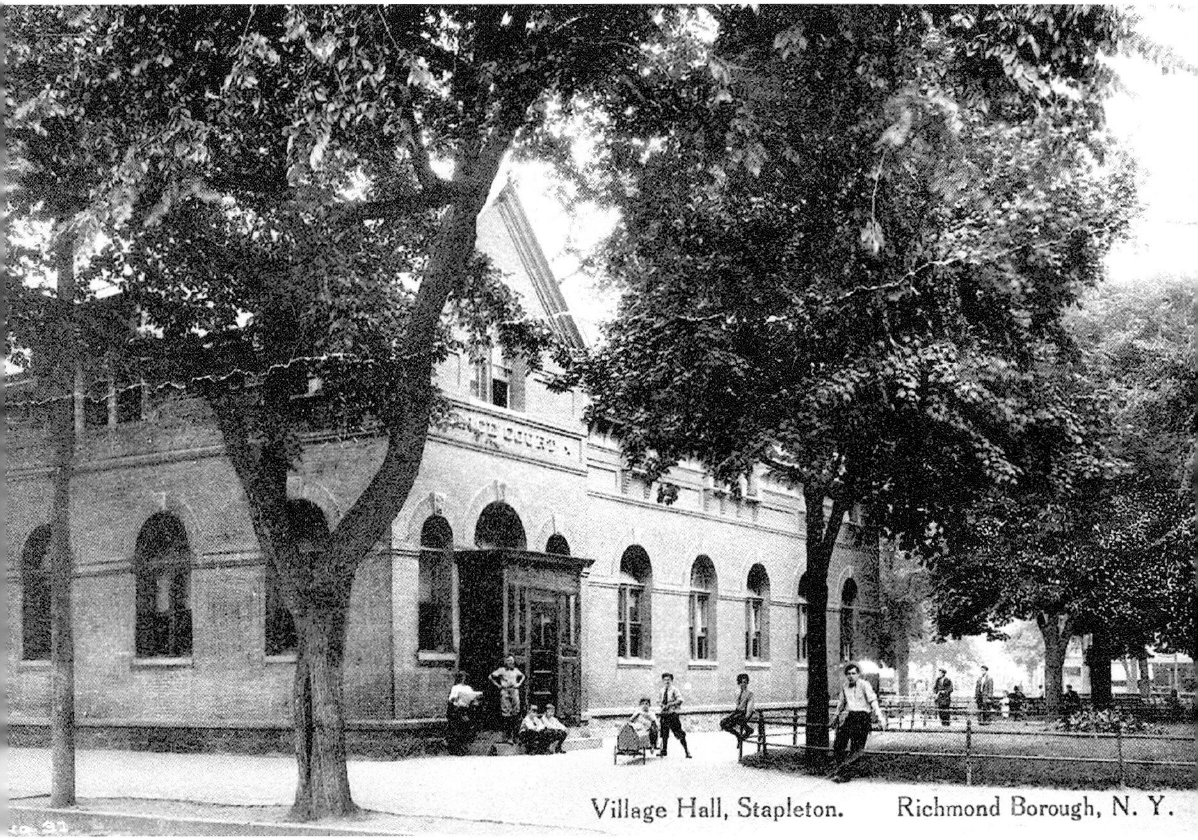

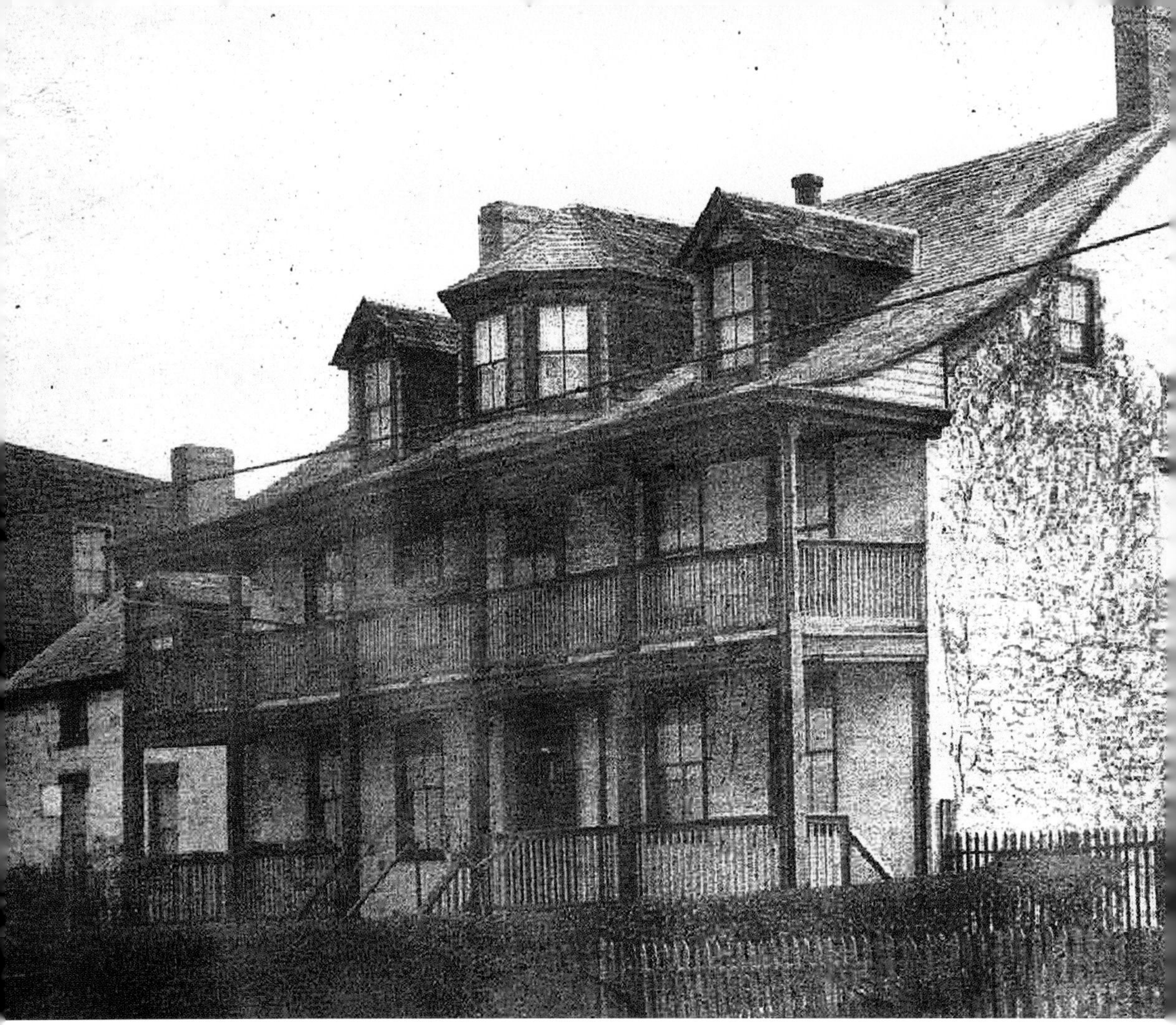

This farmhouse was built around 1800 by Jacob and Mary Tysen at 806 Richmond Terrace. This simple farmhouse underwent several changes through the years, including the addition of a second story and a hexagonal cupola. During the 1800s, the house was used as a tavern known as the Old Stone Jug, catering to sailors living at Snug Harbor. The property was purchased by a retired sea captain named John Neville in the 1870s. Over the years, the house fell into disrepair but was rescued by a coalition of public and private groups working with the owner, Beulah Crute. Today the house is a private residence, a New York City landmark, and on the National Register of Historic Places.

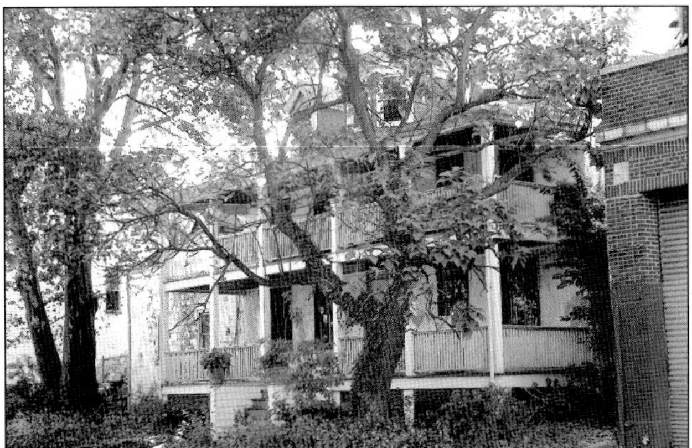

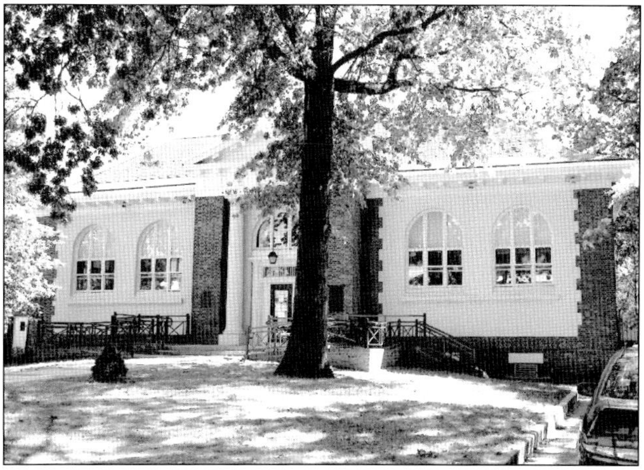

This branch of the New York City Public Library system (made possible by the Carnegie Foundation) was constructed around 1903 at 7430 Amboy Avenue and is the oldest public library on Staten Island. The building was designed by architects John Carrère and Thomas Hastings. Carrère was a Staten Islander who also designed the main New York City Public Library at Fifth Avenue in Manhattan. When this public library opened, Tottenville's small library, financed by the community on Johnson Avenue, was closed. The building was restored in 1993 and was designated a New York City landmark in 1995.

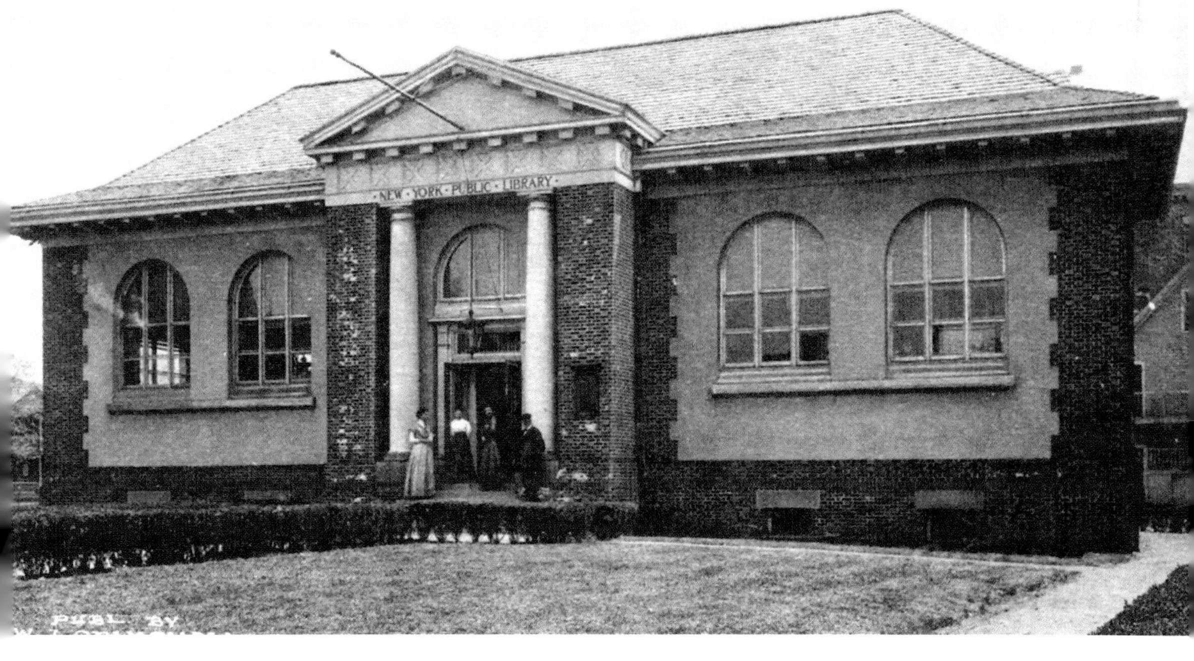

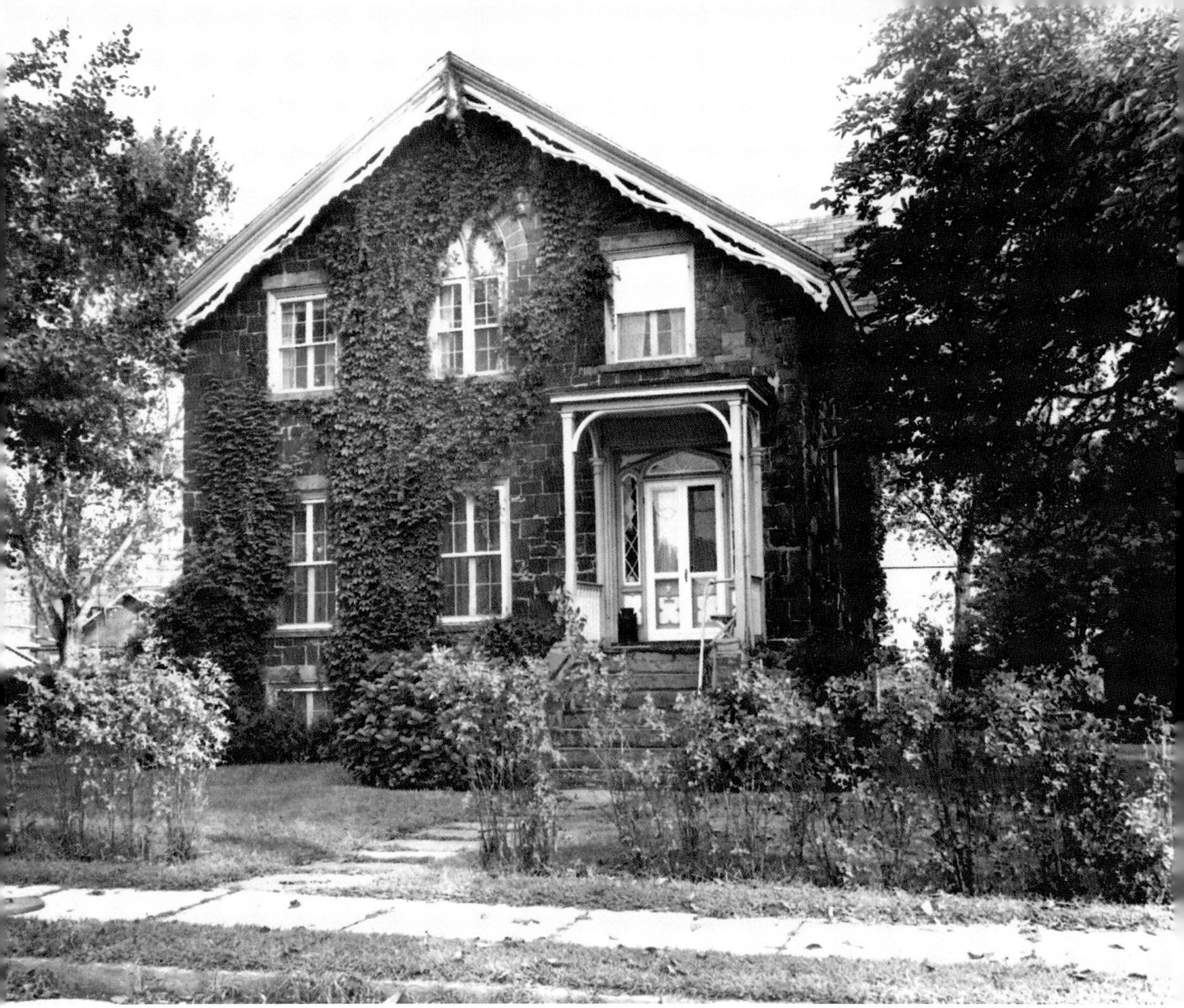

Located at 69 Delafield Place in Livingston is the former home of Dr. Samuel MacKenzie Elliott, a renowned eye doctor and abolitionist. Among his more noted patients were Gen. Winfield Scott, Francis Parkman, Henry Wadsworth Longfellow, and James Russell Lowell. During the Civil War, Dr. Elliott raised an infantry regiment, the 79th New York Highlanders, and led them into battle at Bull Run. In 1839, Dr. Elliott built so many houses in this part of Staten Island that the area became known as Elliottville. The house, built around 1850, is a New York City landmark and is on the state and national registers of historic places. Today the house is a private residence.

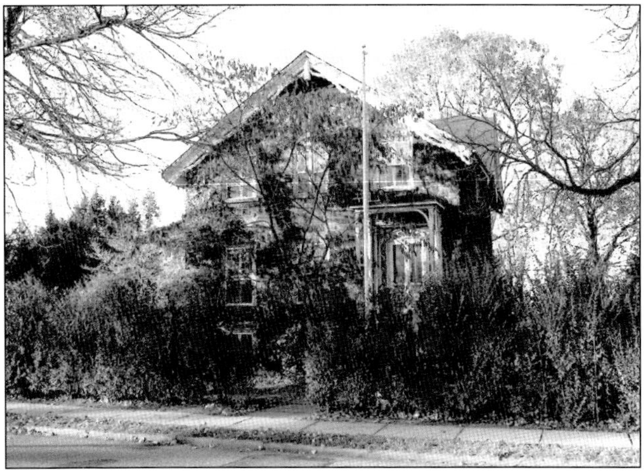

The original farm belonged to Joseph Alston, who built the farmhouse around 1810 and enlarged it around 1840, at the same time the porch was added. Located at 435 Richmond Hill Road, the farm was sold to Sylvanus Decker in 1841, and his family owned and operated the 11-acre farm until 1955. The last Decker to live there, Alberta Decker, willed the property to the Staten Island Historical Society, and it is operated by the Historic Richmond Town Restoration. The farmhouse and its surrounding property was designated a New York City landmark in 1967 and is operated today as a working farm and part of Historic Richmond Town. The farm is open to the public, and the Historic Richmond Town Restoration offers many educational programs for children and adults alike.

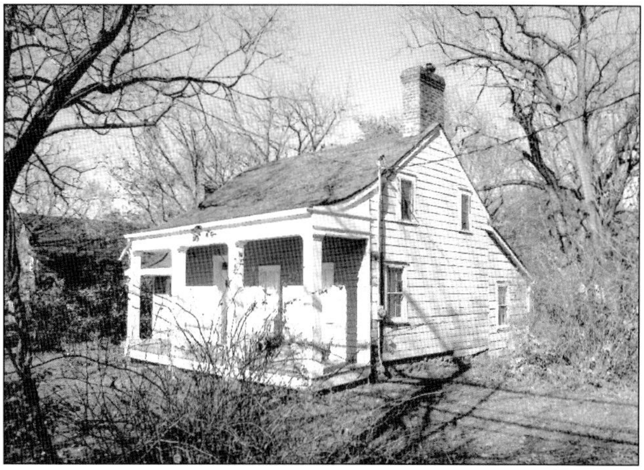

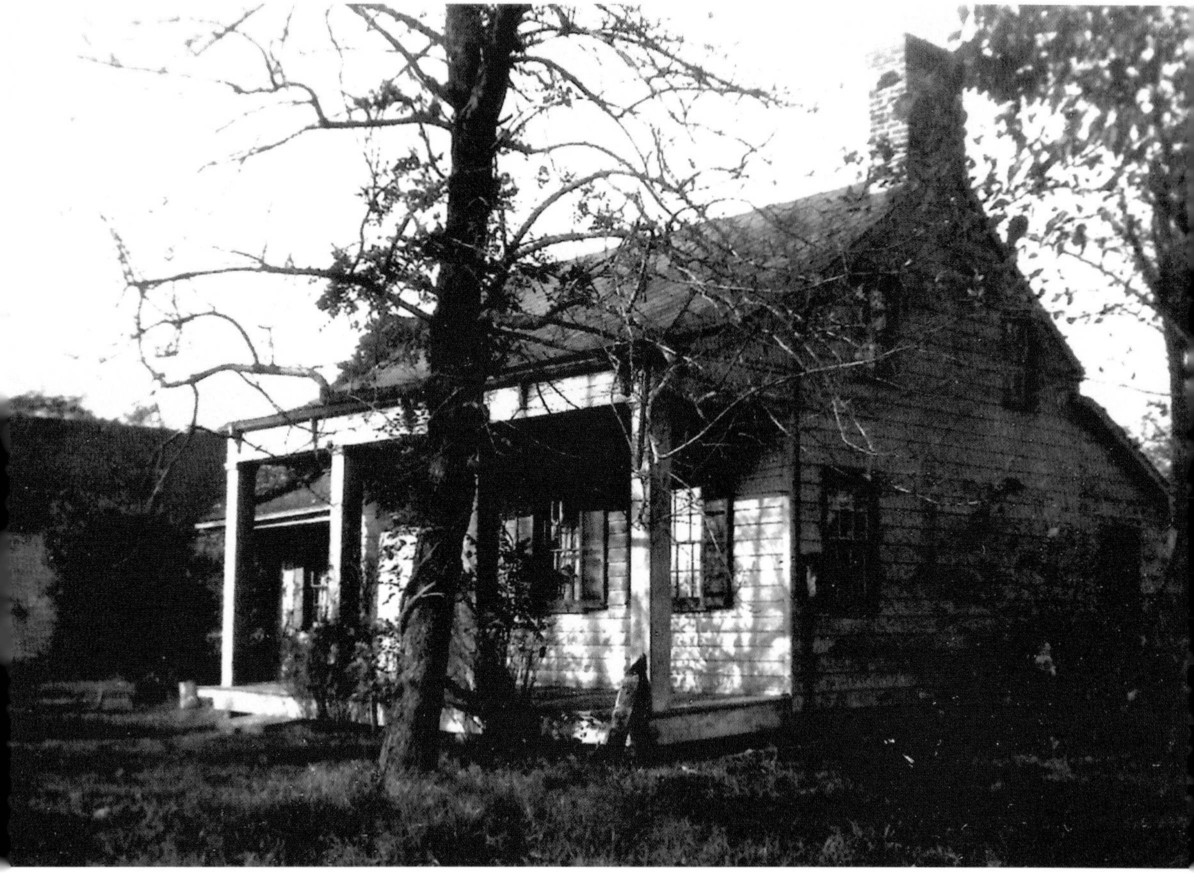

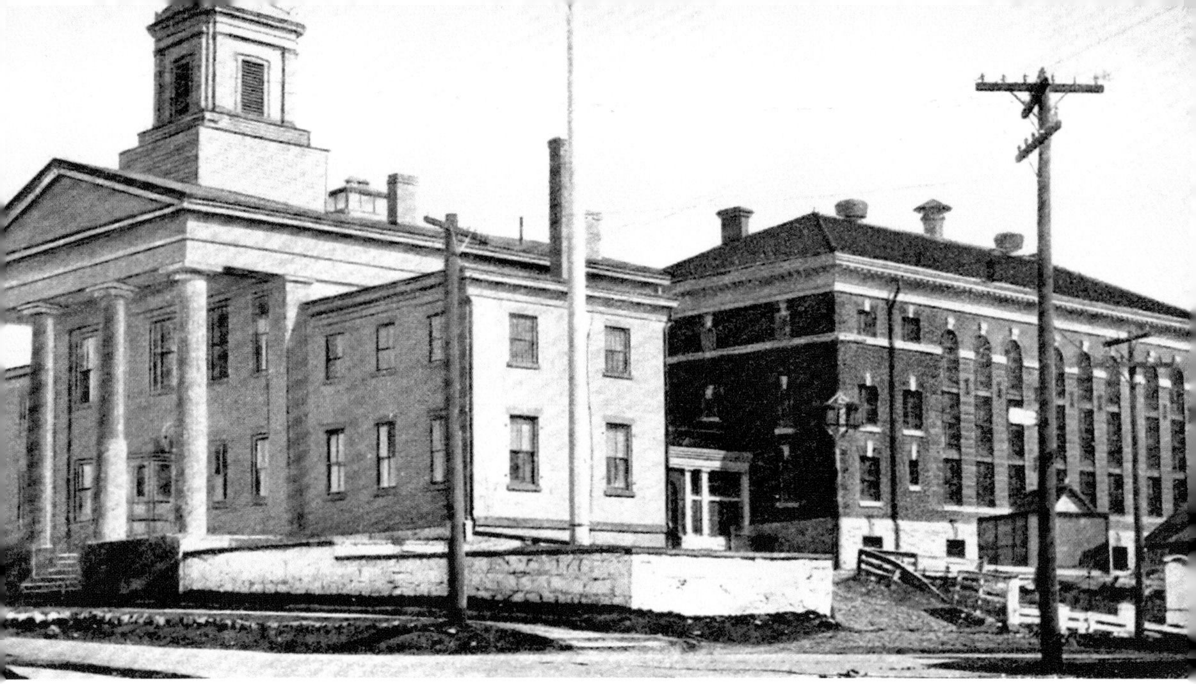

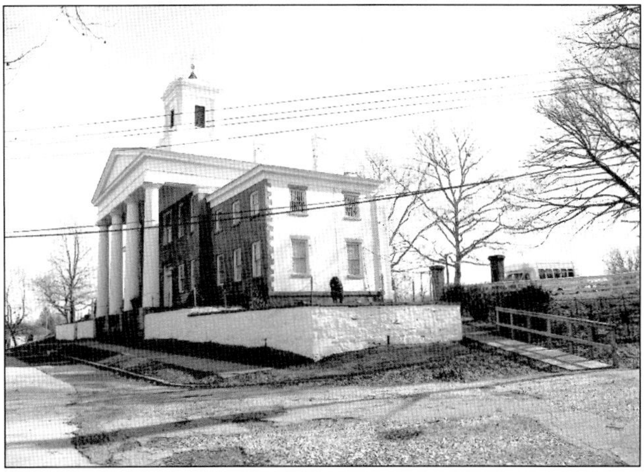

To accommodate the growing population, the state legislature approved the construction of the county's third courthouse. Construction was completed in 1839, and it served as the county courthouse until 1919, when court activities were moved to St. George. The jail was located on the second floor's west wing until 1860, when a larger land facility was built on directly behind the courthouse. This jail was the county's fourth jail and continued in use until 1955, when it was torn down, and the prisoners moved to the jail in the new courthouse in St. George.

The Actors' Fund of America opened the home on the site of Civil War hero Col. Richard Penn Smith's estate in West Brighton in 1902. Built in 1877, the home housed elderly troupers who wished to spend their remaining years in retirement together. The ground floor had a number of salons, a spacious dining hall, a billiard room, and a parlor set up with card tables. The second and third floors had about 50 rooms and a number of private baths. The home moved to Englewood, New Jersey, in 1929 when the Actors' Fund purchased property there, where it still operates to this day. The home remained standing until 1938, and in 1963, it was acquired by the parks department to be used as a parking lot for the Staten Island Zoo.

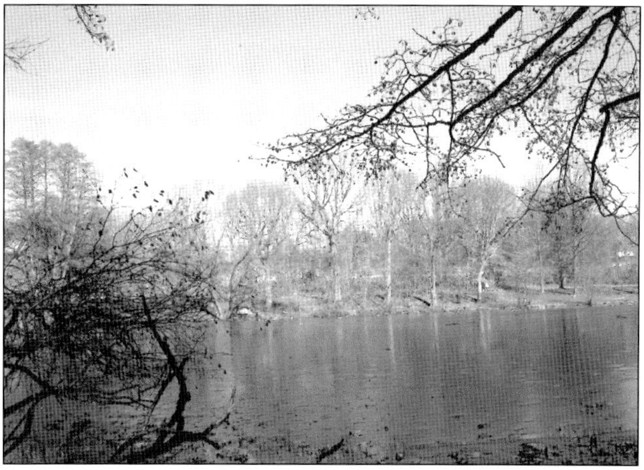

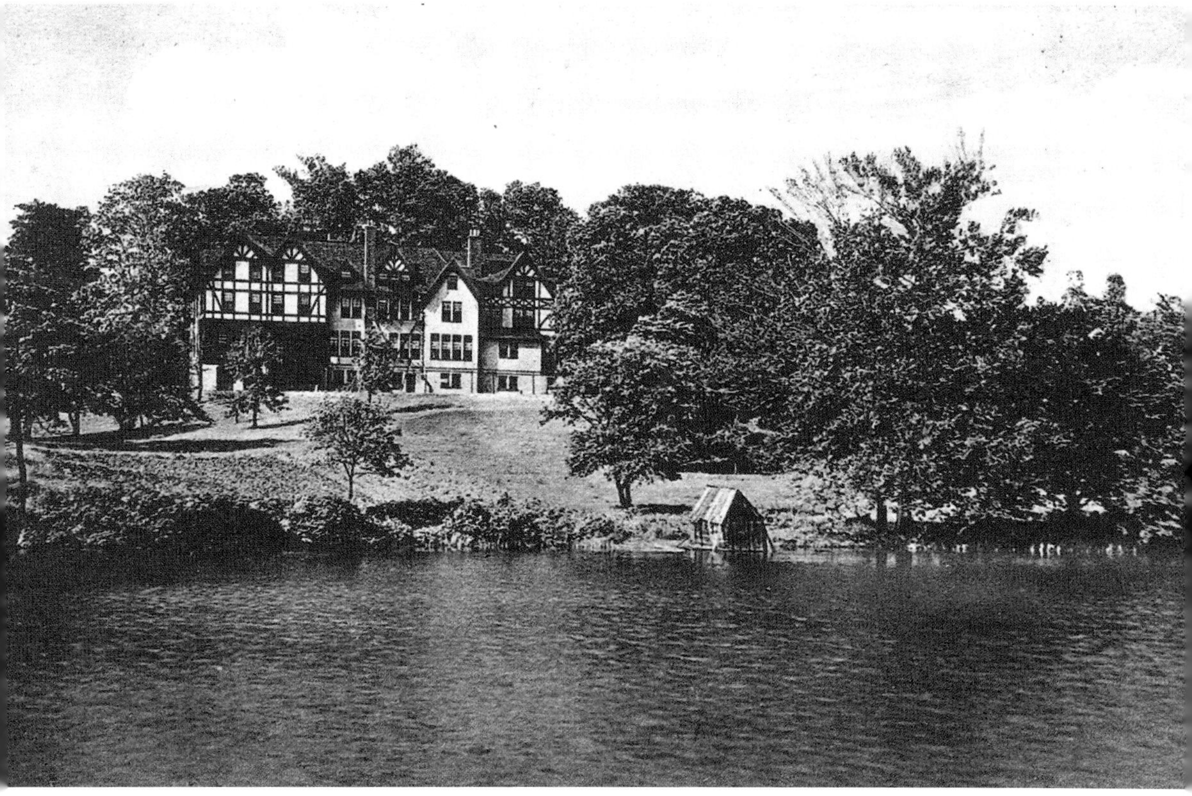

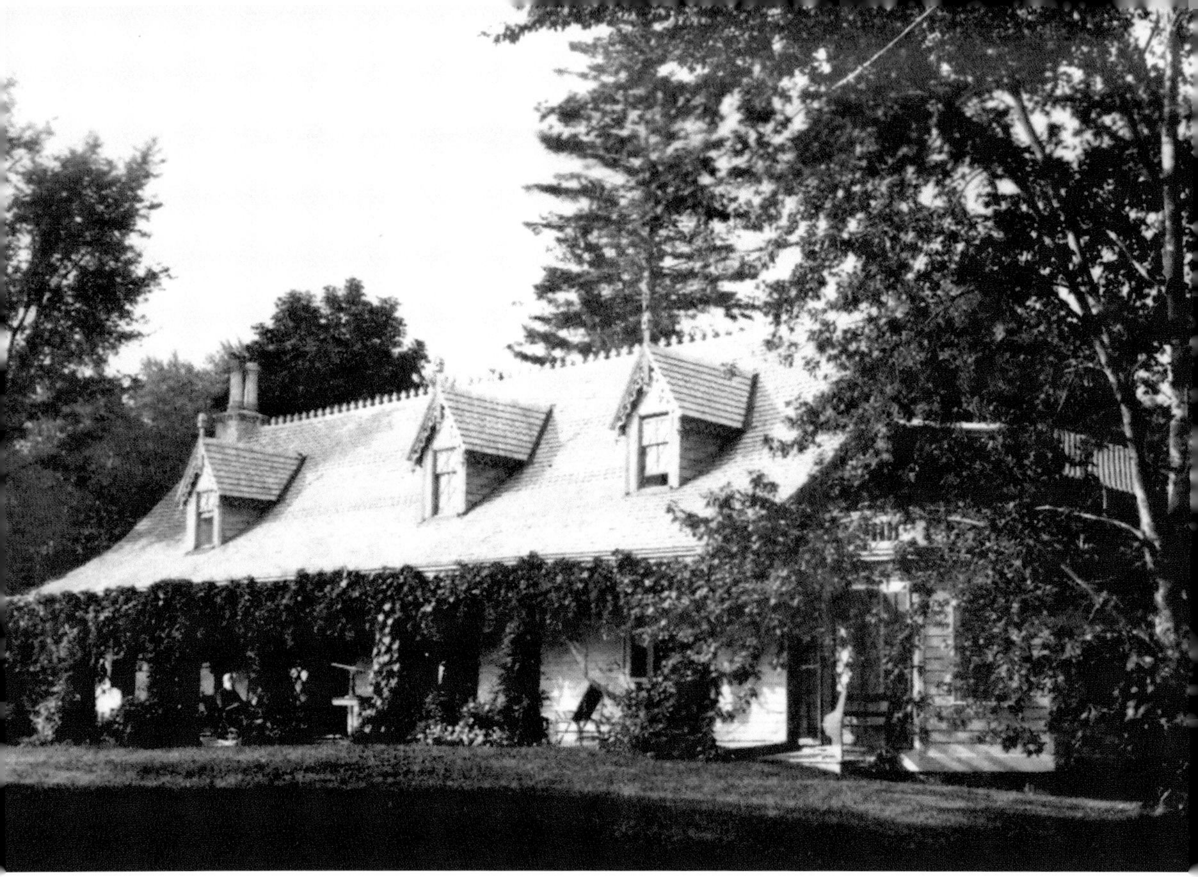

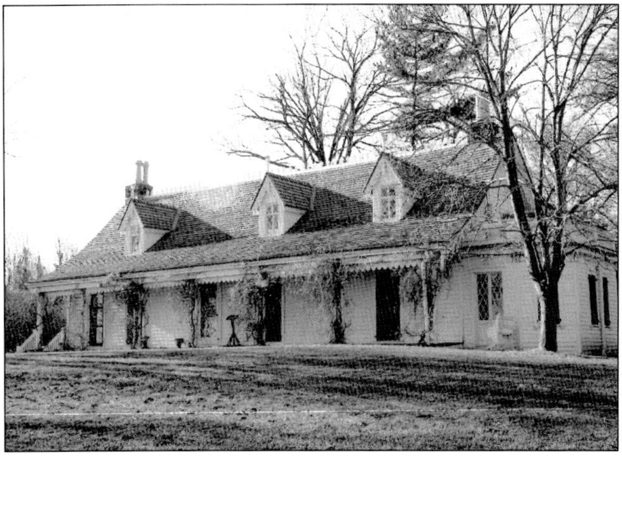

Built during the early 1700s, this one-room Dutch Colonial house (pictured here in 1888) was purchased and enlarged during the 1800s by the Austen family. The most prominent member of the family was Alice. She was one of the country's preeminent photographers of her time. She began taking photographs in 1884 and did so until about 1934—amassing a collection of nearly 8,000 photographs. Her photographs are considered one of the finest works chronicling life in the late 19th and early 20th century in America. Her work and life story became the subject of a *Life* magazine article in the September 24, 1951, issue. In 1971, the house was designated a historic landmark by New York City. Today her home is a museum and open to the public.

The home for the Richmond County Country Club was originally constructed by Junius Brutus Alexander in the late 1800s. Alexander was a wealthy cotton grower and built this as a summer home for his family. Located on Flagg Place on Todt Hill, the house had a rather unique design. Built of brick, the three-story house was encircled by a second structure of wood creating an air space that helped to insulate the house (pictured below in 1885). The grounds were beautifully landscaped with stables, a coach house, and several other outer buildings. In 1894, the house and grounds were acquired by the Richmond County Country Club. For many years, members enjoyed fox hunting, but as time passed, golf became the preferred sport of members.

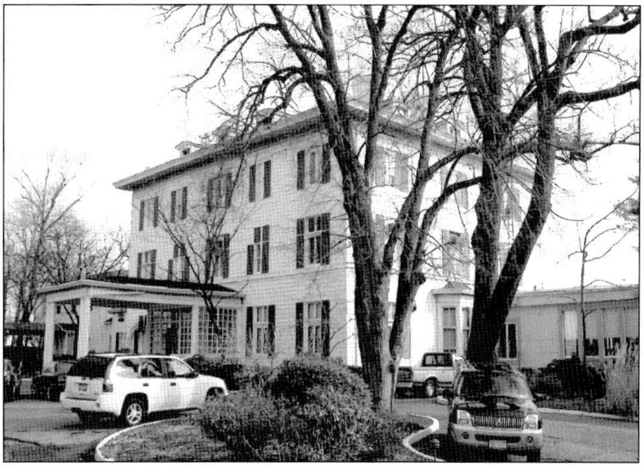

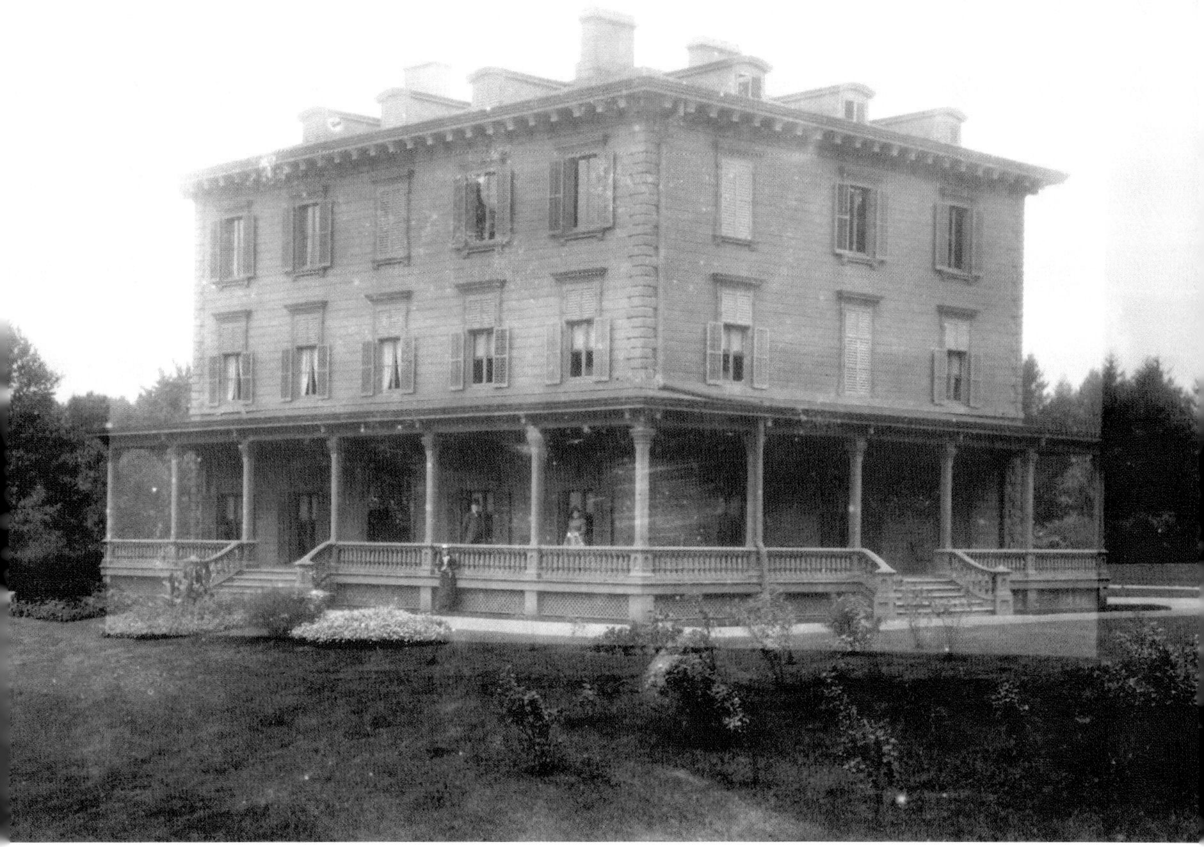

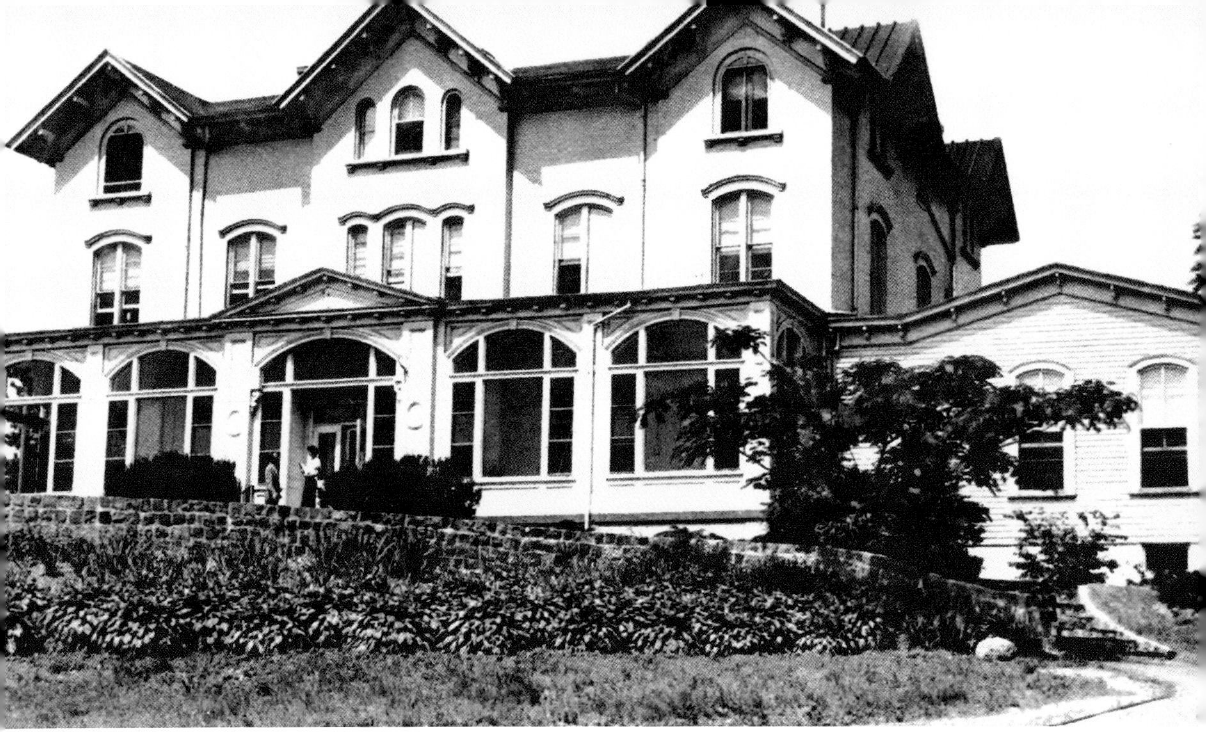

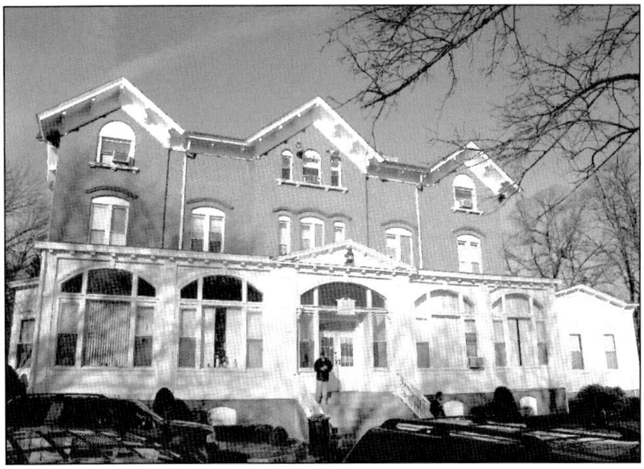

Sir Edward Cunard lived on Grymes Hill in a mansion he built for his family in 1851. He named his property Bellevue (superb view) for its magnificent vistas of New York's harbor. One of Cunard's neighbors was Gen. William Green Ward, whose estate he had named Oneata (kissed by the dawn) was built one year later. Both estates were acquired by Wagner College and are an integral part of its campus today. The Ward mansion serves as the music building, and the old Cunard mansion (Cunard Hall) is home to various administrative offices.

On the left in the photograph is the St. George Theatre. Located at 27 Hyatt Street in St. George, the theater was opened to the public on December 4, 1929, with a seating capacity of 3,000 for patrons to enjoy movies and other theatrical performances. The luxurious decor was second to none with its baroque retractable chandelier, Spanish mission–style light fixtures, and murals. In 1958, the Richmond Opera Company made the St. George Theatre its home, offering professional performances to the island. The building in the center of the picture is Borough Hall, how it looked in 1935.

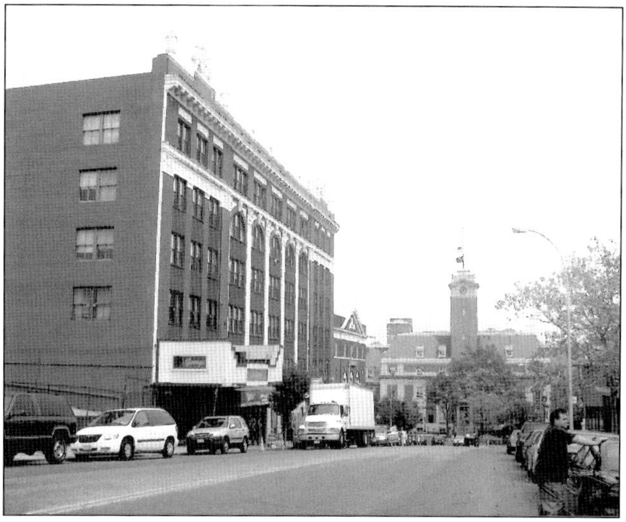

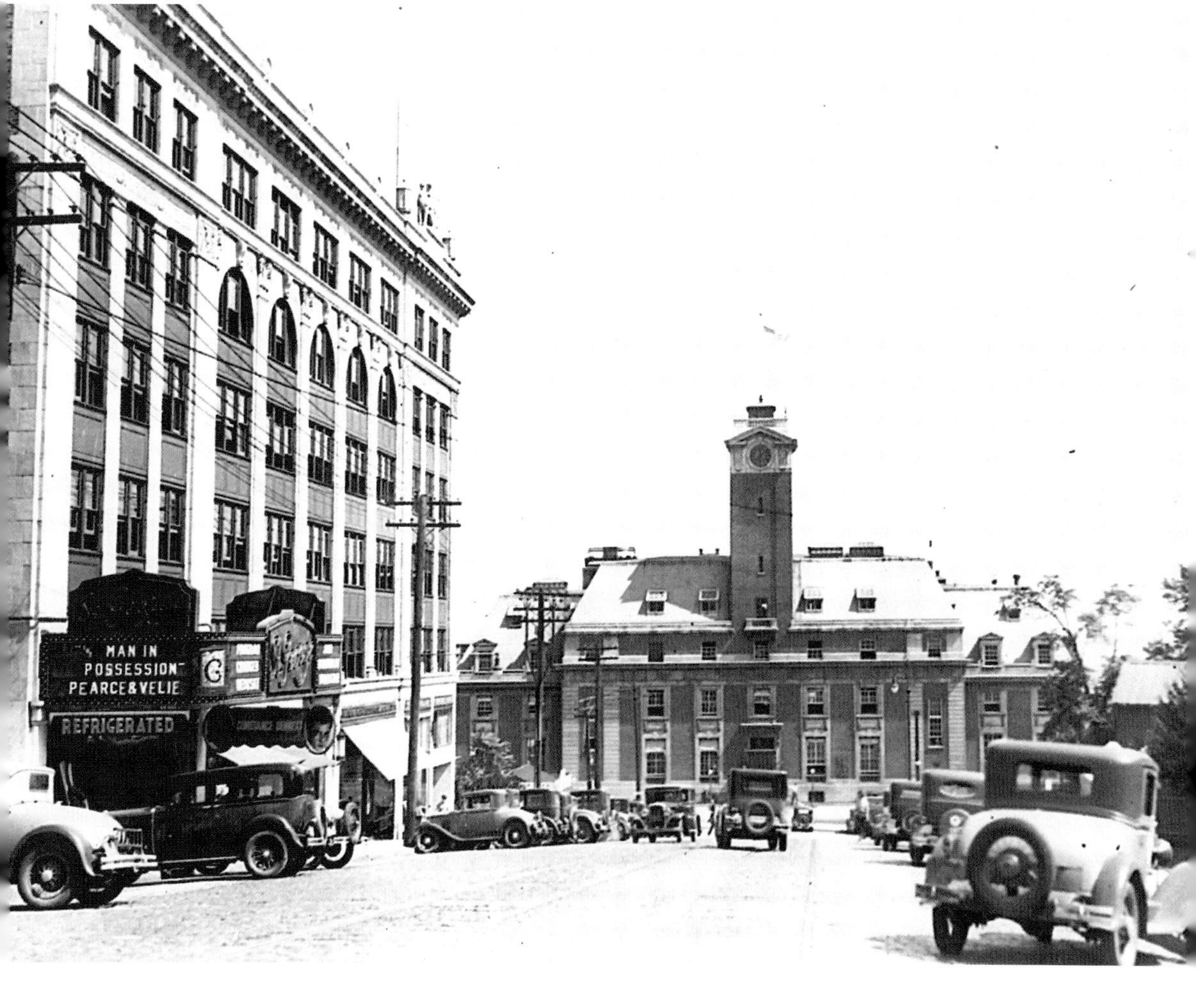

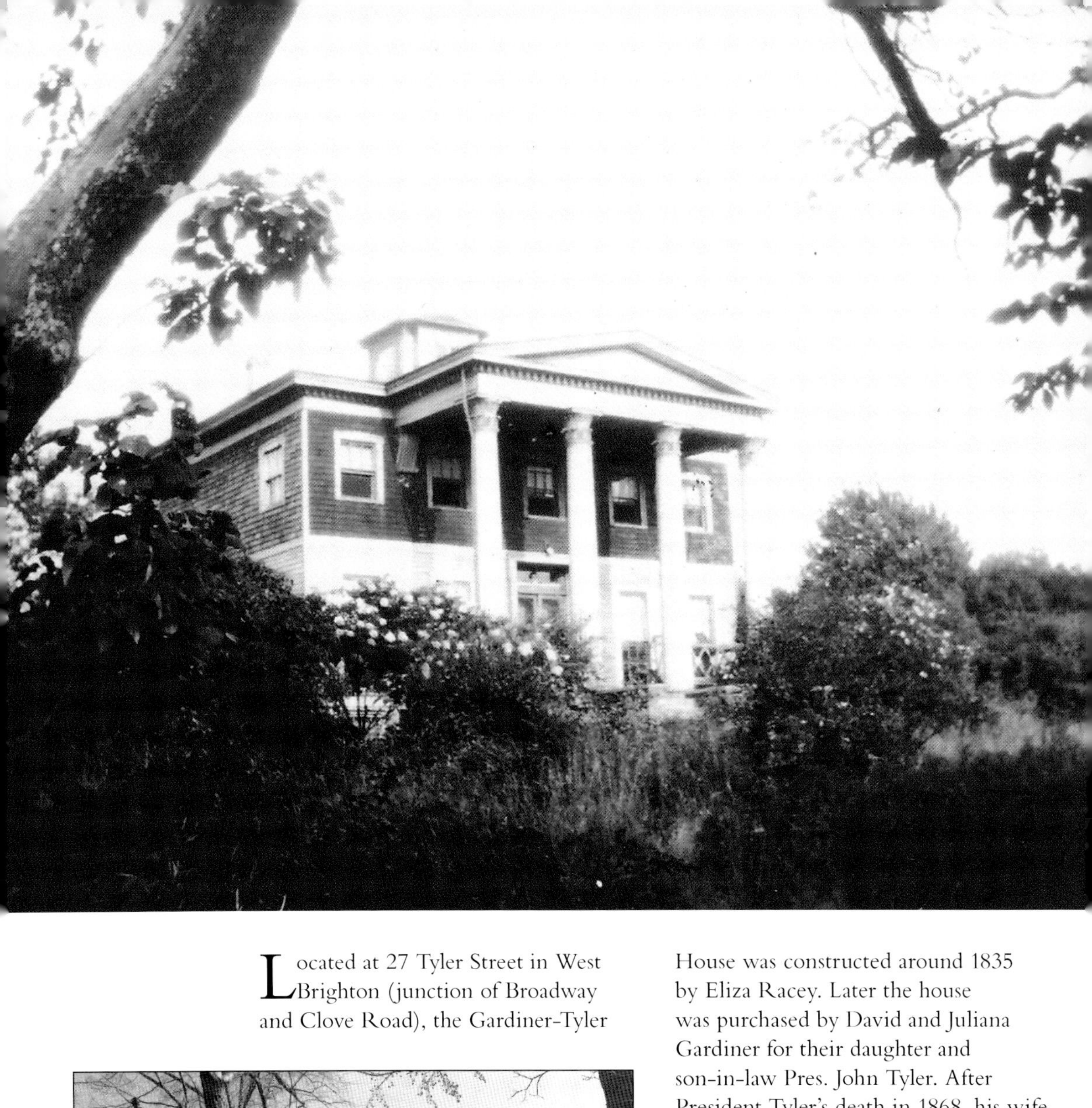

Located at 27 Tyler Street in West Brighton (junction of Broadway and Clove Road), the Gardiner-Tyler House was constructed around 1835 by Eliza Racey. Later the house was purchased by David and Juliana Gardiner for their daughter and son-in-law Pres. John Tyler. After President Tyler's death in 1868, his wife moved to Staten Island with her seven stepchildren and lived there with her mother for 15 years. After Julia's death, the house was purchased by William M. Evarts, who served as attorney general under Pres. Andrew Johnson and as secretary of state for Pres. Rutherford Hayes. Today the house is a New York City landmark, and it continues to be a private residence.

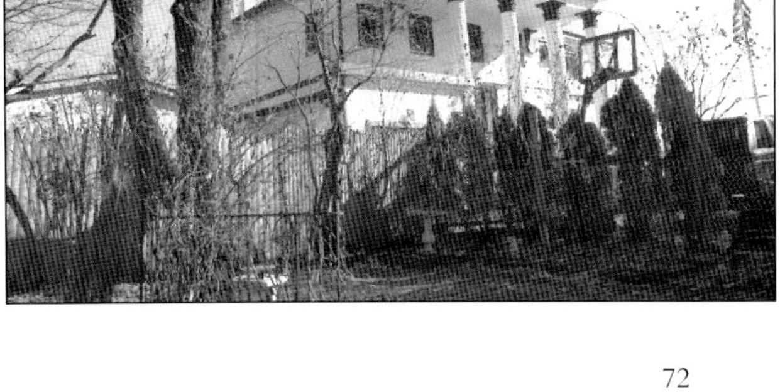

Known as the Henry Hogg Biddle House, the structure was built in the 1840s overlooking the Arthur Kill in Tottenville with commanding views of Raritan Bay. (Originally Henry Biddle Hogg, he changed his name when he moved to Staten Island from New York in 1828.) Its unusual design combined Dutch Colonial with Greek Revival to produce a structure with two-story porticoes on both the front and rear of the house, the only one of its kind built on Staten Island. The house was restored and is a private residence today. Located at 70 Satterlee Street, the house became a New York City landmark in 1990.

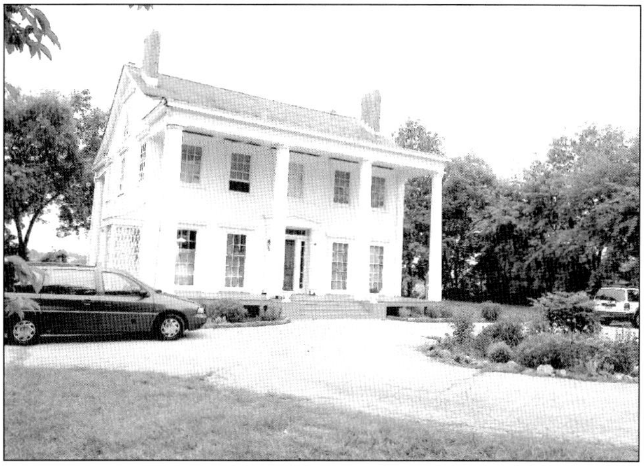

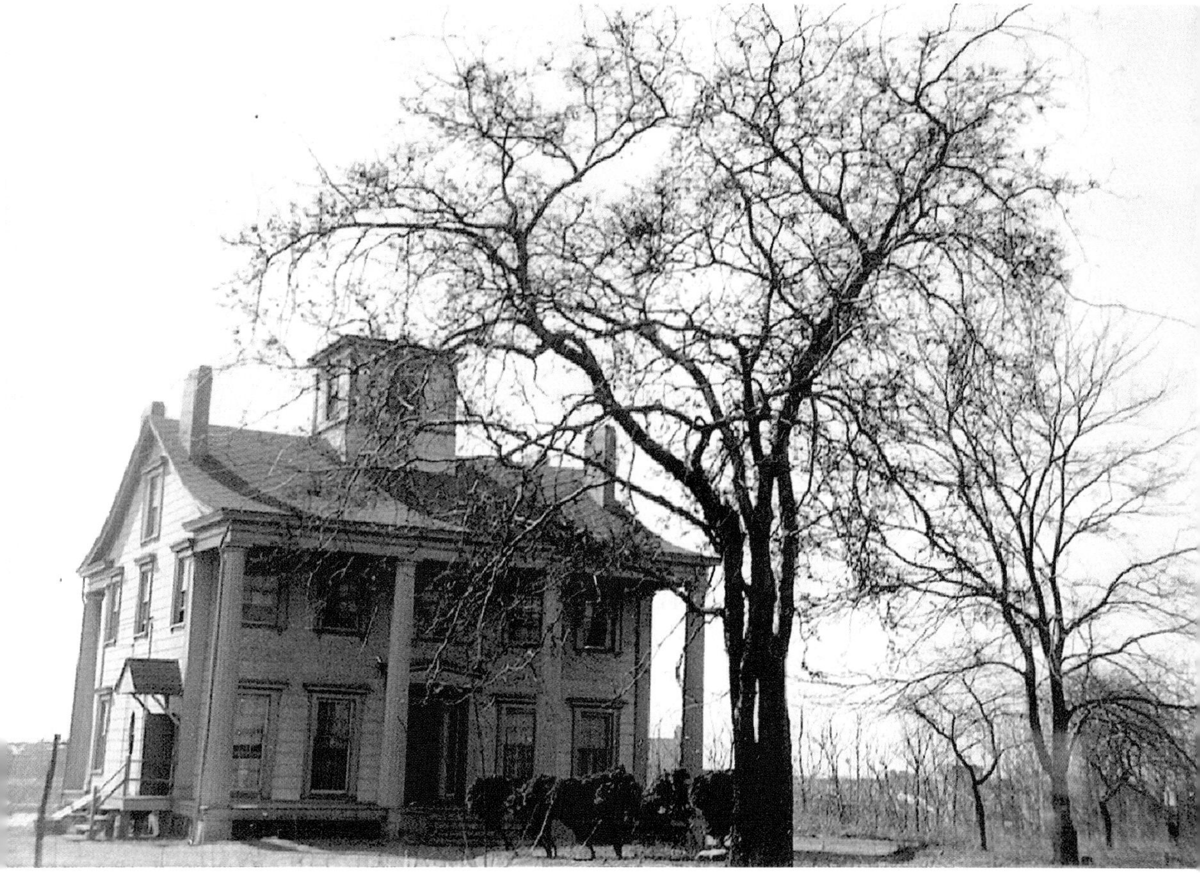

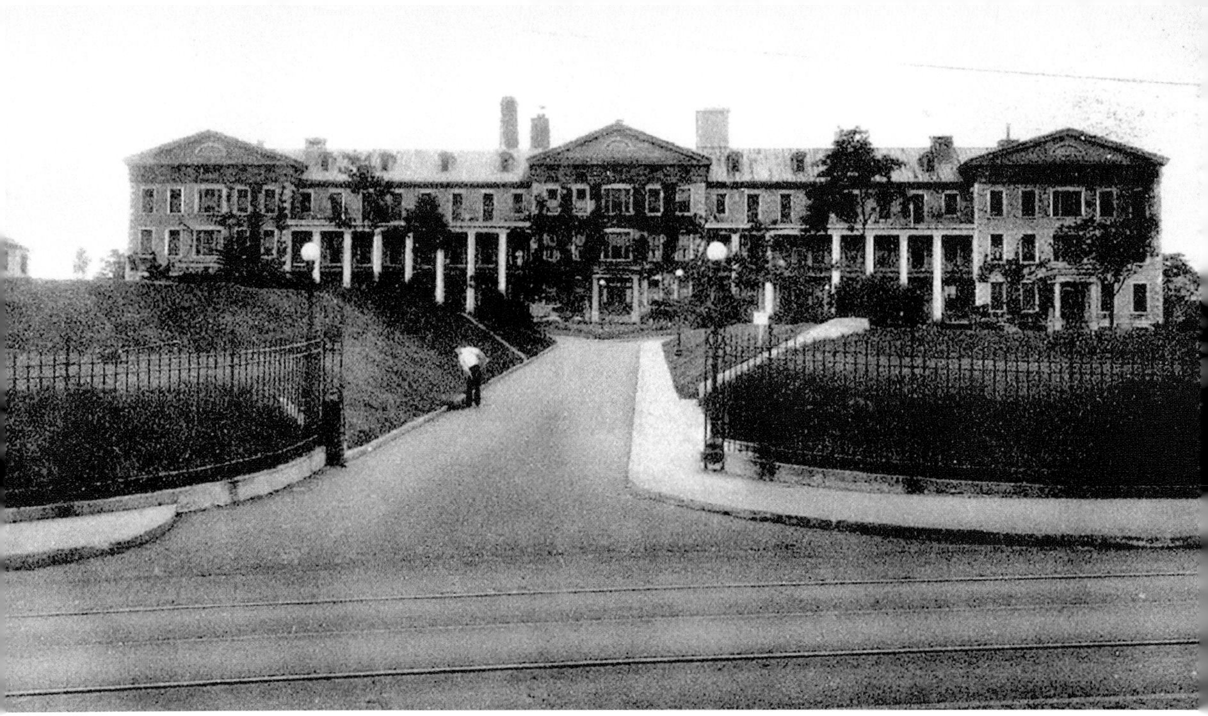

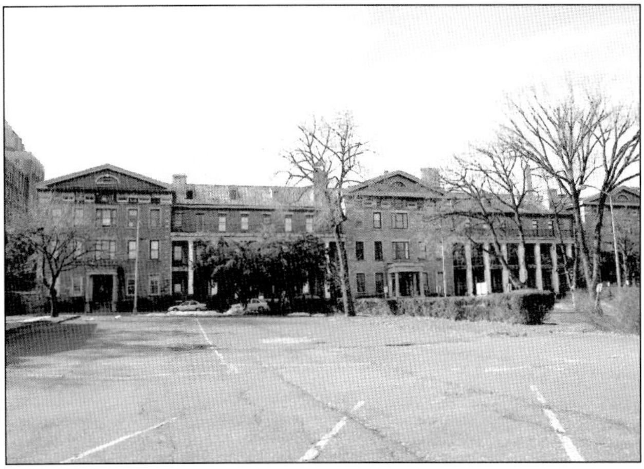

This hospital originally opened in 1831 as the Seamen's Retreat to provide care for 34 sick and disabled merchant seamen and continued until 1882. The property was leased by the federal government for the use as the Marine Hospital and was finally purchased by them in 1903. In 1931, the government purchased additional property from the Vanderbilt family, and the expanded site became the United States Public Health Service Hospital. The government closed the facility, and in 1983, it was acquired by St. Vincent's Medical Center to operate Bayley Seton Hospital as a community hospital. Escalating costs and declining changes in health care has forced the hospital to plan on closing its doors in 2005. Although the facility remains open, its fate is still uncertain.

The Old Mill Restaurant was originally known as the Grasmere Tea Room and Golf Course. Located at the corner of Clove Road and Hylan Boulevard, it was built in 1930. The distinctive twin windmills were added along with a cocktail lounge, banquet hall, and an outdoor dance floor in 1933. It was among the most popular spots on the island until it was destroyed by fire in 1957. Today a Chase Manhattan Bank occupies the site.

Chapter 6
BUSINESS AND INDUSTRY

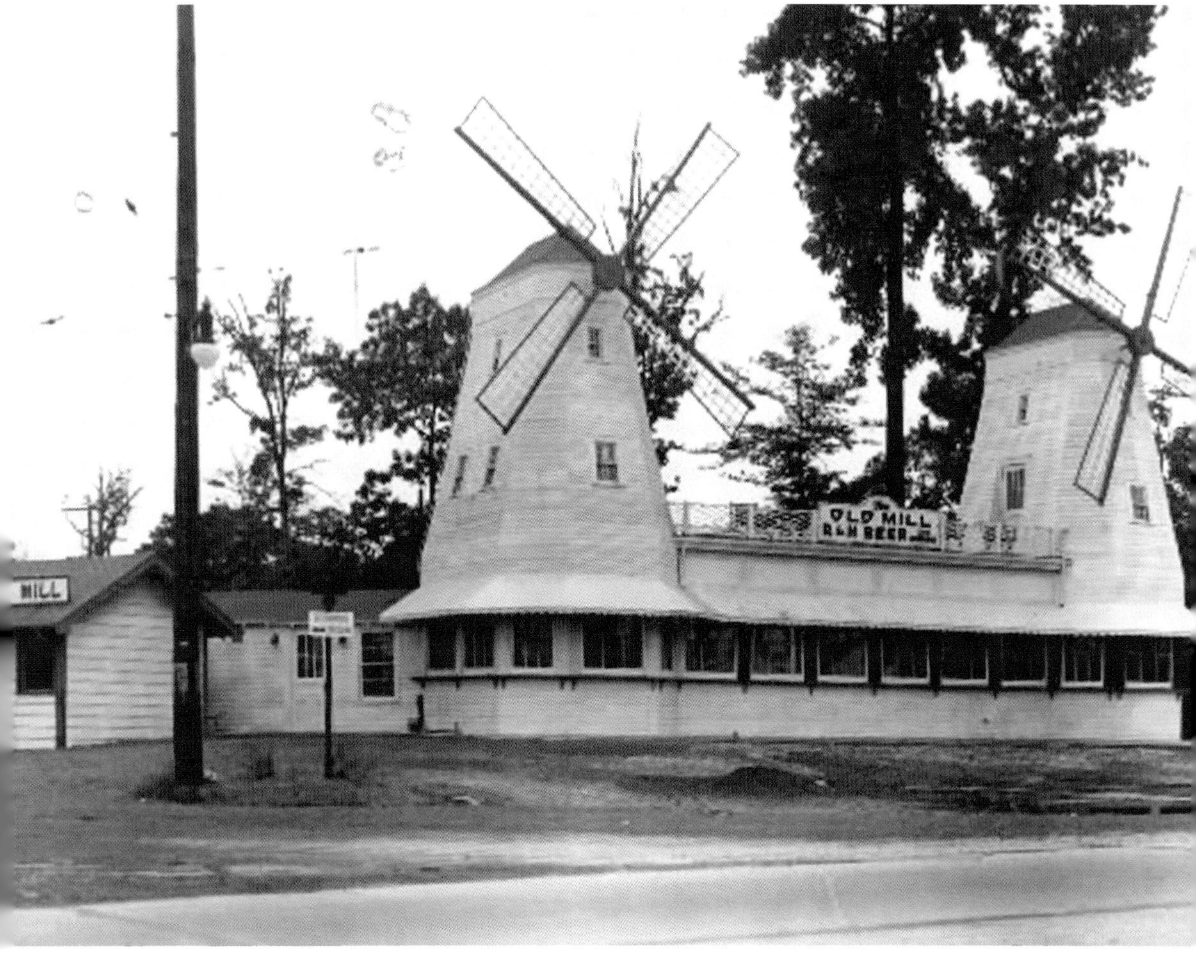

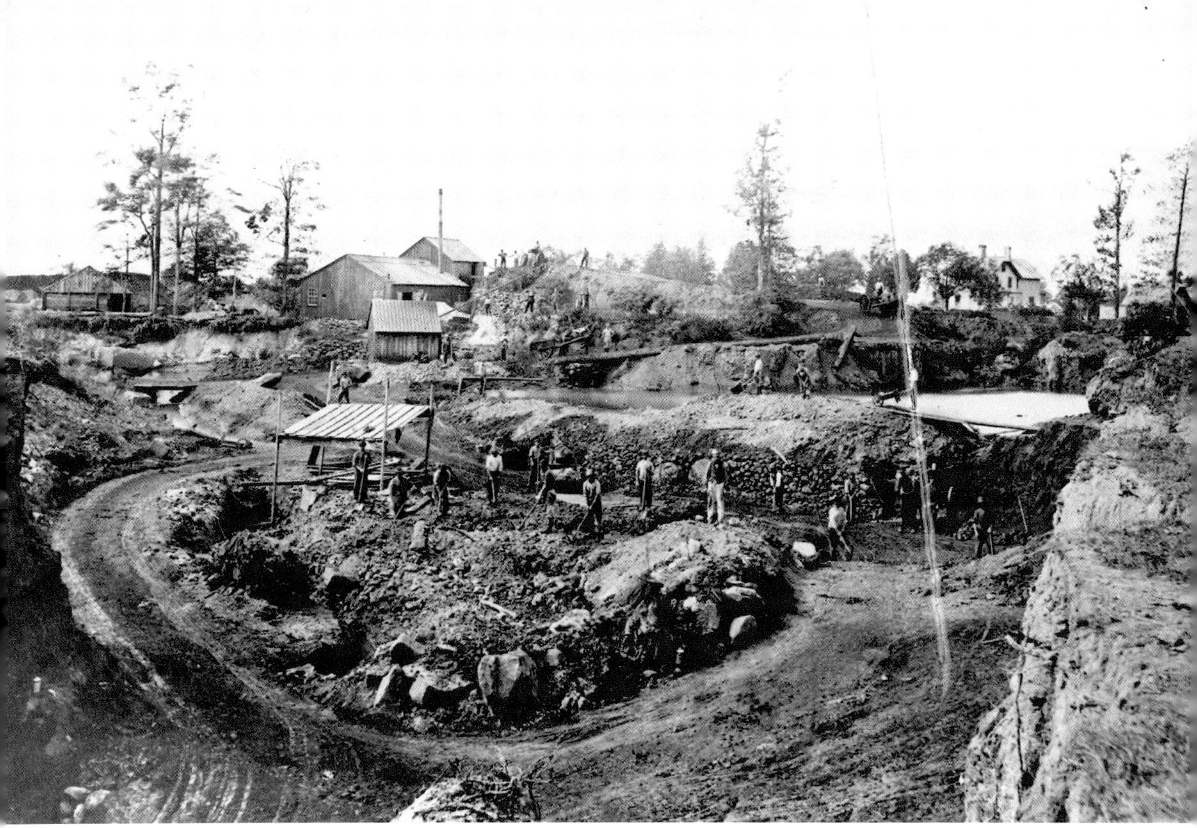

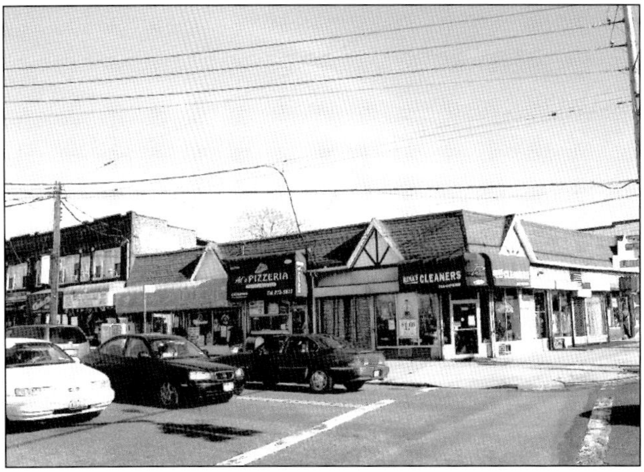

The existence of iron ore on Staten Island was known to the early settlers; however, it was not until the early 1800s that it became important enough to commercially mine. The ore was easily mined from serpentine rock formations left by receding glaciers near the surface. The early Dutch settlers called the area Iron or Yserberg Hill, known today as Todt Hill. This ease of access to the ore simplified the process and gave rise to a number of mines opened in and around Todt Hill, Emerson Hill, and Jewett Avenue (pictured here). The last mine to close was on Jewett Avenue, but before it closed, Staten Island mines had yielded over 300,000 tons of iron ore.

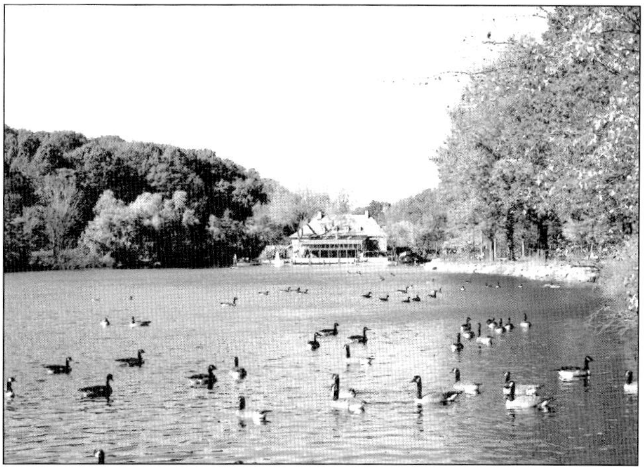

Ice harvesting was a profitable business in the 19th century. Ice was in great demand by the growing beer industry as well as other businesses and homes alike. Ice was harvested from lakes and ponds across the island (both Clove Lake and Silver Lake would freeze to depths of 14 inches and greater). The island's first icehouse was built in 1835 at Britton's Mill Pond (Clove Lake—pictured above), and it became the Richmond Ice Company. With the advent of home refrigeration, the ice industry slowly died, and the last great harvest was during the winter of 1919–1920. Today the Lake Café restaurant is on the site of the icehouse.

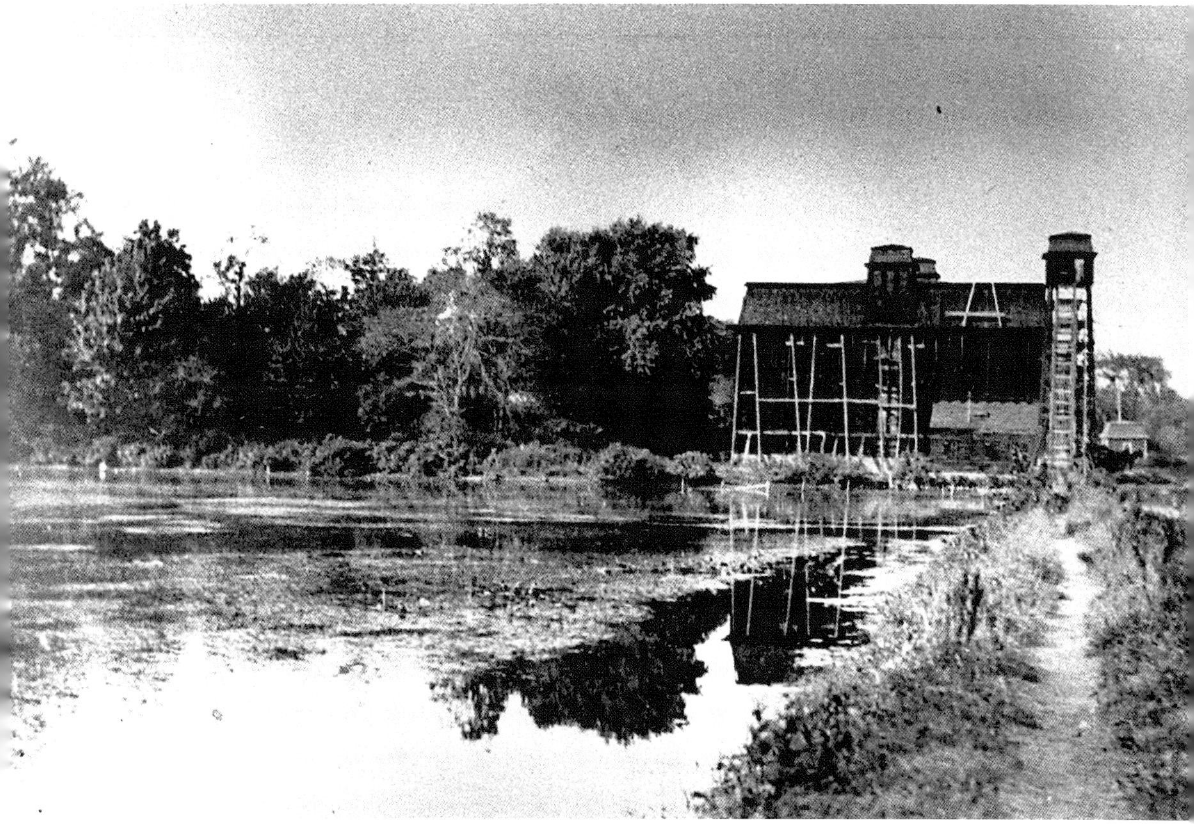

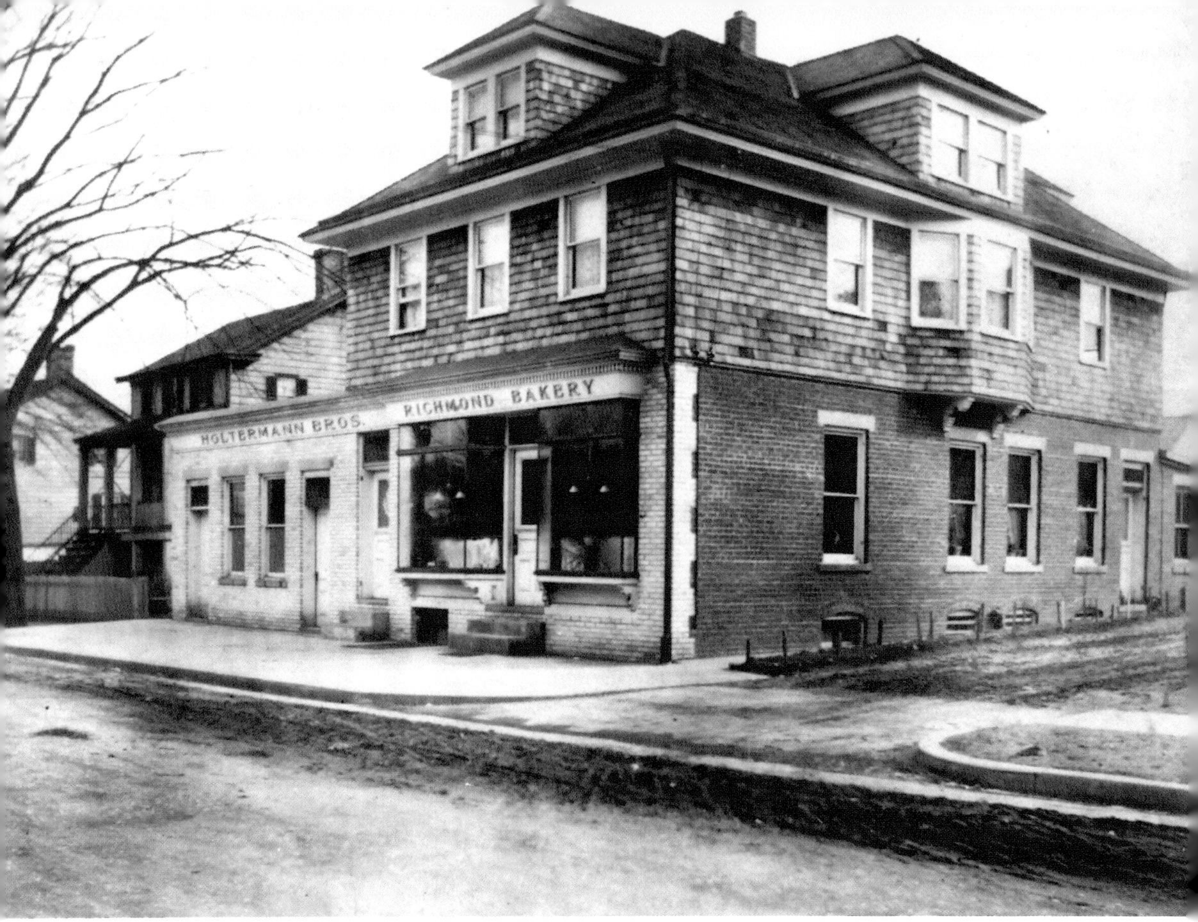

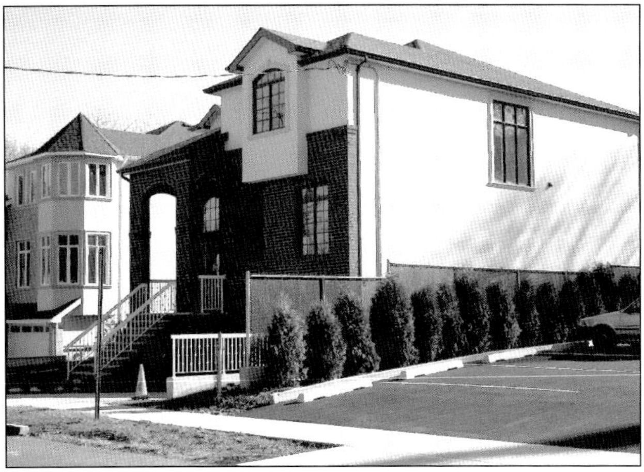

Holtermann's Bakery, a household name for over 100 years, began making bakery goods on Arthur Kill Road in Richmondtown. A German emigrant, Claus Holtermann purchased the Garrett Homan Bakery, which was operating from the old Treasure House, and established Holtermann's Bakery. In 1882, Holtermann moved the bakery into the candy factory (pictured above). Many of his bakers were brought in from Germany and lived in rooms above the bakery. In 1930, Albert Holtermann, Claus's brother, moved the operation to its present location at 405 Arthur Kill Road after he built it himself. Although home delivery ended in 1978, Holtermann's Bakery remains Staten Island's oldest bakery.

Stapleton was considered the financial center of Staten Island in the mid- to late 1800s. Several banks opened during that period, including the Edgewater Cooperative Exchange and Building and Loan Association of Staten Island (1887), the Stapleton National Bank (1902), the Richmond Borough National Bank of Stapleton (1904), and the Staten Island Bank and Trust (1867). The only one remaining is the Staten Island Bank and Trust. Pictured here, around 1878, the bank operated on Beach and Water Streets. In 1925, the current building was erected and still serves the community today.

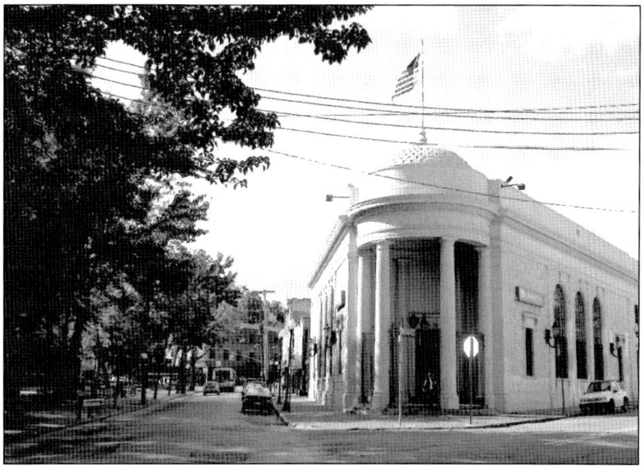

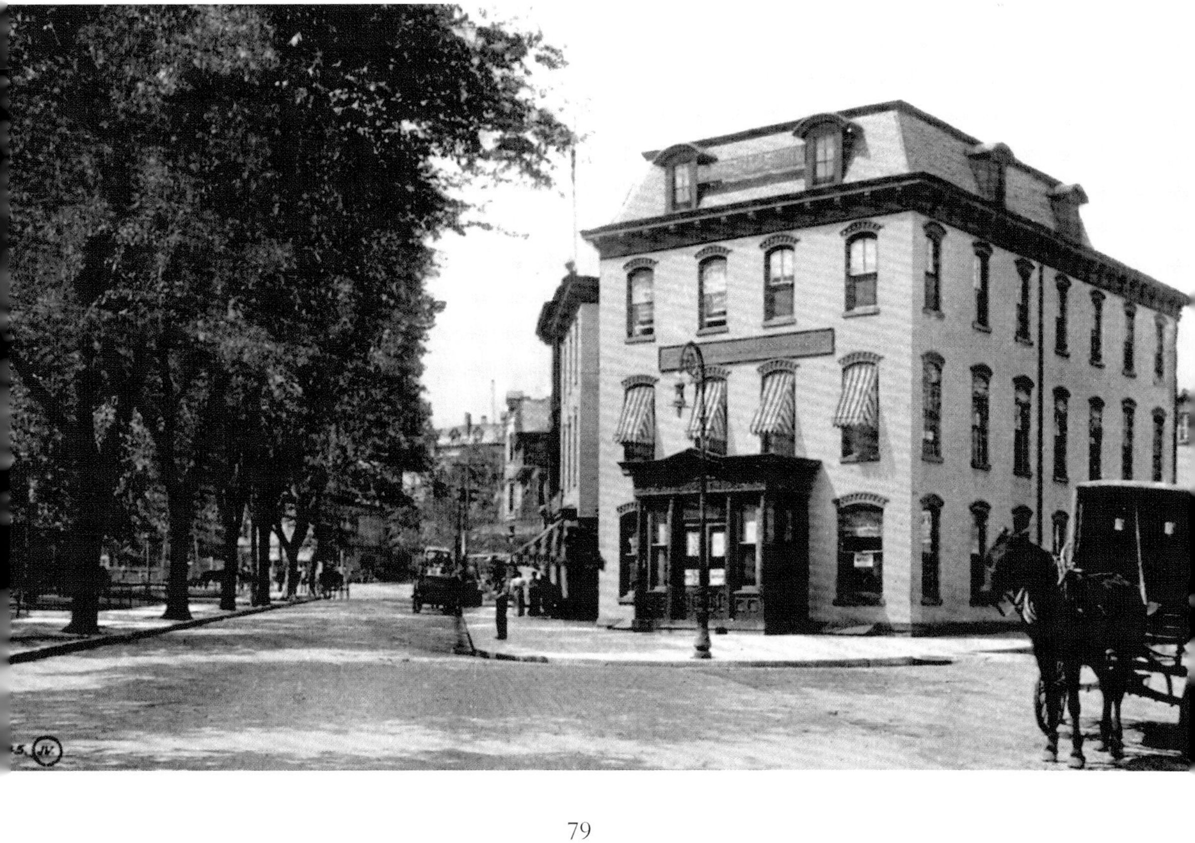

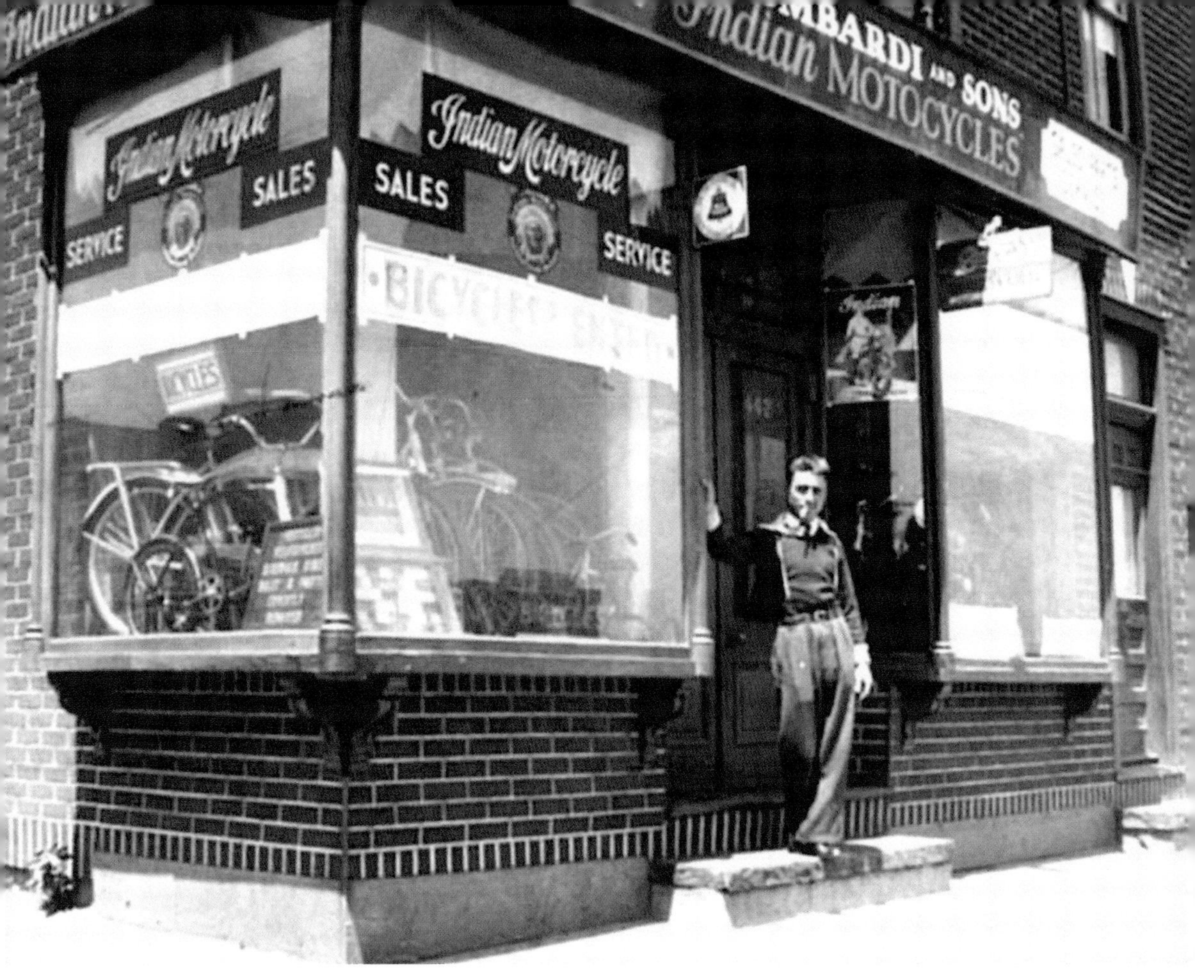

In 1905, Frank Lombardi established a general store in Graniteville where he sold everything from food, to bicycles, to guns, and even farm equipment. Although his main income came from selling pasta, he gradually began concentrating on selling motorcycles. By 1914, he was only featuring American Indian motorcycles and had given up the general store business. In 1927, he moved his business to 457 Bay Street in Stapleton. In 1932, the business was moved across the street to its current address, 440 Bay Street. The business has remained in the Lombardi family for over 100 years and is currently operated by Michael Lombardi Jr. (standing in front of the building), the grandson of the founder, Frank Lombardi. Michael's father, Michael Sr., is seen standing in front of the 420 Bay Street store around 1942.

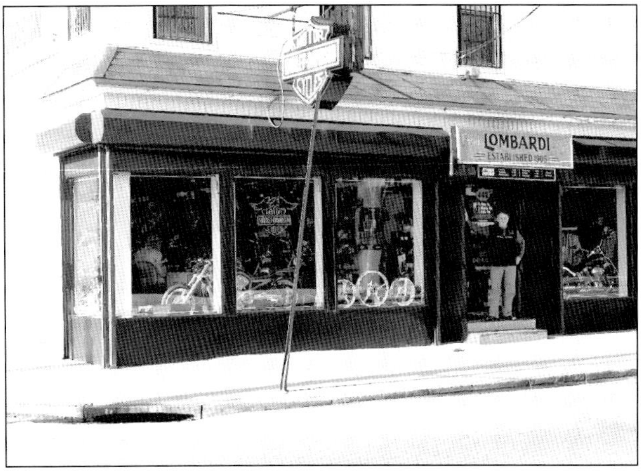

To meet the medical needs of a growing community, the Dreyfus Foundation and the South Shore community came together to open Richmond Memorial Hospital. The hospital began in a converted farmhouse, providing care with 25 beds in 1920. As the popularity of the South Shore grew, so did its need for additional medical care. In 1929, and again in 1935, Louis A. Dreyfus and the community teamed up again and expanded the hospital's facilities, bringing the bed capacity to over 100. Expansions continued through the 1950s and 1960s until the mid-1980s, when a new facility was constructed. In 1989, Richmond Memorial Hospital became part of Staten Island University Hospital System.

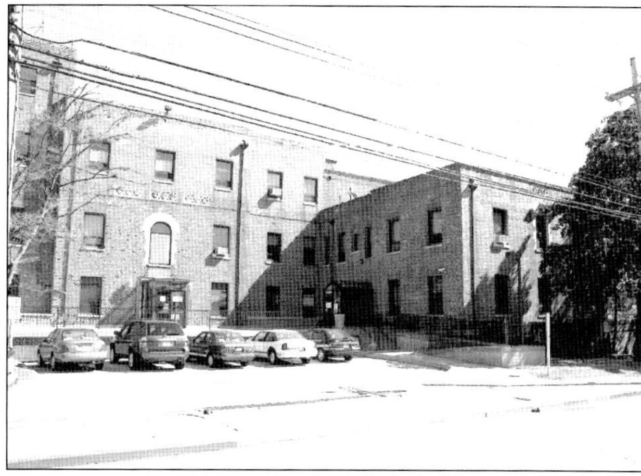

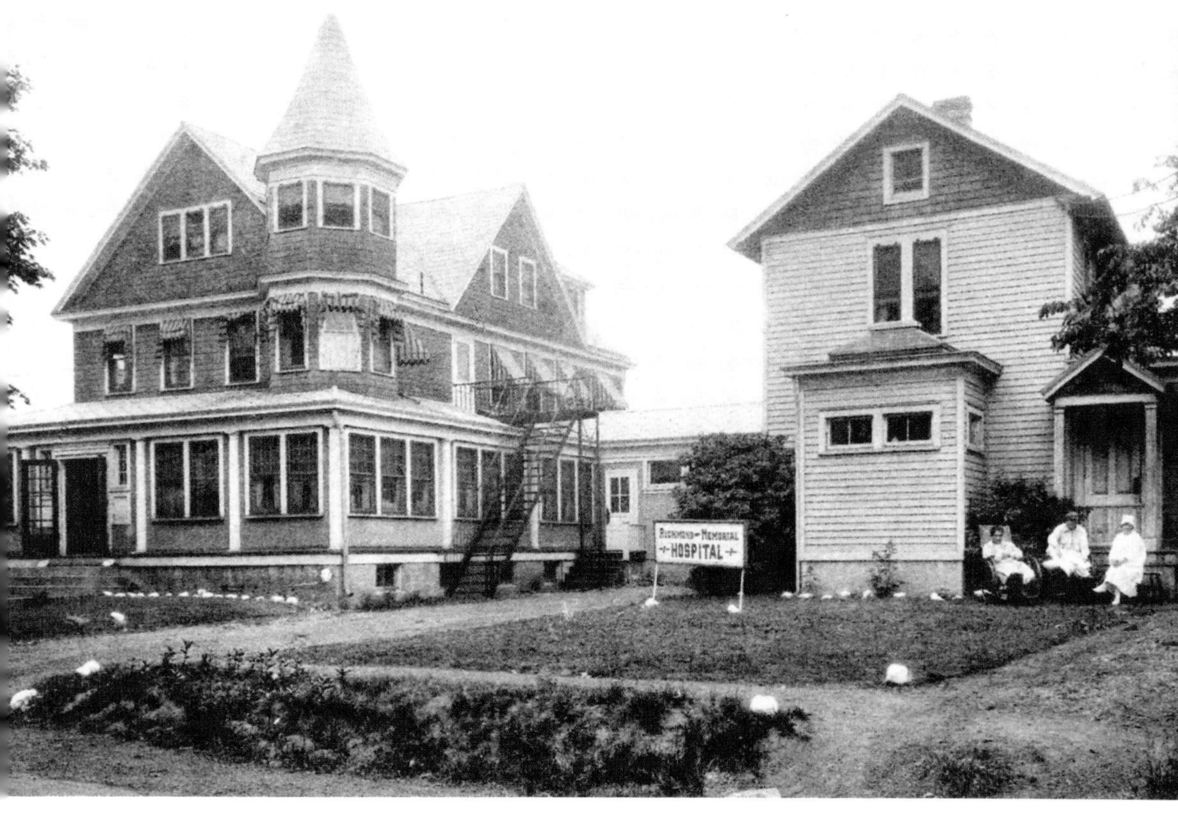

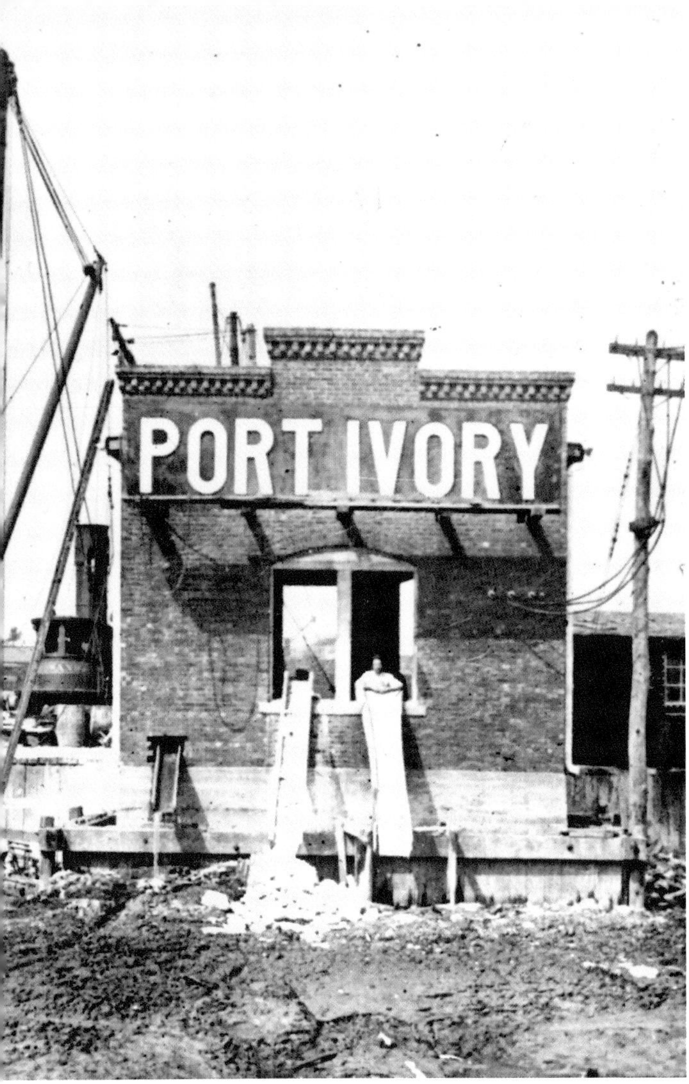

Procter and Gamble was founded in 1837 when William Procter (a candle maker) and James Gamble (a soap maker) formed a partnership. In 1905, the company purchased 77 acres on the Kill Van Kull near Holland Hook and began operations in 1907. The location was named for the products made there by the company, notably Ivory soap and Crisco. Initially the plant produced one million cases of Ivory and Lenox bar soaps, and in its heyday, 1,500 workers were producing packaged soap chips, flakes, granules, and powder soap in addition to its famous bars. The company also made food shortening, oil meal for fertilizer, and animal feed as well as the tubs, barrels, and crates needed for shipping at the Port Ivory location. The plant ceased operation in 1991.

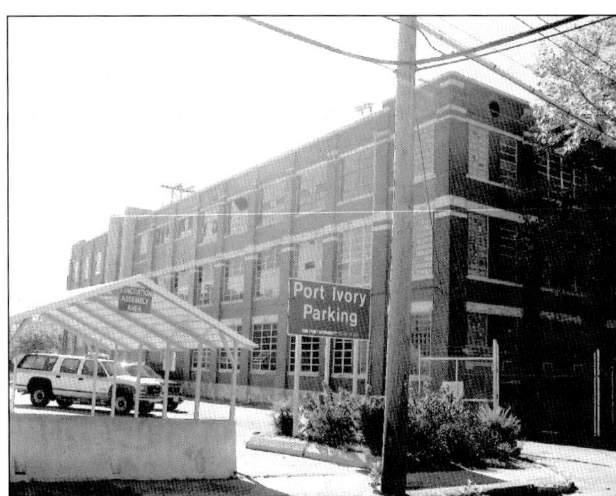

Located at the foot of Broad and Van Duzer Streets in Stapleton, Bechtel was one of several breweries operating on Staten Island. The brewery was known as Schmidt's Constanz Brewery when it opened in 1852 and continued to flourish until Prohibition. The brewery building became Demyan's Hofbrau Restaurant, a favorite of many islanders. It was the caterer for the crew of *The Godfather* during filming on Staten Island. After Demyan's closed, the site was used by a variety of different businesses, including a disco, until it was finally torn down for the construction of residential homes in 2005.

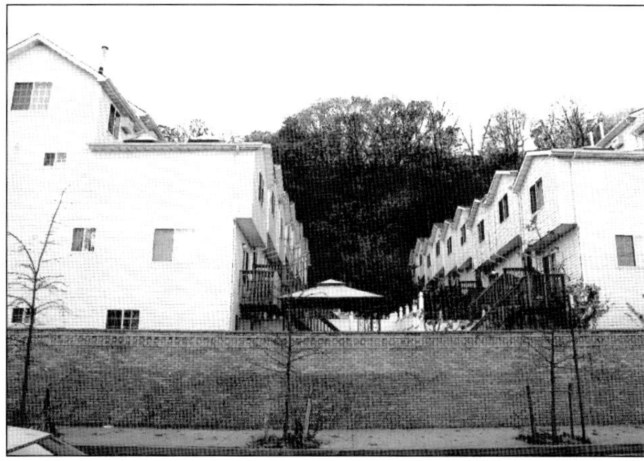

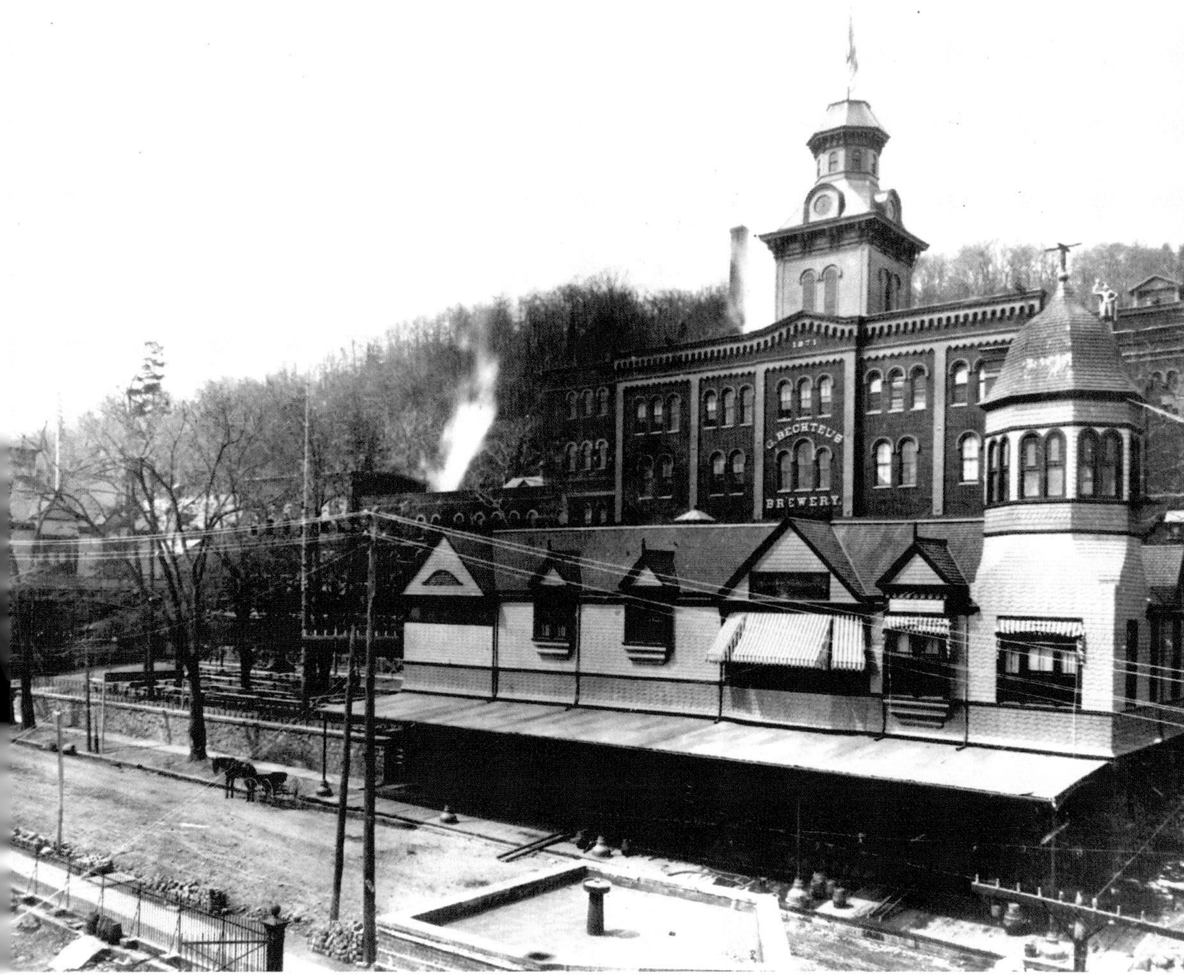

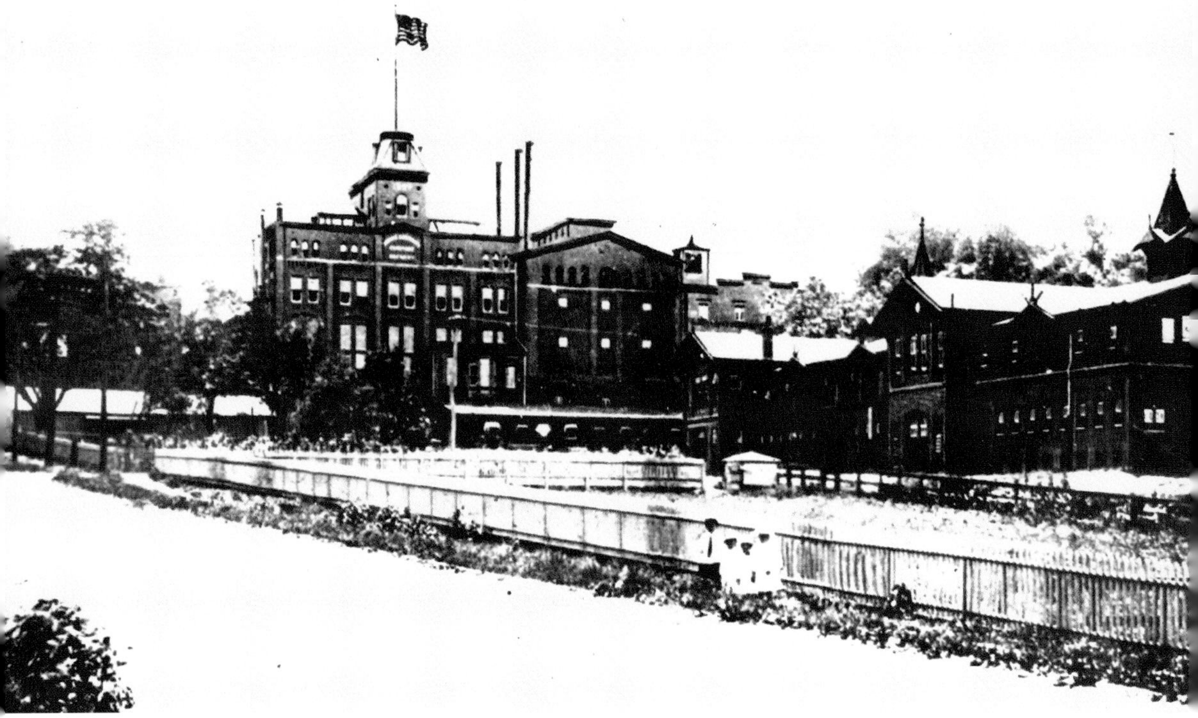

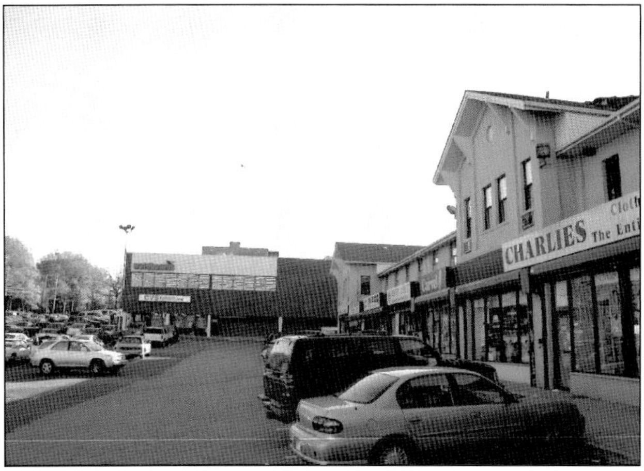

The first commercial breweries were established on Staten Island in the 1850s, and by the 1870s, there were eight commercial breweries competing on Staten Island. One of the first was the Constanz Brewery established by August Schmidt in 1852. In 1875, it became the Monroe Eckstein's Brewery and continued to operate on Manor Road in Four Corners opposite the Todt Hill Houses. Today the property is a mini mall at the intersection of Manor Road and Schmidts Lane. Monroe Eckstein also helped organize the Richmond County Savings Bank in 1886. Although the main building is no longer present, much of the original architecture can still be seen.

At the beginning of the 1900s, civic leaders began talking about constructing a tunnel under the narrows to Brooklyn. A Citizens Tunnel Committee of Staten Island was created to help lobby for the project. Construction of a tunnel actually began at St. George when the digging of a shaft started in 1923. Disputes among interest groups held up the project until in was finally abandoned. In 1950, the shaft was filled in when the new viaduct was constructed at St. George.

Chapter 7
TRANSPORTATION

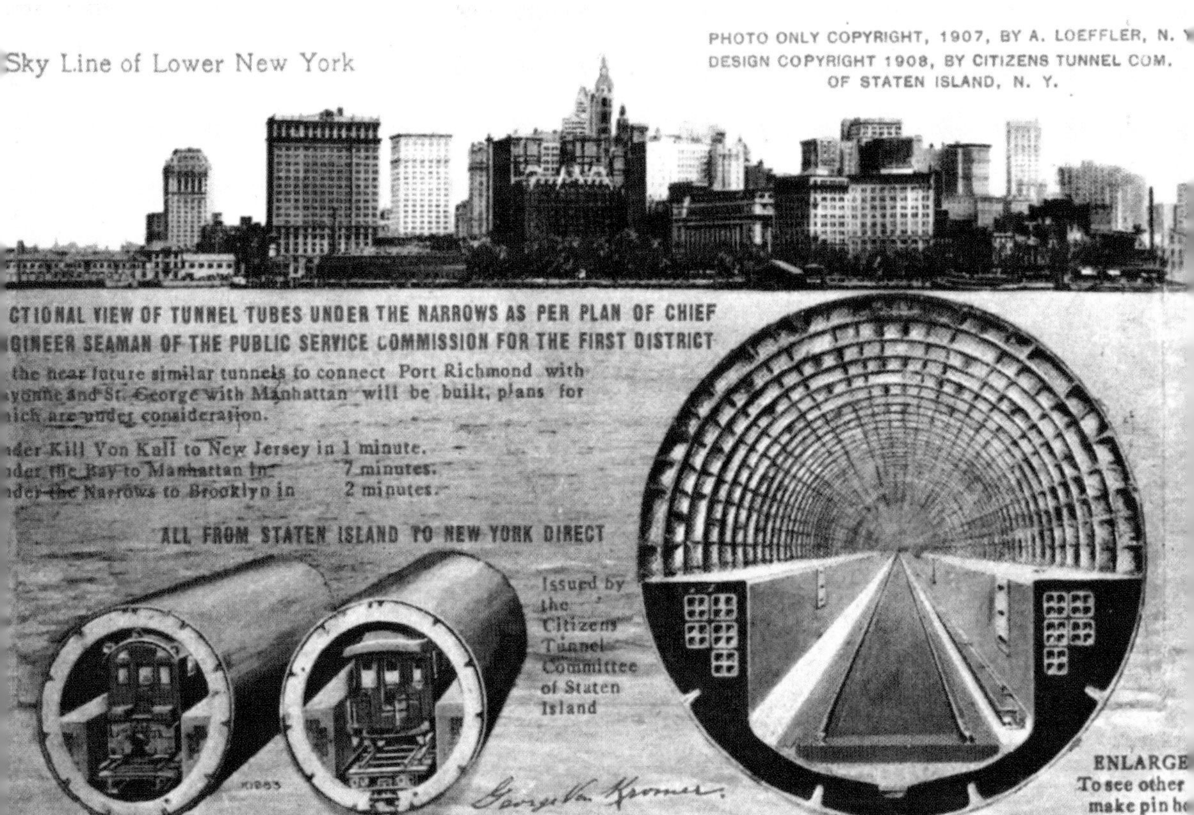

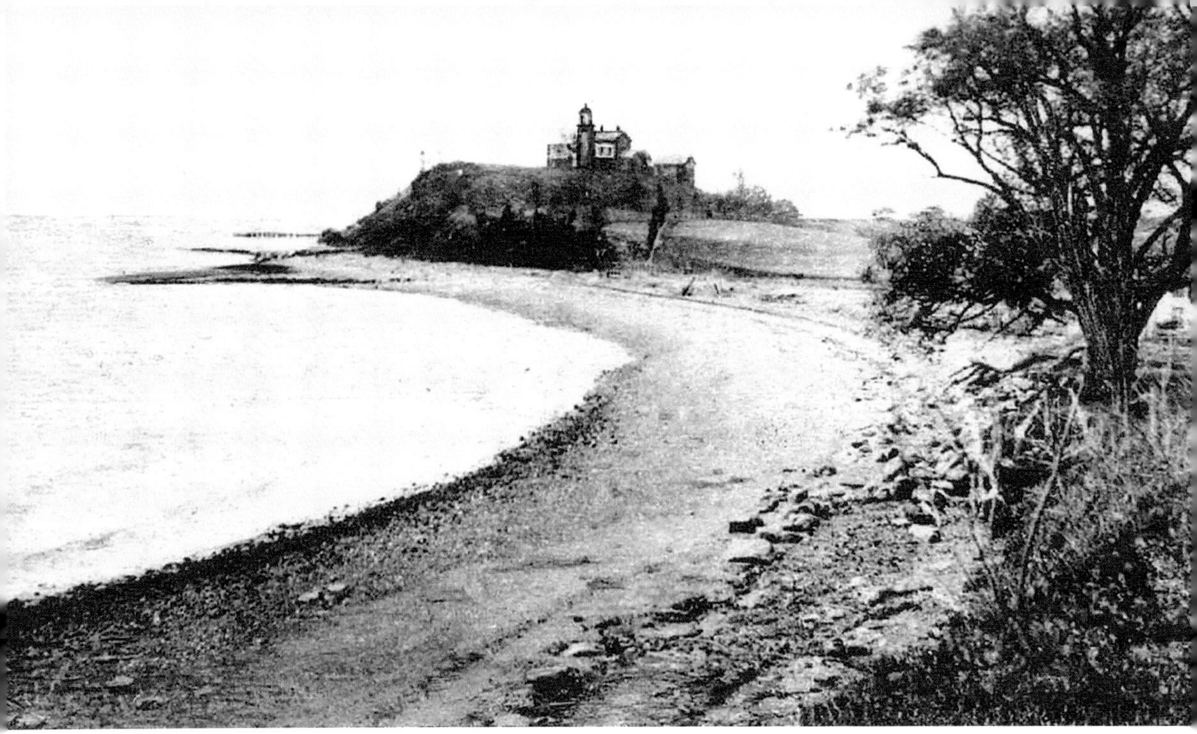

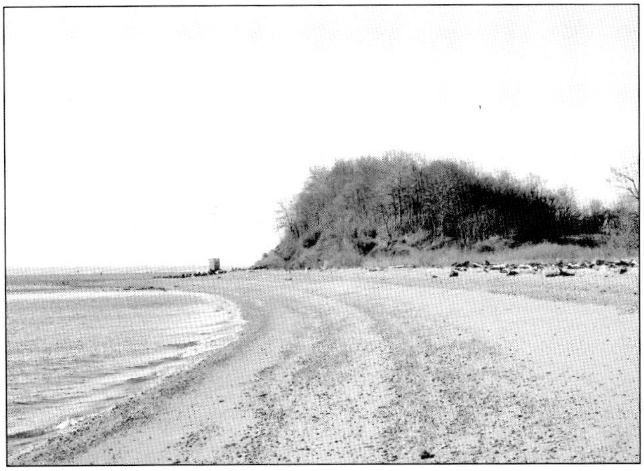

The lighthouse was established in 1828 and constructed on a bluff 85 feet overlooking Princes Bay. The original light was constructed of wood, and after the Civil War, a new light was built of brownstone in 1864. The light assisted ships traveling through the Raritan Bay as well as fishermen working the oyster beds in Raritan Bay until it was decommissioned in 1922. The land was owned by Mount Loretto and was often used as a retreat house for John Cardinal O'Connor prior to its sale to New York State Trust for Public Land. Today an automated beacon, located at sea level below the cliffs, serves as a navigational aid, and the lighthouse is the residence of a park ranger.

In 1750, service between Port Richmond and Bergen Point in New Jersey was called the Corsen Ferry. During the Revolutionary War, it was called Decker's Ferry. In August 1777, rebel units, under the command of Major Irving, crossed the Arthur Kill from Bergen Point and landed at Decker's Ferry in Port Richmond. A brief skirmish ensued at St. Andrew's Church, and after British reinforcements arrived, the rebels retreated back to New Jersey. This was the second attack on St. Andrew's, and it is depicted on a mural in Borough Hall. The original ferry landing at Ferry Street was moved to the foot of Richmond Avenue in 1879, when a new ferry house was built. Service continued under several operators until 1961.

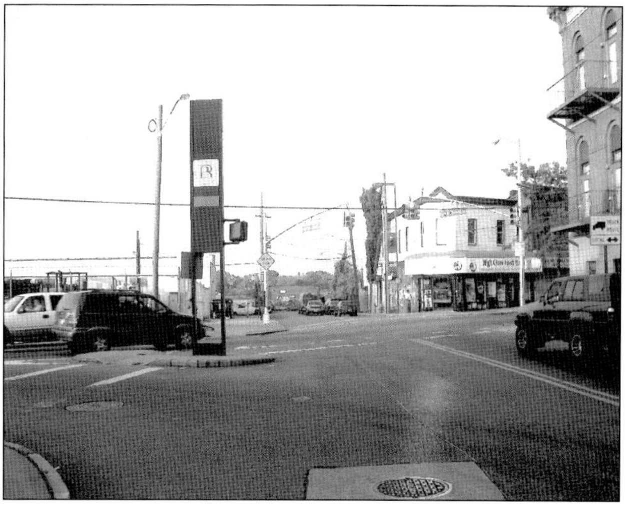

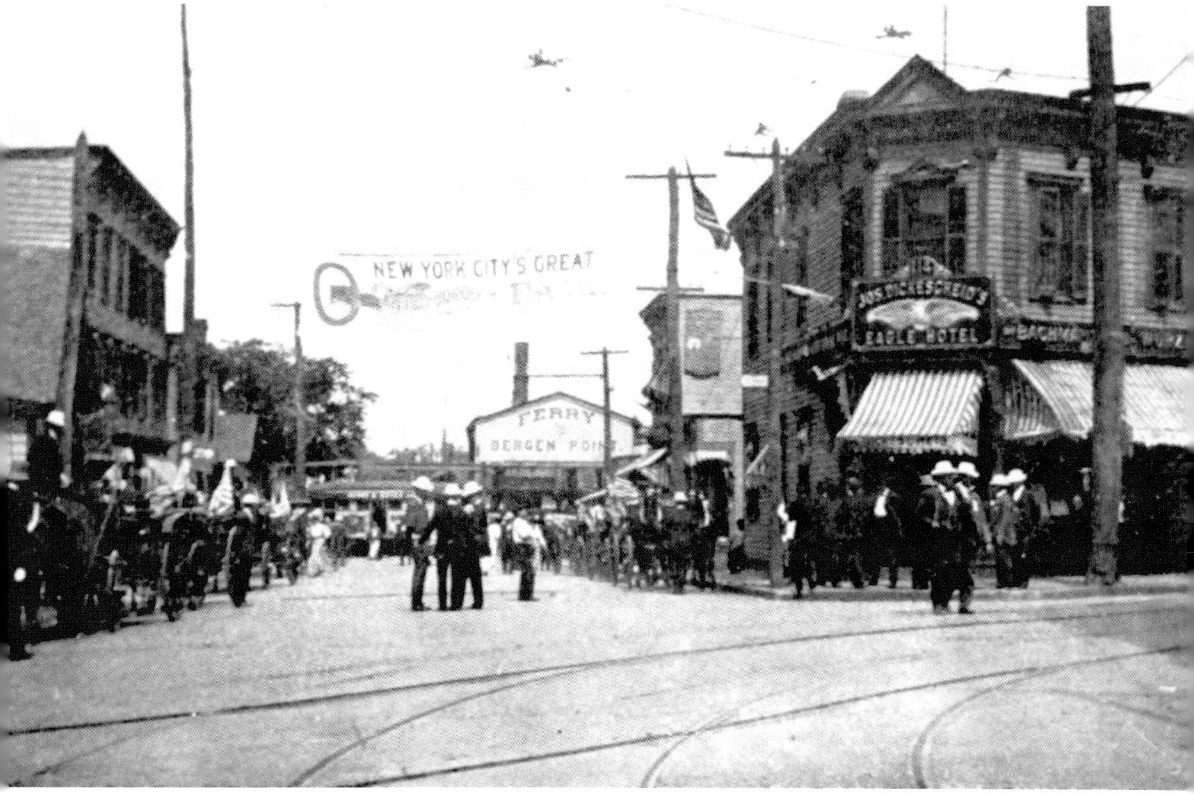

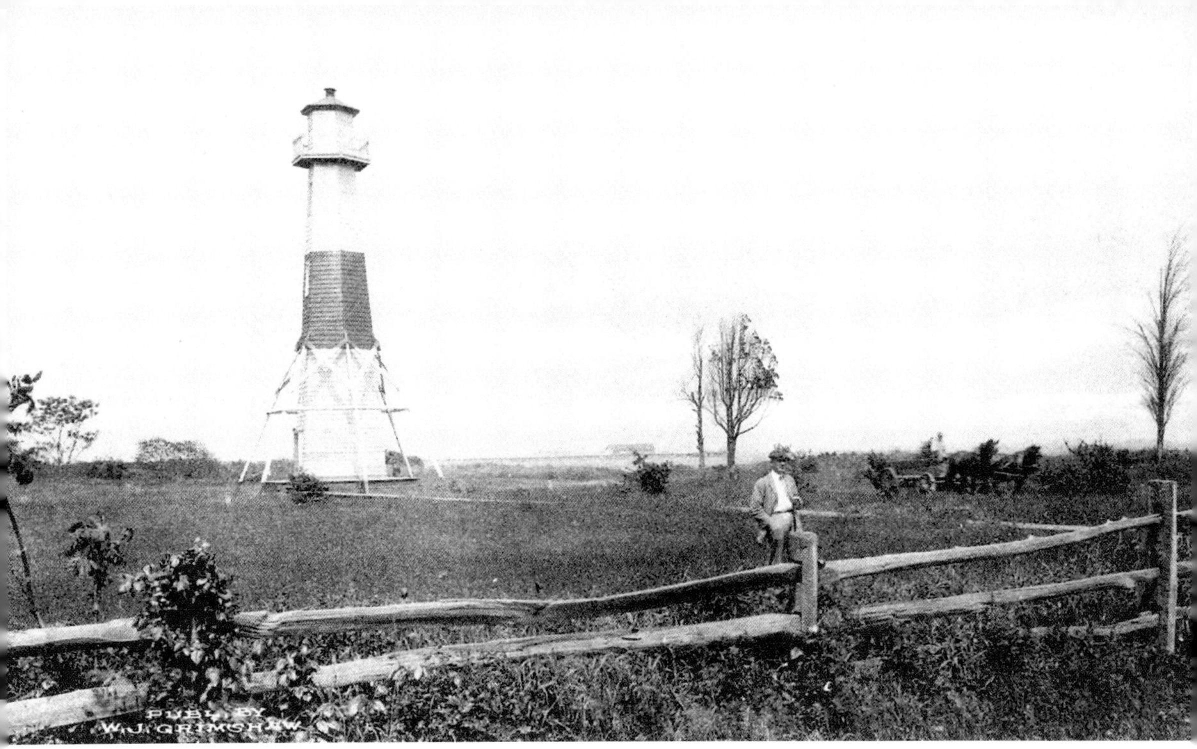

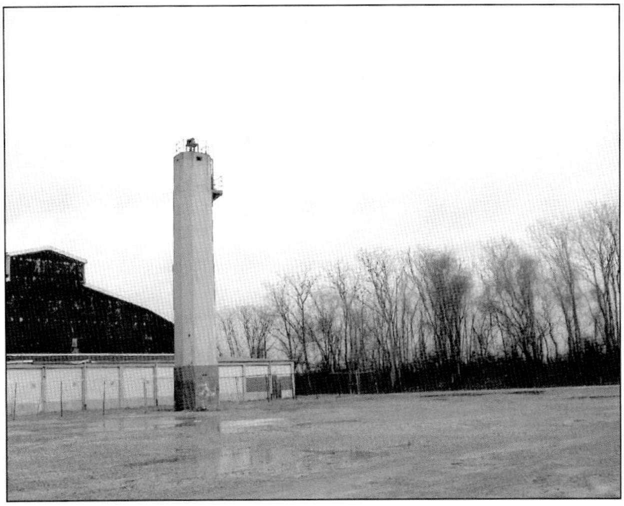

Commissioned in 1856, the Elm Tree Beacon worked in conjunction with the New Dorp Lighthouse at 25 Boyle Street to provide range for ships in the Swash Channel. Built on the old William Vanderbilt estate on New Dorp Lane, the Elm Tree Beacon got its name from an old elm tree Dutch sailors used as a landmark to navigate waters off Staten Island. The original wooden structure was replaced by a 65-foot tower constructed of concrete in 1939. The estate gave way to a military air base, Miller Field, in 1919, and after it was decommissioned in 1969, the property became part of the National Gateway Park system. The lighthouse was decommissioned; however, the concrete tower remains at the southeast end of the field adjacent to one of the remaining hangars.

The Aero Defense Base at Miller Field was established by the government in 1919 and became the home of the 27th Division Air Corps of the National Guard and the U.S. Army. The airport was named for Capt. James Ely Miller, the first American pilot killed in World War I combat over France, and was a landing site for such famous fliers as Charles Lindbergh, Francesco De Pinedo, and Adm. Richard Byrd. During World War II, it served as a holding facility for prisoners of war before they were assigned to prison camps. Originally the property of the Vanderbilt family, the field was decommissioned in 1969, and became home to local sports teams for soccer, football, baseball, and so on.

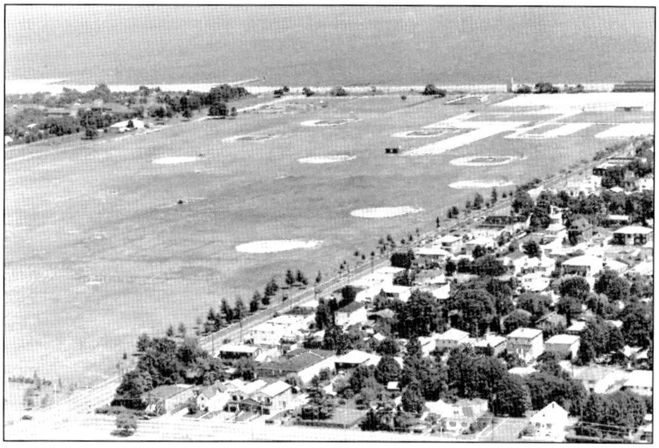

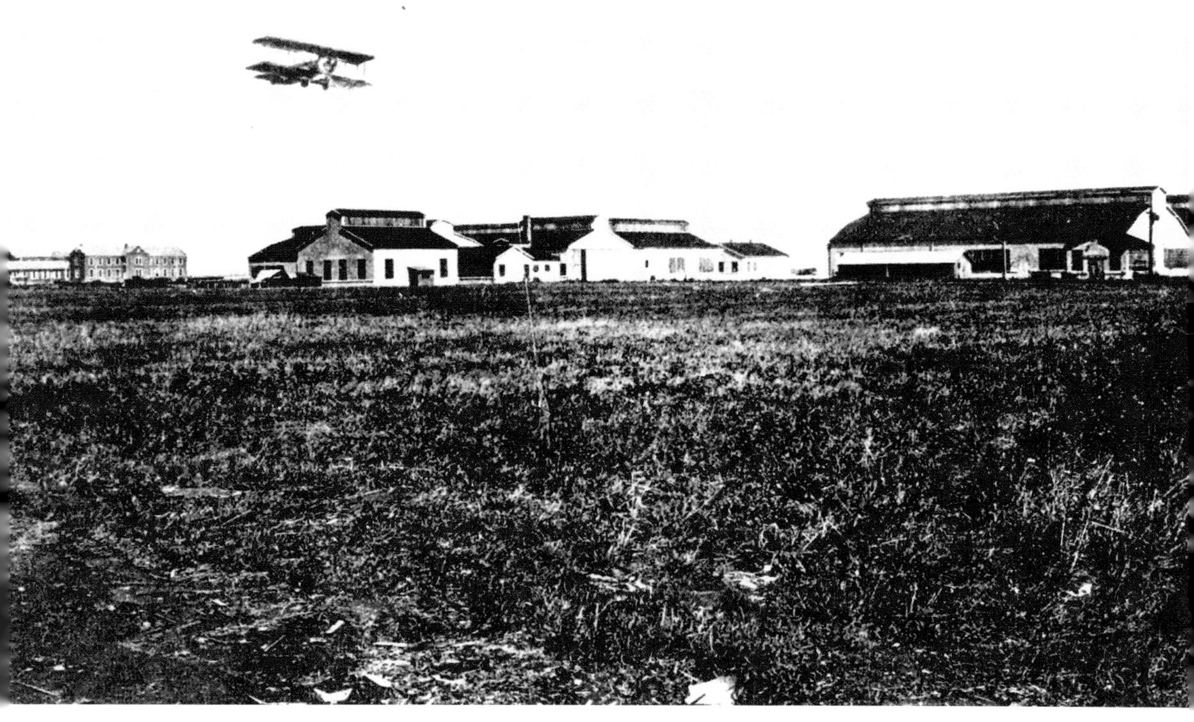

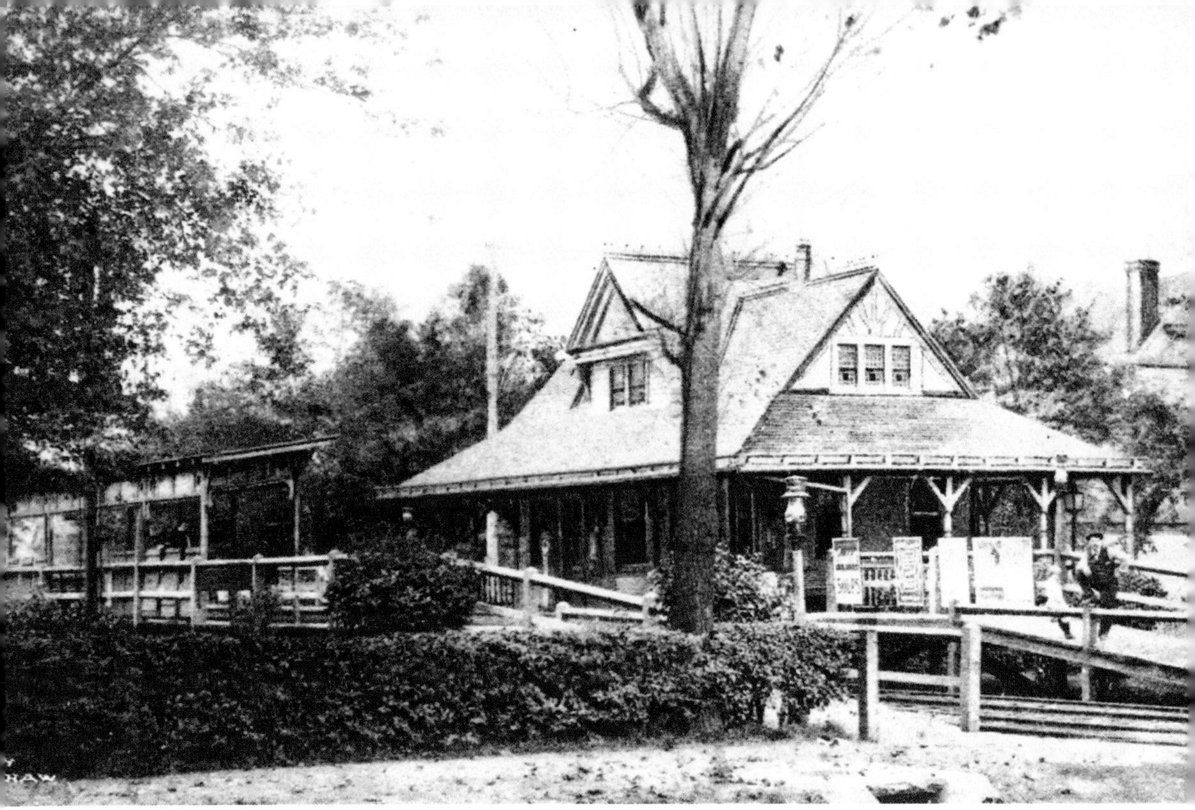

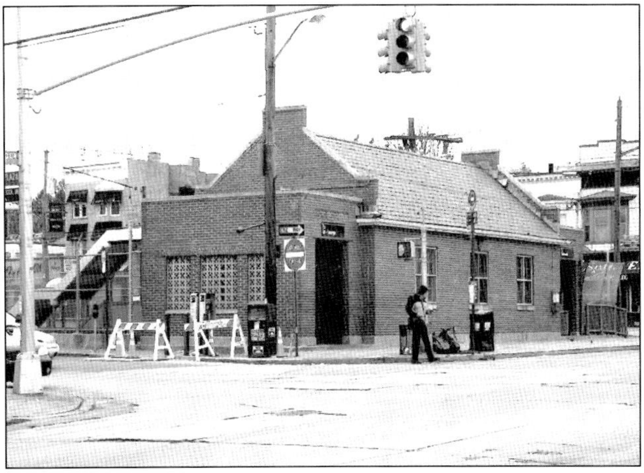

One of the more popular destinations on Staten Island was New Dorp Lane. Many racing enthusiasts were drawn to New Dorp Lane to watch the races that took place there. There trip used to take three hours from New Brighton, but once the railroad was built, the trip was reduced to a manageable one hour. Built in 1888, the station served as the depot for the village of New Dorp until 1965, when it was replaced by a more modern structure. In 1967, the station was moved to Historic Richmond Town, and today it serves as a wood shop for the restoration.

The New Dorp Lighthouse first came into service in 1856 and served as a beacon for ships entering New York Harbor for over 100 years. Officially called the Swash Channel Rear Range Light, the light is 192 feet above sea level and worked in tandem with the Elm Street Beacon, closer to the water's edge, at the end of New Dorp Lane on the old William Vanderbilt estate. Located at 25 Boyle Street, the lighthouse was decommissioned in 1964 and was designated a New York City landmark in 1967, then again in 1973 to include the surrounding property. After years of neglect, the lighthouse was purchased by John Volkral in 1974 and saved from further deterioration. The property is not open to the public and is still under private ownership.

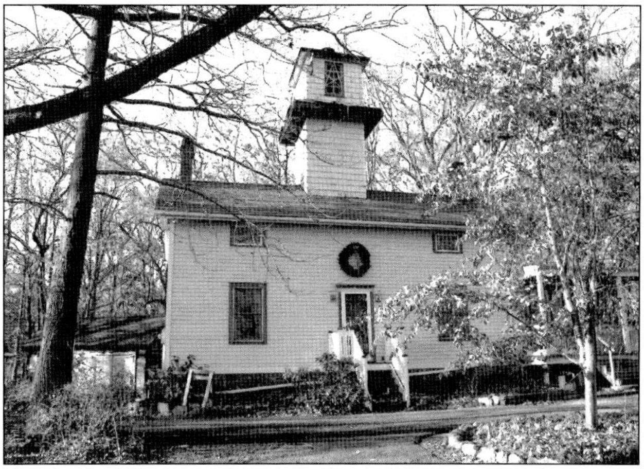

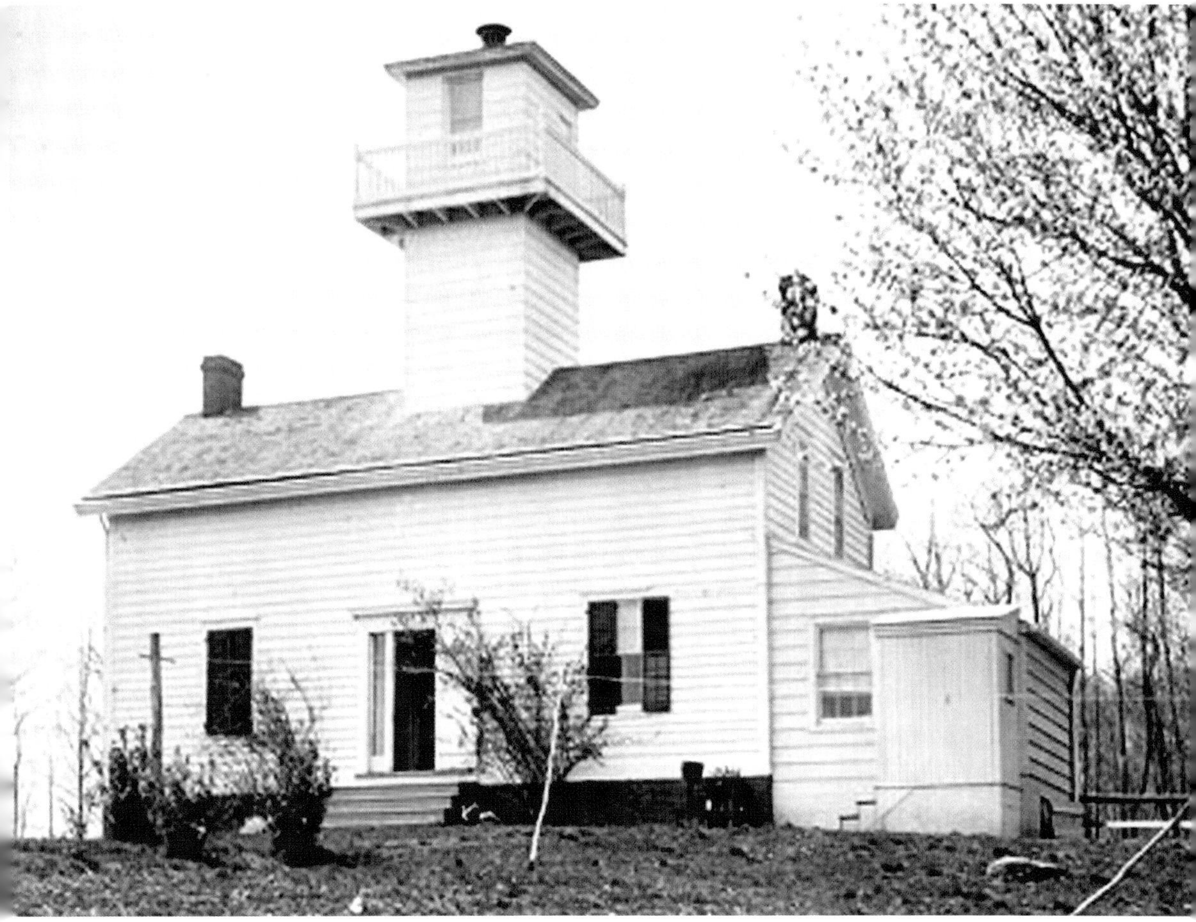

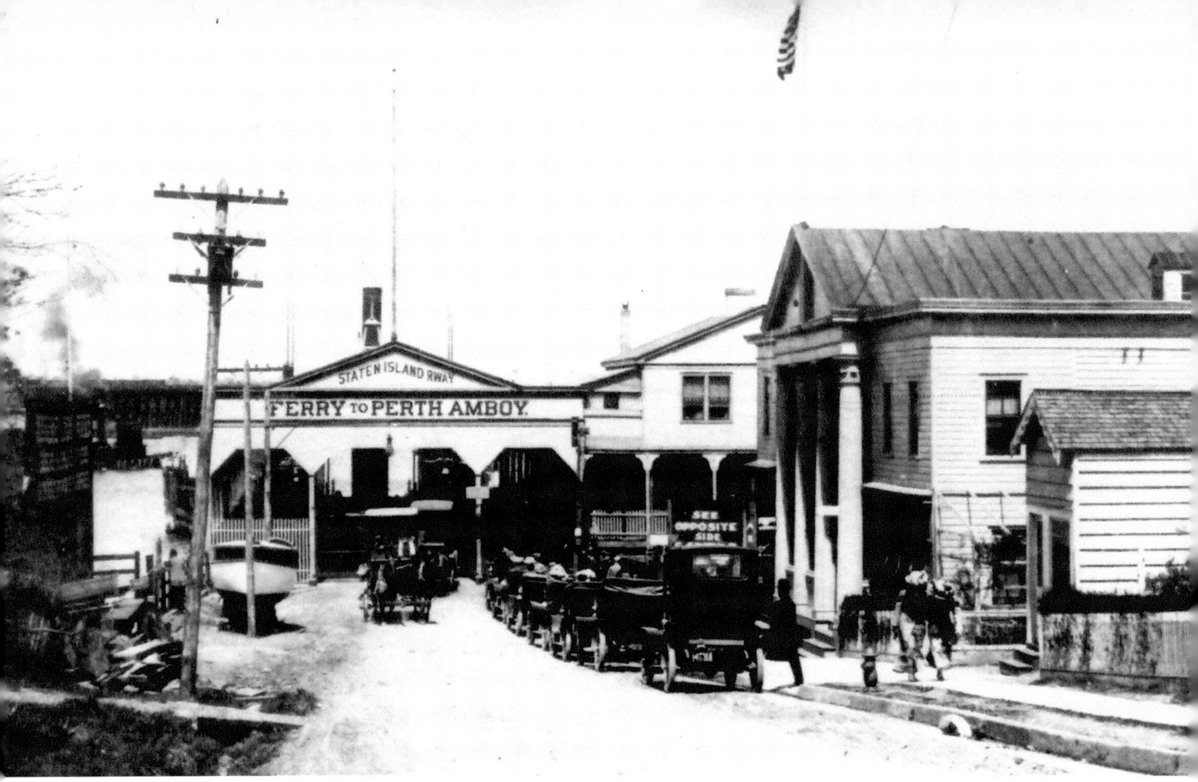

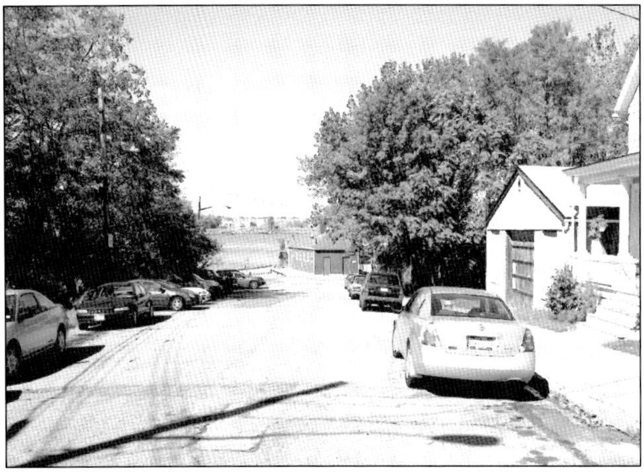

The Perth Amboy/Tottenville Ferry was operated by the Staten Island Railroad from 1867 until 1884 at the foot of Bentley Avenue. At that time, it became part of the consolidated railway operations created by Wiman, Pendleton and Garrett into the Staten Island Rapid Transit. As a subsidiary of the Baltimore and Ohio, the Staten Island Rapid Transit system continued to operate the ferry line until 1948. The service was taken over and operated by the Sunrise Ferry Corporation until the Outerbridge Crossing made it unprofitable. Finally, in 1963, ferry service between Tottenville in Staten Island and Perth Amboy in New Jersey closed for good.

The advent of rail service on Staten Island was a boom for many communities. Railway stations sprang up throughout the island, helping to populate otherwise very remote areas. The rural nature of the communities did not always require crossing gates as pictured here in Eltingville. A watchman would halt traffic whenever a train would enter or leave the station. As vehicular and pedestrian traffic increased, additional safety measures were added. In 1939, as part of the great public works projects, an overpass was constructed to enable the trains to maintain their schedule without impeding local traffic.

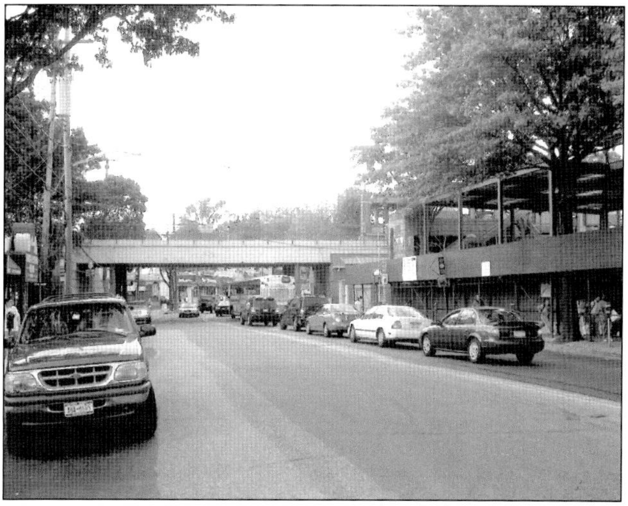

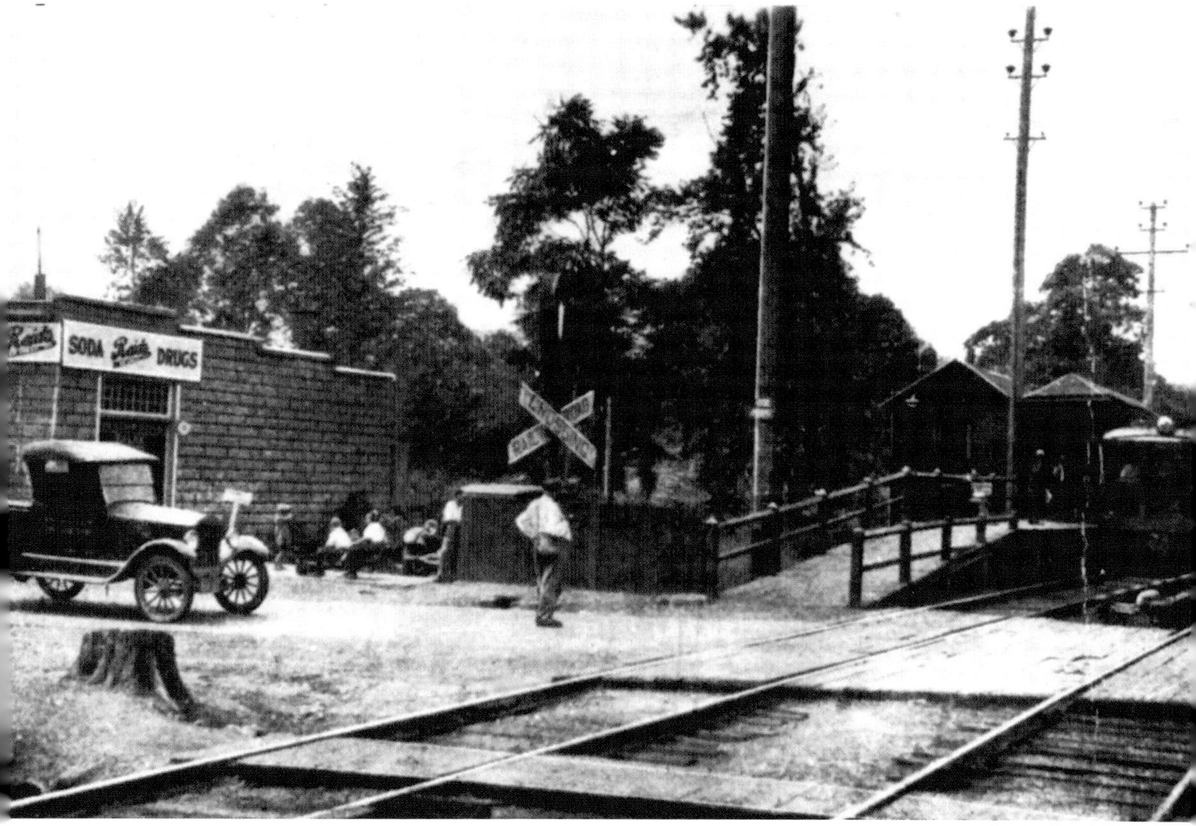

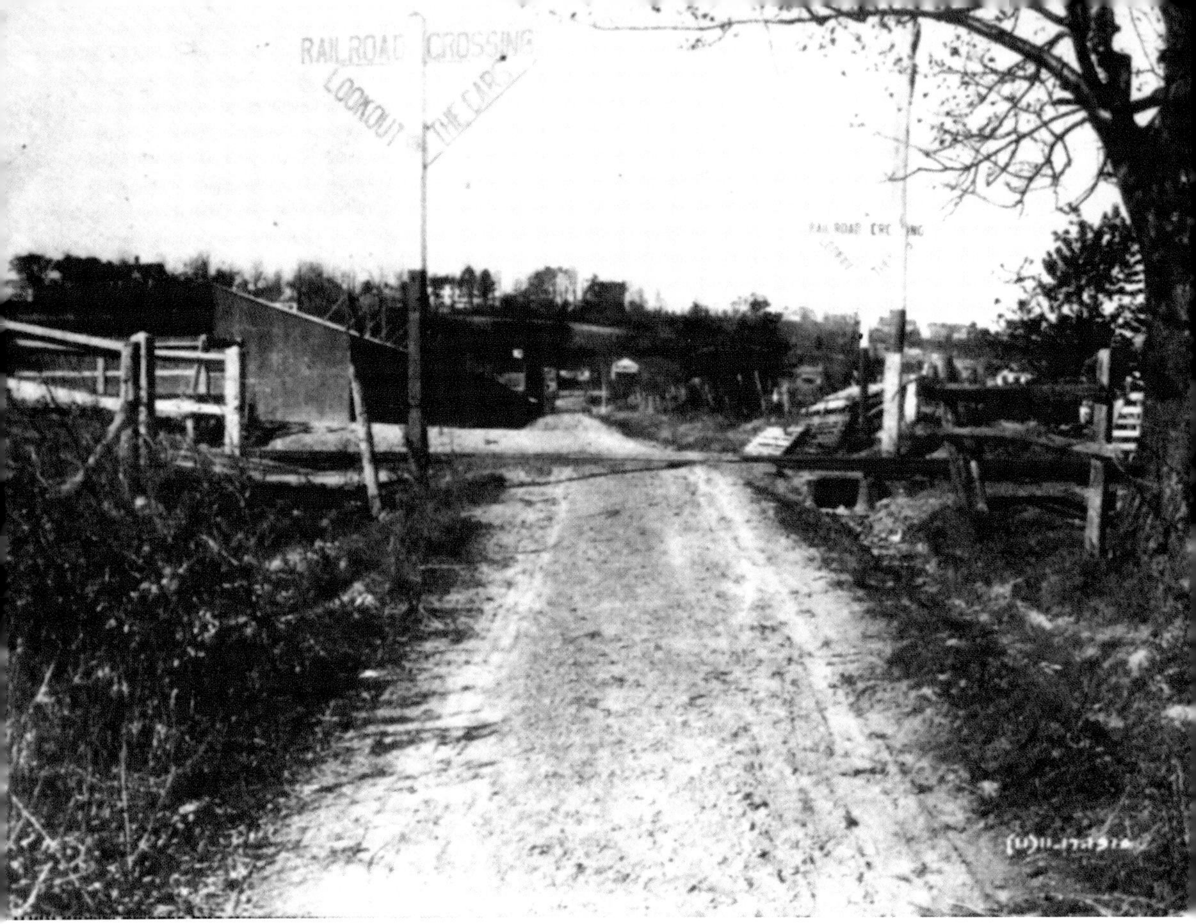

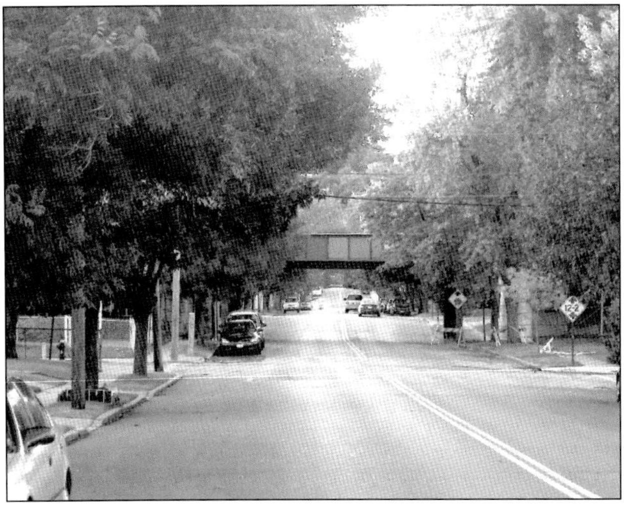

After the Civil War, railroads were built to improve the island's transportation system. While railroads helped, the island's roads were considered the worst in the state. In the 1890s, broken stone and water-bound macadam began to be used, and eventually concrete and asphalt macadam were used to pave the streets. In this photograph of Buel Avenue, looking north in the early 1900s, the road surface had not been paved, and there were no crossing gates to protect traffic. With the exception of major thoroughfares such as Victory Boulevard, most roads were narrow and built mostly of dirt or clay. Eventually the roads were upgraded, and in the 1930s, the railway was elevated to permit traffic to move safely.

Staten Island's first railroad was first built in 1860 when the island's population was about 26,000. The single-track line ran from Vanderbilt's Landing in St. George to Tottenville, connecting the ferries to New York and Perth Amboy in New Jersey. The trip took nearly two hours. The operation was plagued with problems and in 1866 was leased to the Rapid Transit Company. The new operating company made many improvements, including a bridge over the Arthur Kill, and freight traffic to and from the St. George docks increased to about one million tons a year. Today the Staten Island Rapid Transit Company operates the line, and the

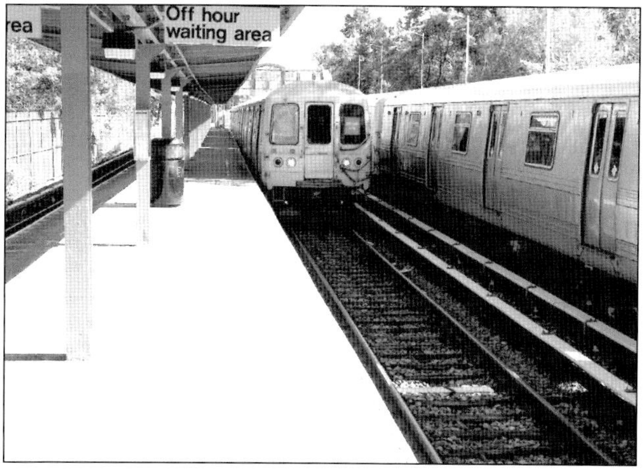

trip from St. George to Tottenville now only takes about 45 minutes.

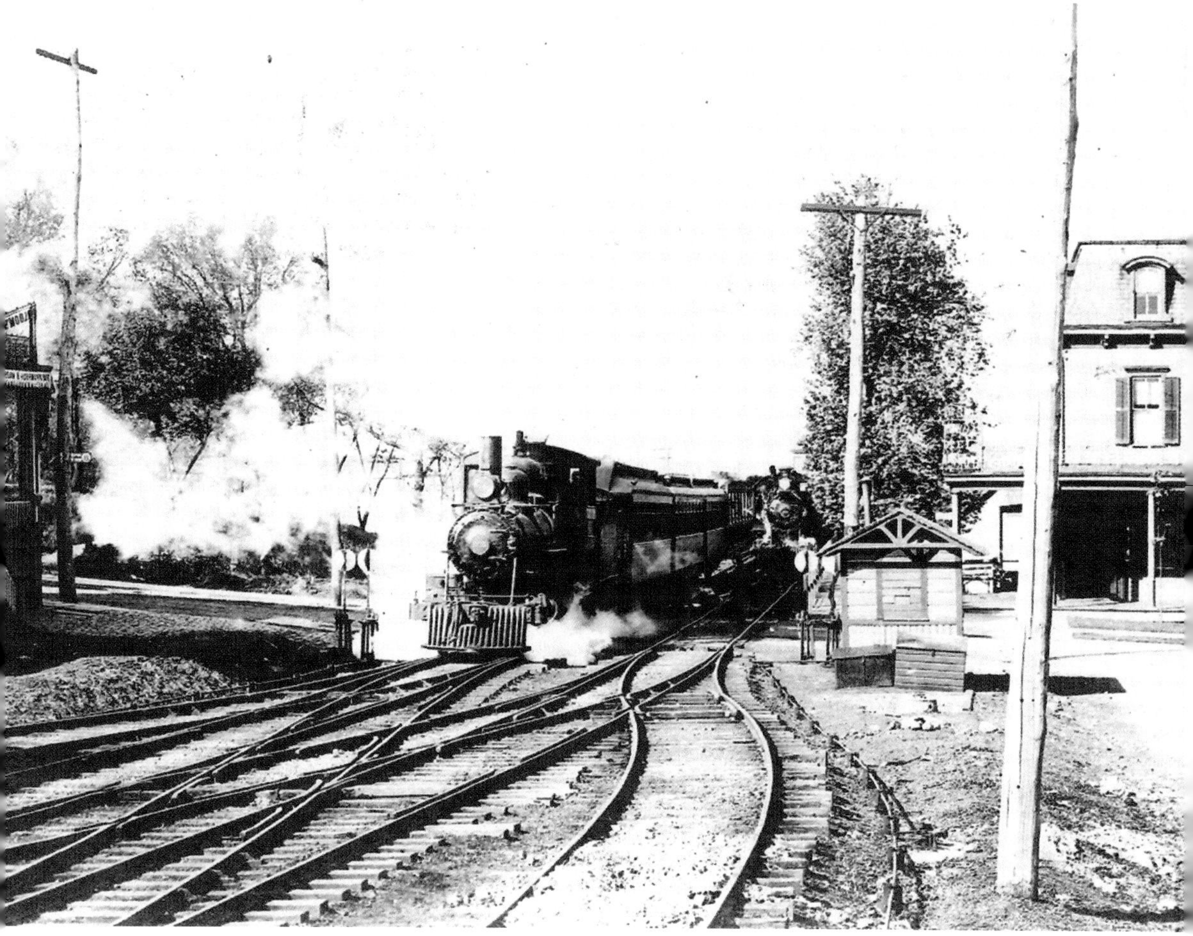

Consistent with our mission to preserve history on a local level, this book was printed in South Carolina on American-made paper and manufactured entirely in the United States. Products carrying the accredited Forest Stewardship Council (FSC) label are printed on 100 percent FSC-certified paper.

MADE IN THE USA